NEXT YEAR WILL BE BETTER

The huts, Dining-Room on the left, Bedroom on the right.

NEXT YEAR WILL BE BETTER

HYLDA M. RICHARDS

University of Nebraska Press
Lincoln and London

Copyright 1952 by Howard B. Timmins Publishers
Foreword copyright 1985 by the University of Nebraska Press
All rights reserved
Manufactured in the United States of America

First Bison Book printing: June 1985
Most recent printing indicated by the first digit below:
1   2   3   4   5   6   7   8   9   10

Library of Congress Cataloging in Publication Data
Richards, Hylda M., 1898–
    Next year will be better.
    Reprint. Originally published: London: Hodder &
Stoughton, 1952.
    1. Richards, Hylda M., 1898–   —Biography.
2. Authors, Zimbabwean—20th century—Biography.
3. Farm life—Zimbabwe. I. Title.
PR9390.9.R5Z47 1985   821 [B]   84-24029
ISBN 0-8032-3869-X
ISBN 0-8032-8915-4 (pbk.)

All characters in this book are real people, except the Very
Efficient Woman who is a composite character made up of
all the many efficient housewives who gave me advice.

CONTENTS

PART I

The Years Before

PART II

The Crowded days

PART III

The Busy Weeks

PART IV

The Anxious Months

PART V

The Hard Years

PART VI

The Better Years

PART VII

The War Years

Foreword to the Bison Book Edition
By Elspeth Huxley

These reminiscences by Hylda Richards show her to be the English counterpart of the pioneer woman of the American West. After nearly starving on a farm in Kent, she and her husband and their two small sons sailed for Capetown, South Africa, in 1928. Starting with very little capital, they acquired a block of virgin land in Rhodesia (present-day Zimbabwe), cleared the bush, ploughed with untrained oxen, and learned to work with the native African labor. The Richardses were faced with the deadly combination of the early 1930s: drought, locusts, and the collapse of prices for their produce. They experienced poverty, hardship, sickness, at times despair, but ultimately won out.

Hylda Richards tells the truth about life in Africa as her family experienced it—at the opposite pole from the scene often presented in romantic fiction of gallant pioneers, bold white hunters, and brave little women facing the perils of the jungle with a love affair now and then to bolster their spirits. Emerging in these pages as a sympathetic figure, she writes with humor and endures with courage, finding some compensation in the interest and beauty of the African landscape. Her specification of time and place makes her story convincing. Having the virtues of first-hand-ness and honesty, *Next Year Will Be Better* provides a valuable view of colonial history, and of one woman's experience of it.

To the country women of Rhodesia

PART I

THE YEARS BEFORE.

Chapter 1 — There they go!

I HAVE burnt my novel, I think there were 250,000 words. Anyhow, it has made a great mess in the fireplace, but the boys will clear it away. Lupenga will bring his half-petrol tin, scoop it up and carry it to the rubbish pit .... well, not quite so far as that, because a native cannot steel himself to take the last step, but invariably shoots the débris within a foot of the hole.

I have watched the flames creeping over each sheet until nothing is left of this ponderous work; but I know that the wind will carry little charred bits all over the garden and for weeks I shall come upon odd sentences from my novel, *"Frances stood looking,"* and *" 'No', snapped Hugh,"* and I shall remember. It would have been the dawn at which Frances was looking; she made a habit of it. She also looked wistfully at the sunset and silently at the dark velvety sky. She was always standing looking at something, somehow, because this gave me a chance of describing her. No real-life character situated as Frances was in the early part of my novel would have had time to brush her hair or mend a stocking .... and this brings me to my point: You cannot take incidents that happened to yourself and pin them on to Fictitious Characters. Nkosi (as he was later to be called by the natives) and I suffered so many ordeals and excitements when we came to Rhodesia that I decided to write a book about it. Since neither of us was anything like a hero or heroine, I created Hugh and Frances and then the trouble started.

Frances' character had to be moulded to the things I had done. I had to find good reasons why I had acted in a certain way, why I had made certain mistakes and seldom could I find any reason at all; and when I did it was most unheroic and utterly unfitting a heroine. In furnishing good reasons for her behaviour, Frances had to be made young, inexperienced and childish. On the other hand, Hugh, who acted Nkosi's part, could not help being likeable, and this showed Frances up rather badly. I did my best to blacken him. I made him elderly, shortsighted, with a stoop and hairy legs, but he still stole the limelight.

Then we came out with two lusty children, and how could Frances, aged eighteen, have two children of six and three? I fixed it. It entailed a great deal of planning and the introduction of stepmothers and deceased wives, but in the end Frances was provided with two children she loved dearly. She was young, innocent, without relations, and there was plenty of scope for lonely pangs .... but she was a little fool. As the story went on I learned to despise her. This is what happens when true incidents are pinned on a Fictitious Character.

I enjoyed myself on her personal appearance. I made her everything I should have liked to have been myself .... petite, with fair, curling hair and grey eyes. I gave her a heart-shaped face, though I believe such things look better in print than in the flesh. I gave her a glorious voice and wistful charm, but try as I would I could not give her a brain. It appeared that if Frances had had a brain and commonsense, either she would not have had the experiences I had, or she would have risen above them: and as for the sake of present and future settlers, I want to write of what happened to the four of us in Rhodesia, it seemed the only thing I could do was to write our story and consign that of Frances and Hugh to the flames. This I have done.

My friends tell me that I should not bring Hugh and Frances into this book, but I should feel guilty if I had not mentioned them. After all, they were with me for eight hundred odd pages and deserve some recognition.

So this story is without a heroine, though Nkosi is certainly the hero, and Bryan and Peter are two ordinary little boys for whose sake we cut away from our Home ties and made a home in Rhodesia.

Oh, I forgot .... you are waiting to go, Frances. You must have a decent exit. What about walking with Hugh into the sunset? I think you would like that. Your curly head could rest against his shoulder and we could have a few nightjars swooping around for atmosphere. Goodbye, Frances. The Big Red Sun is waiting for you. Off you go into the Future .... into the Past .... the land of Romance .... the land that never was, the land that we women long to visit but suddenly find, with the chill wind of nightfall, that we passed through unknowingly long ago.

I am sorry I made such a mess of you, Frances. I did my best, but you would never have been popular. I shall be popular because readers will say, "If that foolish creature managed, how much better I could manage myself."

Away with you, eyes fixed on the sunset, beautiful gleaming skies of red and gold, turning grey. Be careful how you walk. Hugh is so shortsighted, and I should not like you to stumble into an antbear-hole and spoil your exit as no doubt I should do. Goodbye, Frances! Goodbye, Hugh!

There they go . . . . two grey figures, arms entwined, husband and wife, an old-fashioned conception of marriage perhaps but one I think we all wanted . . . . once. Not two individual personalities, each picking his separate way over the veld, but together, making a home, making a country.

Chapter 2 — *Of we went!*

Our attempt to farm in Kent was a failure. We grew good crops but while the Continental trains flashed through our little country station, bearing produce to the London markets, our own baskets and sacks were pushed on to the siding to wait for the Slow Goods which took them leisurely to market when all the buyers had gone home to breakfast.

Nkosi and I had spent eight years on that farm. We put his army gratuity into fruit trees and worked from dawn to dusk, seven days a week to make a living while they grew to maturity. I, a London girl and only capable of frying bacon on a gas stove, had to tackle many things, learning by experience. Among other things I set fire to the cellar: rather an achievement when you consider there was nothing inflammable inside it, and I poisoned Nkosi with an unventilated rabbit-pie; but once the gripes were over he rather enjoyed the experience because it has provided him with an anecdote which he is never tired of telling.

We worked strenuously and very happily. In the soft-fruit season we started work at 4 a.m. and ended at ten in the evening. Often we were so tired that we sat on the bottom step and pushed each other upstairs to bed. But we were happy because we were young and strong and were making a home.

Each year began in hope and ended in bitter disappointment for our crops were either unsaleable or sold at a minimum price.

Both our babies, Bryan and Peter, were ugly skinny little

things and refused to put on weight or stop crying, which made life more complicated.

To save Peter's life, my father prescribed goat's milk. The first goat we bought, Mrs. Edmonton, was a horned and bearded old lady, and of a most provoking disposition. When milked she had to stand on a box, and directly the milker approached her, she turned round and offered the wrong end. Mrs. Bethnal Green, the next goat, had an undercarriage of completely different design which necessitated an entirely different method of milking, one I never mastered. Nkosi milked both ladies blasphemously, and I remember the way he used to bang the fruits of his labour down on the kitchen table. However, Peter decided to live, so it was worth while. As I was always apt to overdo things, Peter grew so heavy that he became bandy when, at an early age, he insisted on standing. I was told to keep him off his feet but he was a powerful child and when strapped in the pram he used to plant his feet firmly against the end and deliberately bend his legs out of the true. He had to wear splints.

Once out of the pram he found Bryan's tricycle and rode it before he could walk and was doing stunts before other children could manage the pedals. I never knew one moment's peace with Peter. In one single day he burned a good shawl on top of an oil-heating lamp, took the telephone receiver to pieces and pulled off the hands of the clock. Once I found him hanging by his feet over the iron gate and twice he was bitten on the face by a dog. Another time he cleaned his teeth with green paint and shortly afterwards ate some poisoned berries.

Bryan, the elder, had also been a starveling baby, had also been overfed, become bandy and worn splints. Again, I had persevered to such an extent that he became knock-kneed and had to wear another kind of splint before his legs were as they should be.

He loved Mrs. Edmonton and it must have been from her he derived my nickname, "Mummie-Goat." "Mummie-Goat" I have been ever since, though in later years it became plain "Goat."

Bryan lived in a world of his own, a world of flowers. He knew each flower in our large rambling garden, and every morning when he was turned out of doors he went round to see how they were getting on. Unobserved, I used to watch him gently touching a flower-head and looking deep into it. He always had gentle hands. He would not talk but knew the

Latin name of every flower. The Relations, all garden-lovers liked this and used to take him round their gardens asking him to name the flowers.... montbretia, gladiola, hydrangea and viola-cornuta; he used to roll them off, but still refused to talk. When he sat in his high-chair he used to spend hours with flowers and jam-jars and on his third birthday all the Relations and many of the villagers sent him bouquets. Everyone talked flowers to him and gave him picture books on flowers and one day he went into the garden in a rage and pulled off all the heads of all the flowers and threw them on the lawn.

As life without any relaxation or outside interest is rather blighting, I had started an amateur dramatic society in the village which became a great success. As ours was a Dickens village, we did sketches from his works and my favourite part was 'Tilda Price, which I had to play to Nkosi's Nicholas Nickleby which was rather difficult as by that time he knew me too well to be impressed by the feminine fascinations and coyness of 'Tilda.

About the third year of these winter activities, I asked my mother down to see our show. The first half was Dickens and the second a farce which I had written. In order to be on the stage to help with the scene-shifting, I took the part of a miserable little servant-girl and to my great surprise found that I had a funny face. My mother had always told me that I must keep smiling because my face in repose was either miserable or worried-looking and it was very cheering to discover that I could use this drawback to make people laugh. My mother was surprised and pleased and that evening we went home rejoicing. I remember lying awake that night unable to sleep because I was so happy. I had put over a good show, and I had all those I loved best in the world under my roof and I wondered if I should ever feel so completely happy again. I did not want to sleep but to lie and savour this perfect happiness.

The next morning Nkosi had an interview with the Relations. They had been very generous to us when we started farming, and once or twice when we were in a very bad way they had lent a helping hand. They now had decided to look into our affairs as all farmers at that time were losing money. Nkosi came back very white and strained. We were to leave at once, there was no future for us in our fifty acres. Our debts would be paid up and we should have to Go Abroad and be given Another Chance. I was glad then that I had lain awake and been happy, for now I felt we should never be happy again. First of all, it was the failure to make good when we had worked so hard; then the parting with our home, our bits of furniture, our garden, our growing fruit-trees and for me, the parting with my friends the Dramatic Society and the break with my mother and family.

On the day of the sale, the pots and pans were laid out on the concrete yard, an attractive farmhouse yard edged with grass and holding an old-fashioned well which I had painted white with a red roof. Pots and pans, each with a history. They had often been more my masters than my servants but they looked pathetic waiting there. At the last moment I snatched up the thick aluminium saucepan in which daily I had heated the children's milk and hid it away. I could not part with it.

During the war when the Rhodesian Government asked us to sacrifice our aluminium saucepans for war material, Lupenga and I took the saucepans outside and with a brick dashed them to shapeless masses on the granite rock, but I rescued this saucepan and it is still with me. I shall probably have it placed on my grave, as the natives do with their prized pots and pans.

Another incident was the armchair of shabby brown corduroy. We two had sat in it together when we were first married and the babies, when of manageable size had been laid on it while we had meals. Later on two little boys had, when unobserved, done their best to break the springs.

In the cruel light of day it stood waiting to be sold. Someone offered ten shillings and there were no more bids. The buyers of course saw only a dilapidated armchair. I turned away while I wiped my eyes. However, when I came back I was delighted to find two people running each other up over my coffee-set. It had cost three shillings at Woolworths and the winner, the milkman, paid 12/6 for it. This made up for a lot of unhappiness.

So we left the farm. Leaving the soft-fruit bearing well and the hard fruit just about to yield the longed-for return. We left the garden broken in, the house clean with its Woolworth paints and I think we were the last of the ex-Service couples "put on the land" to go broke.

The Relations were very good to us, they not only paid our debts but gave us money for another start. We felt like remittance people and rather guilty at not having made good but were determined that we would prove that their belief in us was justified. So, after eight years of unceasing effort

we left our home, feeling that all we had gained was the
ability to work hard, to laugh at ourselves and, of course, our
two nice children.

Nkosi went to Rhodesia in April, and the children and I
moved over to Westcliff to be near my mother until he
could send for us.

We could not find a flat. Time after time I was on the
verge of being accepted as a tenant when the fact that I had
two children disqualified me. I began to blush furiously
whenever I was asked if I had any children. At last a woman
overlooked my shame and rented me her flat. There was,
of course, no garden and the road was alive with traffic.
Peter used to ride the tricycle round the tiny flat and I
was in constant fear of the white paint, but he never touched
it. He was only three but an expert rider.

Once when we were out he put his feet up and dashed
down an asphalt slope. To my horror I saw an invalid lady
in a bath-chair being pushed up the incline by an old man,
who finding it tough going, had buried his head in his arms
and was pushing blindly. There was no way of stopping
Peter, and the invalid lady and I could see a head-on crash.
She rose to her feet, waved her sunshade and screamed.
Within a yard of the bath-chair my little darling suddenly
swerved round a lamp-post and came to rest facing uphill,
completely unperturbed.

During the last winter on the farm, Bryan had started
chronic bronchial-asthma, attack after attack, and he was
frequently in bed. This persisted through the spring and
my father advised me to have the child's tonsils out before
we went to Rhodesia. This was done but Bryan was very
ill and had not quite recovered when Peter had a mastoid
on his ear. To complicate matters Nkosi's cable came sum-
moning us to Africa. Luckily, I was able to engage an old
family who took charge of both invalids while I raced about
getting ready.

I spent the last evening in my sister's flat in London. All
the family came to see me and I cried and cried. It would
not have been so bad if Nkosi had been with me but as I
was alone I felt very homesick. They said afterwards all they
remembered was my bathing my eyes at the basin. The next
day July 19th 1928 we sailed for Cape Town.

The devoted friends who witnessed Frances' last hours in
her native land had no memories of a blotched face in a

basin but of eyes, dark-rimmed, in a small wistful face. She also made a more interesting departure.

"Soon after dawn Frances woke to the beat of the engines and looking through her porthole saw that the ship was slipping quietly down the Thames. Everything was still and grey in the early morning and she lay watching the riverside with its wharves and factory chimneys gliding by. Goodbye England!"

My own comment was less romantic. "We must have started very late, as we are only just going down the river. It smells filthy."

The voyage was interesting but uneventful. Peter felt very seasick the first day and explained that he could not pick up his toys as he was "not a strong boy."

When he recovered his strength, I never had a moment free from anxiety. Passengers and members of the crew were always bringing him back from the jaws of death. It was, therefore, a relief when, with the Cape Rollers, his strength was again impaired, and I had a reasonable hope of being able to hand over to Nkosi his two sons intact. Once this was done my responsibilities would be over.

On Monday August 13th, just as the sun was sinking, we sighted land, a long, low haze (just as the novels describe). After dark we could see the lights of Cape Town stretched like a sequin trimming to a black velvet curtain. At nine o'clock the engines stopped suddenly. It seemed strange after three weeks of constant beating (it reminded me of times when the music failed in a silent film). We anchored outside the harbour for the night. Before I went to bed I leaned over the rail and watched the twinkling lights. It was peaceful and beautiful but a dreadful wave of home-sickness came over me, seeing the strange new land, and thinking of the new life before me.

The next morning very early while it was dark, I heard a puffing outside and putting my head through the porthole saw the little pilot steamer alongside and lay and watched the pilot climb on board. I was struggling to dress myself and the boys, when a friend rushed in and said my husband was on the quay and had been there before dawn. I ran up on deck in my dressing-gown to see him. Our meeting was not the glad reunion I expected. With several yards between us we could not even shake hands so I said "Hallo!" and he said "Hallo! Had a good trip?" and I said, "Yes, thank you," and then, as conversation seemed to flag, I went back to dress.

It was late afternoon and pelting with rain when we started off for Rhodesia. The outskirts of Cape Town are not inspiring, and there are stations and stations of cemeteries. This depressed me for I realised that, like thousands of others, my bones would lie mouldering in this new land.

I had never slept in a train before and the thought of spending five days in one was exciting. The compartment reminded me of those useful pocket-knives containing blades, chisel, saw and corkscrew, of which only one can be used at a time. We had just battled with bananas and blankets, sponges and spirit-stoves (strictly illegal on trains), shapeless masses of coats and rugs rolled together with boots and coathangers dropping out, and had made some semblance of order when it was time to put the children to bed, and from little room we changed to no room at all. There were three tiers of bunks on each side and we had to have all six out because of the quantities of hand-luggage. Peter, because he would be certain to fall out of bed, had a lower bunk: Bryan the middle, a mere slit, and we two adults decided on the top berths. As Nkosi lifted Bryan up in his arms to put him in his narrow bunk, he said, "Post me, Daddy."

When we reached Bulawayo I was astonished that there could be such a civilised modern town so far north. It was quite unexpected.

The train for Salisbury left at 10 p.m. and we thought that if we hired a room in a hotel and tired Peter out, he would sleep all the afternoon and be fresh for the evening. Although I had brought overalls for the children to wear in the train they had not a clean suit between them, and it was necessary to buy something for them to arrive in. Bryan was easily fixed, but no child's suit would stretch over Peter's burliness and we had to buy him a khaki shirt and shorts with a belt. Peter had not the figure for a belt; it went round him like the ribbon on an Easter egg.

After our shopping we had lunch and put the children to rest. This they refused to do.

Worn out with trying to relax, I tidied my most unlovable little sons and the room and took them to tea.

After tea we found to our dismay that unless we vacated the room at six, we should be charged for the night. This we certainly could not afford to do, so we sat in the lounge.

It was then that we repented that we had tried to tire them out; they were exhausted, but refused to sleep in my arms or on a chair.

People were having sundowners and looked with dislike at two restless, querulous little boys. Dinner was a nightmare; they were sleepy and cross and, knowing that Peter would howl if I spoke sharply to him, I had to bear with this outrageous behaviour. Glad as we had been to bring the children in to dinner we were more than relieved to take them out. After another miserable, interminable hour we took them to the station and begged to be allowed to put them to bed in the waiting train. This was refused. Finally, at ten-thirty we put our perfectly fiendish children to bed and they fell asleep immediately.

We arrived in Salisbury the next evening just before sunset. Crowds of people were waiting. No familiar faces for us, I thought, but the manager of the farm at which we were to stay was there with a friend and we had a drink. This was very cheering.

We were able to have some washing done at the hotel and when Peter's coloured suits came back I was glad to think he would no longer have to wear the khaki shirts but he refused to wear his suits; he had been raised to the dignity of shirts and would not give them up. We had a battle, but as he had the bellow of a bull and we were in an hotel, I gave way, but how I longed to get him in a home of my own to restore a little discipline.

Nkosi had been accepted as a farm pupil for a year and it had been agreed that we should stay with the farm-owner until an empty house on the estate was prepared for us.

After a few days our host called for us in his new open two-seater. The children were given a lift by another farmer in the district.

I thought my first drive through the veld would be my last. It seemed a pity to have come so far quite safely, and then to be dashed to pieces on the boulders within twenty miles of our destination. The track was just beaten earth covered with sand and in it were ruts and holes and hillocks, roots of trees and great boulders. Sometimes it sloped sideways down to a deep donga, and we travelled at an average speed of 45 m.p.h. On better stretches we touched 55 but

when we skidded we slowed down to 40. I was perched on
Nkosi's knees to begin with, but was halfway over the
windscreen most of the time. As we sped along, our host
told us that three accidents had occurred on that road
during Show Week and it did not ease my mind when we
saw a derelict car which had started to climb a tree.

When Nkosi asked a question, which necessitated the
driver's leaving the wheel and fumbling in his pocket, I
nearly screamed.

Thus we arrived at the farm on which we were to spend
our first year.

Chapter 3 — Where we came to.

I had been prepared for anything except what I found.
I had imagined mud-huts, grass-shelters or, at best, a primitive
sort of house. Instead I found a long, low, white bungalow,
with antique furniture and Persian rugs on the highly polished
floor.

Our host dressed for dinner every evening and we had to
follow his example. Nkosi swore nightly as he struggled into
his boiled shirt, but I loved changing.

It was so like a scene in a play. The brightly lighted room
and through the uncurtained french-windows the black night
and wonderfully bright stars. The contrast between light and
darkness, veld and evening dress was most pleasing, and I
felt almost like Frances in my (one only) evening frock,
leaning back in the deep armchair, while Nkosi chatted with
his host over coffee and liqueurs.

We found that the farm was run by a most efficient
manager and that the owner was seldom at home.

He asked me to take over the housekeeping and, as the
native servants had been without supervision for so long, he
would be grateful if I would take complete charge.

The staff consisted of five houseboys and a picannin and
at first I was amazed at their efficiency. Everything shone
brightly and the meals were served daintily. Tea in a silver
pot on a silver tray, was brought punctually at eleven and
four o'clock, with a silver dish of expensive imported biscuits.

But when I began to look round, I found that the efficiency
was only on the surface and that behind it was dirt and
shocking extravagance.

In this way I first came upon Darkest Africa — the

ignorance, natural and acquired, of the African native. In the kitchen I found two sinks rivalling each other in filthiness. I was introduced to cockroaches and found the dressers woven to the wall by cobwebs. Luckily my dreams of "marble halls" and "vassals and serfs at my feet" were soon shattered. I realised that native labour is what you make of it, and whereas you may have a clean house with one servant you may have twelve servants and a dirty house. I found I could do little, for whenever I wanted a job of work to be done in a different manner, I always seemed to arrive just after it was done or when it could not be attempted for another hour. When I tried to show by example, the natives would watch my efforts for a moment and then turn away and get on with another job and leave me to it. Nothing I could say or do would make them take the slightest notice of me. The houseboy was completely elusive: he did what he considered his work and then disappeared and I could never see him go or find him once he had gone. Sam, the butler, was dirty and stole on a lavish scale. He ordered pounds of tinned food, secure in the knowledge that his master would not make him account for it.

The cook, a native steeped in grime, would brook no interference and I felt that if I was to eat at all, I had better not watch the food being prepared. He had two boys under him to wash up, but every piece of china had to be rewashed before it appeared on the table. This extra work was undertaken quite willingly, anything rather than spend a little extra time washing a thing properly in the first place.

The wash-boy did about one day's work a week, but that excellently. The garden boy grew no vegetables at all, but managed to show a promise of vegetables to come. The flower-garden-boys, their watering finished, squatted together over a weed. Cuticura soap, then half-a-crown a tablet, was used all over the house and in the kitchen. Large quantities of milk were brought in every day, though a larger quantity, I imagine, found its way to the native compound.

Natives have the sense, when they are employed by an absentee master, to give him what he wants so that ways, means and thefts are never considered. Clean white suits, bought by the master, highly polished furniture and floors, plenty of hot water and dinner served in the right way with gleaming silver and glass and clean linen, all these must be forthcoming, and then the rest of their lives is their own, plus perquisites.

Breaking in new houseboys is, I think, one of the hardest jobs of the Rhodesian housewife. Like most settlers I had come to the country full of love for my black brothers. I had thought of them as faithful "Poor old Joe's" and motherly "Coal-black Mammies," willing to serve and, if necessary, to lay down their lives for their white masters. I found ignorance, dirt and quiet indifference. It has taken years for me to begin to understand the native, appreciate his good points and realise that the difficulty is caused by different standards of right and wrong; that there is a certain limit of efficiency with each native, beyond which one cannot go. When one reaches this limit one can either take it seriously and grow bitter with chagrin, or take it lightly and laugh.

The proverb "A new broom sweeps clean" could have been invented whilst watching a native servant. A "new broom" sweeps furiously clean. It goes into every corner and up the walls. It cracks against furniture and knocks off lumps of plaster. New dusters dust clean, they rub and polish, they concentrate on chair legs and smudge over pictures. A room when "done" by a new broom looks like "After the Battle."

While the mistress is standing by to tell the boy what his next job is, he keeps her waiting while he concentrates on some minute and unnecessary detail. This is to show her how thorough he is, so that having realised this she will never again trouble to inspect closely. This feverish activity lasts three days, during which the New Broom never rests a moment. Then comes the slump and he will sweep and dust round a thing, see no cobwebs, observe no corners, will put photographs upside-down, cloths inside out, lay sauce and pickles for breakfast and marmalade for dinner. At this critical moment the woman of experience will pounce.

Sometimes the boy will allow himself to be trained; or finding he cannot train his mistress, he will give notice. When he has gone the mistress tells herself that the next boy shall concentrate on the things the other boy refused to do. Usually the new boy takes kindly to these particular jobs; and then, a week later, it is found that the very things the last boy did without being told are anathema to the new one. So it goes on; boys come and go, each turned out on a different point of housecraft, until the mistress realises what things are most vital to her peace of mind, and when a boy suits her in these respects she compromises with the things he cannot or will not do. This is why the boy you found utterly hopeless goes to your next door neighbour and becomes a Joy. Similarly their outcasts may just as easily become your Joys. Only the years teach one how to cope with native servants, so that during their first day of office one knows which brand they are; the intelligent, quick boy who will later on use that intelligence for evading work, or the apparent idiot who may, with patience, become a strict routiner. You must yourself decide whether you will battle with profound ignorance for many months and risk seeing the finished product going off elsewhere to earn better wages, or whether you prefer to have the Bright Boy and spend time daily jumping on him. Expect no Old Joes or Black Mammies, but realise that the boys will tolerate you and sometimes try to please you, but are not in the least fond of you. Only when they have lived and worked for you for many years do they become attached to you, and then they are very tolerant and loyal.

My hope of being the Beloved Mistress of devoted slaves received a nasty shock. Like all newcomers, at first I tried to spoil them so that they would love me, but they just took advantage of my kindness and made Incredible Demands while the sun shone or the iron was hot.

Natives are neither downtrodden slaves nor insolent upstarts, but just Africans .... children of a continent that goes its own way watching with good humour Man's futile attempts to change her face. Africa knows that directly Man tires or she gets tired of him she can very easily cover up his little efforts and carry on as she has always done.

Chapter 4 — Where we lived.

The farmhouse into which we moved, was built in the shape of an "L" with rondavels at each end and in the middle. Between these were smaller, lower rooms whose purpose we found out later seemed to be to receive all the rain from the round, thatched roofs. Not knowing this we were able to select from the many rooms those that pleased us most.

We could afford only a minimum of furniture .... four iron beds, six secondhand bentwood chairs which always gave a jarring rasp on the cement floors, and a plain round table which was reduced in price because it had a crack in it. We also bought a chest-of-drawers for Nkosi's clothes. Looking back, I can see no reason other than that of sheer stupidity for giving him the luxury of smoothly-sliding drawers while my clothes lived in a petrol-box cupboard of my own making.

Our host had a wonderful workshop, and while we were there Nkosi made two Morris chairs, and even to-day the sticks that support the back fall out unexpectedly with a clang and leave one suspended. Then he made a sideboard out of petrol-boxes and a plank. He carved a crude pattern on the little doors with a chisel and a hammer and I stained it and gave it antique drop handles. He said there was no need to put a back to the cupboard part as it could be pushed flush with the wall, which it would have done had not our walls been curved. However, I managed to keep the glasses from falling out, and one day we really will provide a back.

I made wardrobes and cupboards with petrol-boxes and covered them with cretonne; they looked quite nice. Petrol-box furniture may be called quaint or artistic, but it really is a great nuisance to the people who live with it. First of all, it harbours fish-moths and cockroaches. Once these pests have taken up residence, and that is simultaneously with your own, you cannot get rid of them. They are as safe as the defenders of Gibraltar Rock. Another disadvantage of the petrol-box furniture is that nobody but yourself ever draws the curtains. Finally, the boxes need constant restaining and the curtains washing and renewing, for shabby petrol-box furniture is most depressing.

Then rondavels. How newcomers love them! So quaint! So Rhodesian! To me, to live in a perfectly round room is a means to insanity, though many people do not find this so. First of all, suppose you have only two doors to the room and that is few for a Rhodesian house; you come in and you do not know which is the quicker way to the sideboard, so you hesitate thinking it out. When you reach the sideboard, which stands out from the curved wall, you can never be sure what is directly behind you as you would be in a square room. The houseboy may have moved the wretched piece of furniture, so that whereas it was the fireplace that was behind you, you find it is now the armchair, and then all your calculations as to which is the nearer way are useless. I can never rest in a rondavel because I can never be sure just where I am.

The sitting-room looked very attractive. The good pictures brought from England hung on the white-limed walls. One of our dearest possessions was, and still is, a huge picture of the sea, no sight of a sail, no smoke on the horizon, not even a gull, just blue sea, and during our landlocked years this has given us great joy. I put royal blue curtains up at the windows and a little runner to match along the rail of the sideboard. The bentwood chairs were re-stained and given little blue cushion seats tied with tape. The fat Peeps in wriggling from his chair used to break the tapes regularly, but I kept on mending them. Our cherished brass candlesticks shed brightness by day as well as light by night, and as the round table became impregnated with raw linseed oil it took on a gloss which reflected the candlelight on its surface. The Morris chairs with cushions to match at least looked comfortable, and when drawn to a blazing log fire one could almost persuade oneself they were. One other piece of furniture Nkosi made with pride was a small bookcase. This had the habit, and still has, of suddenly diving forward and spilling its contents. We have never discovered the reason.

But I have described the furnishing too soon. Before we could move we had to get as much as possible done in the way of staining and painting, but as the house could not be locked up we did not like to leave anything of value, nor could we unpack the eleven crates we had brought from England.

The day of the move was fixed. We borrowed a waggon which we loaded the night before, for we planned to start directly after breakfast. Our host was bringing out guests from town and wanted our rooms. Unfortunately, Bryan woke up with a cold which would inevitably turn to bronchitis and Nkosi with a touch of the malaria which he had contracted years before in Brazil.

We wrapped Bryan up warmly and all four walked the long mile to our new home.

On arrival I put Bryan straight to bed and poor Nkosi collapsed and he also had to go to bed. This was a shattering blow as he was chief removal man, carpenter, spiritual comforter, besides being sole interpreter.

Our host had promised to bring us some meat from town, but when we sent over, we found he had forgotten it.

Oozing with the Pioneer spirit, I interviewed my cook, a sulky-looking boy named Myros, who did not understand one word of English, not even "kitchen kaffir."

I explained with my hands how to make soup from a packet which with potatoes would be enough for me and the children. I also showed him how to make a vanilla blancmange. He intimated to me with impatience that the meal was as good as cooked, so I left him, marvelling at the way natives could cope with primitive and inconvenient kitchens. My kitchen was both. It was very small and dark and had three doors. The only wall that was not full of doors was given over to a dark, dilapidated, sinister-looking stove. There was a chimney, but that was the last exit the smoke considered. It belched into the room, down the passage, and all over the house. The oven door did not fit at all and a large wad of newspaper had to be shut into it to get the oven even partly warm. There were no firebars or grating. Huge logs of wood were rammed into the cavity and stuck out, dropping ash and cinders on to the cement floor. Only too glad to leave this abomination to the capable Myros, I went to look at my invalids and save Peter from whatever danger threatened. Luckily, that first day I did not know the place was infested with snakes. Somebody might have told us to clear the undergrowth which had advanced upon the unoccupied house and buildings. It was only a week later, after shooting four five-foot snakes during one short Sunday afternoon, that we realised this must be done.

Settling my invalids I went to see what Dick, my houseboy was doing. I had already summed him up while we had been getting the house ready, as a boy of willing incompetence and freakish imagination. His ambition was to do anybody's work but his own. Directly a job found its way on to his routine it lost its charm. I spent a busy morning unpacking, reclaiming Peeps and trying to cheer poor Bryan, who was always so good and patient, and in reassuring an almost delirious Nkosi that everything was under control. Tired out I was glad when Dick, changed into spotless white, announced that lunch was served. He had laid the table unaided and had put on everything that we could conceivably want and I was so tired I could not bother to eliminate, but smiled wanly, pushed Peter's chair in, and sat down feeling really hungry. Then, with a flourish of cloths Dick brought my mammoth meat dish on which was a lumpy brown mass, the soup, with potatoes dotted about like half submerged rocks. A mistake, but never mind it would taste all right. But it didn't. Peter said it was "Disgustingoo" and having told him he was wrong, I found he was only too right. The mess was sweet and then I realised that my chef had mixed soup, potatoes and vanilla blancmange together. It was too disgusting, so we had bread and jam. My faith in Myros was destroyed.

None of the five servants Nkosi, in his kindly ignorance had

engaged for me, was trained. They were just ambitious farm-
boys who were out to get what they could from a "newone
boss". In achieving this ambition they were greatly aided by
our not understanding their language.

Kitchen Kaffir is a bastard language which has to be
learned by master and servant alike. When one realises the
different accents brought from the Old Country, it seems a
wonder that any means of verbal communication can be
found. The natives soon learn however, that it pays to try
to understand Nkosi, but with a mere Nkosikas, whose only
weapon is words, it is safe to assume complete blankness.

My Nkosi is clever at languages and when he first arrived
he bought a book on Chiswina, the language of the indigenous
native; but he soon found that many of the boys came from
Nyasaland and spoke Chinyanja. He bought a book on
Chinyanja and then found that it still served only a few
because the boys came from different tribes. In spite of his
good intentions, therefore, he had to fall back on Kitchen
Kaffir. We were able to buy a book and even I, a fool at
languages, managed to grasp a few words. This with a pair
of mobile hands sufficed, for I could always ask the children
who in a few weeks could converse easily with the boys.

My third boy was paid by me but really belonged to Myros.
Myros demanded a picannin to help him.

Evidently he thought that washing up was a waste of his
skilled time. This picannin did all the washing up, chopped
the wood, made the fire and carried the water. He also
washed and ironed Myros' clothes. Myros did nothing at all
but smoke by the fire and when he went for his afternoon's
rest from one until six he left the kitchen in a filthy state.

The fourth boy was a washboy who, having been engaged,
had gone off to collect his wife and family. A washboy was
what I needed most as I had not liked to give our host's boy
much washing and there was still an accumulation of soiled
clothes. Myros refused to help me over this and Dick running
round and doing everything breathlessly wrong all day had
no time at all. The fifth boy was a garden boy who out of
the tangled undergrowth had excavated three or four beds in
which he had sown many packets of seeds while we were up
at the other house. These beds were hailed with delight by
every insect for miles around and the birds watched anxiously
on the trees ready to pounce on anything the insects could
not manage to consume.

This boy was a genius at managing to look busy. If I came

upon him suddenly he would pick up a water-can and trail along with it giving out long groans, so proving that it was only sheer exhaustion that had caused him to pause in his work. If he was discovered bending over a bed presumably asleep, he would point out the insect he was watching. When you could not find him and waited for his return he would embarrass you by telling you he had "gone into the veld", and when you ventured to say that he had been a long time, he intimated that if that were so it was Nature's fault, not his. Now I can deal with such as he, but in those days I was completely at his mercy.

At this time every boy brought a diminutive picannin who he suggested should "boss-up" *lo picannin boss.* I did not take kindly to the idea of allowing a dirty little picannin to have control of white children, nor did I wish my children to have a picannin to order about, so I decided to bring up my children myself and use the African for house-work. My Picannin Bosses should not become lazy and dependent on a native's help and should learn to take care of themselves. Anyway Peter was too independent to be bossed up, and Bryan did not like the natives near him.

I managed to cure my two patients and get fairly straight but was still frightened when left alone, though I did not let Nkosi know this.

One morning I was sitting machining at a rickety table on the front veranda when I was aware of a tall black figure wrapped in a blanket, standing on the other side of the wire-netting, a foot away, gazing at me fixedly. I caught my breath! I felt sure he was a local chief who had come to demand that I surrender my money or have my throat cut. I jumped up, flushed, my heart racing as I heard the slow solemn words he repeated over and over again. Then Peter said calmly, "He wants soap," and I realised the fatal words were "Me want Seep." It was Samson the washboy, and when I greeted him his huge black face broke into a cheery grin. Samson was the first boy I liked. He was good with the children, taught them what dangers to avoid and amused them by making them strange toys. He used to play with Peter, pounce out on him and chase him, and I would hear shrieks of laughter and see Samson giving Peter a wild ride on his back. It was Samson who discovered the snakes, and so the awful anxiety I had over the children's safety abated.

We settled in and soon the house was running fairly smoothly. The Staff was twice the size it should have been, but that is not a bad fault to begin with. One has to learn to manage native labour and use it to the best advantage. I soon accepted the Black Magic which abounds in an ordinary Rhodesian house. How things disappear, are asked for, and reappear in strange places. How the natives walk from the kitchen door into the fourth dimension. How twelve spoons turn out to be ten spoons, how tea and coffee sink in their tins and sugar disintegrates without human aid. Now I realise the magic is a combination of a few facts. First, the dozens of doors; second, lack of understanding of language; third, the habit a native has of half stealing and fourth, the white woman's faulty memory, which seems to come with the sun.

However, I got along and was able to continue teaching Bryan, for there was no hope of a school even had he been strong enough to go. Bryan was a slender boy with fair, curly hair and big grey eyes, blacklashed; he had a fine white skin and pink cheeks. Just before we left England he had been a page at the wedding of one of my friends, and had worn pink velvet knickers and a white silk shirt. I had made Peter knickers and smock to match, and the first time we were asked out for Sunday afternoon I dressed both my little darlings in their velvet and silk suits. I had a great tussle with Peter and only the threat of being left behind made him consent to wear the hated garb. Bryan wore the tie pin he had "won at a wedding for holding up the train the best." They both looked lovely in their mother's eyes. Peter, his gold hair brushed down in front until it shone and fluffed up behind in its own peculiar way looked decidedly cross. That was the last time they wore silk and velvet, the last time the clothes were fit to wear; they saw to that. Afterwards they wore khaki every day, with white or coloured shirts and grey flannels for best. That was the end of my pretty little darlings.

Housekeeping was very difficult. All groceries had to be ordered by post a week before and on the day they were supposed to arrive a native had to walk the six miles to the siding to fetch them back. If they did not arrive we had to send the next day that the train came out. Naturally, packages could not be above a certain weight and the native took the whole day for the journey. The Official who had interviewed us when we arrived had told us that it was quite unnecessary for a settler to have a car, but we found he did not know what he was talking about. Trains went to Salisbury only three days a week reaching town at one o'clock if there was

no delay. The train back left town at 6 the following morning
so even if we could have walked to the siding it meant that
we should have to spend three nights in town every time we
went. The expenses of this would soon pay for an old car.
Sometimes neighbours gave us a lift, but we could not rely
on this and had to buy most of our groceries at the little store
run by a Jew when the boy went to the siding for the mail.
He was a very nice, obliging man but his charges were high.

We soon realised, therefore, that the first need of a settler
is to have some form of transport of his own and decided to
buy a car. Through neighbours we managed to get one for
£30 and were given a lift to town to collect it.

As Nkosi had never driven in his life, a young man took
us as far as the siding and then left Nkosi to manage on
his own.

His face set, Nkosi wrestled with the gears. I remember
so well the agonised jerks and the family's tactful silence.
The calm of the level road brought smiles of joy and relief
which turned to breathless silence when we skidded through
sand, plunged through the river, and crawled up the steep
bank. It never struck me that Nkosi would not be able to
manage and I am sure I never thought to congratulate him
on this achievement. The car was a great blessing and meant
that we could go to the siding once a week, to town once a
month, and out visiting on Sundays. Nkosi tried to teach me
to drive, but, like most husbands, found it irritating, and after
we narrowly escaped an accident by his insane order,
"Quick put your foot on the what's-its-name," he asked a
friend to teach me.

There were very few neighbours and I found them difficult
to get on with. Looking back I think it must have been my
own fault because I did not like Rhodesia. My heart was in
England, and instead of trying to understand the people, I
was angry they were not like those I had left behind.

However, I met Margaret, a young English girl staying
about six miles away, who later on when she married and
lived in Salisbury became our best and most loyal friend
through all the years.

The few neighbours who called told me how to make
yeast and how to preserve the very disappointing fruit
Rhodesia has to offer. The methods I had used in Kent were
either wrong or impossible. My neighbours were full of
advice and, as each woman held opposite views on each
subject, I was worried which view to take and seemed always

in the wrong. Nkosi was also given advice but he took it with
bags of salt, for he said he would only listen to farmers who
were making their farms pay, and these were very few in
those days. However, he learned how Not to Do many things.
Each farmer told us that he was the only good farmer in the
district; that those who earned more were lucky and those
who earned less were fools. We soon found that the only
thing agreed on was that the roads were frightful and that
something ought to be done about them. At the same time
no-one was going to fill in a hole so that "old So-and-so"
should benefit: rather than that they would swerve away
from the hole and swear till the road became one long twist
of evasions. We learned that if you stuck on somebody else's
road it was your bad driving but if they stuck on yours it
was your bad road.

The rains broke suddenly. Though we had been warned
of the fury of the tropical storms, we had not visualised
their ferocity. In a few minutes the sitting-room was
marooned from the rest of the house by the water that had
run off the roofs of the rondavels into the little adjoining
rooms and passages. There was intense activity, while everyone rushed around pushing furniture about, catching drips
and diverting cascades. The passage was a foot deep in water
and the kitchen received its first real cleaning but unfortunately (I know now inevitably) Myros had not a dry
stick saved for emergencies, so there was no hot water for
tea and no prospect of anything hot or cooked for dinner.

As Rhodesian houses are all built for sunny days the
sudden darkening of the skies makes a sort of extra night.
This, of course, does not matter for one is usually far too
busy salvaging and protecting one's belongings to notice it.
One good thing about storms is that they never last long;
nearly always they clear up before sunset; very seldom we
are not cheered by the last gleams of a watery sun. If there
is time before the sun goes down we always go out and
measure the rain, view the damage, smell the freshly washed
earth and watch the uprising of the thousands of little fairy-
like flying ants into the air. The children always love playing
with the washed sand and paddling in the clean puddles.
After this we had to change our suite of rooms.

The waiting period between two chapters of life is difficult.
After the first interest of the new country had worn off I was
very unhappy and took little pleasure in anything. Nkosi

was discontented, hated an inactive life and had counted on the rains bringing him more work, but there was not enough to keep even the manager very busy.

Nkosi, who always rose at dawn, finished his work by ten o'clock and was bored and morose. Sometimes he hardly spoke all day. I was peeved about this, but now I see that it was because he was longing to get on to his own farm and start wiping out the previous failure. In my youth and lack of wisdom I thought it was selfishness, and pitied myself immensely. I was very homesick, too, because I had been used to a busy creative sort of life. Being Home-born and white-skinned I found that any exposure to the sun brought on a bilious attack. I took little pleasure in the children because I was worried to death whenever they were out of sight. The warnings about snakes, scorpions, tarantulas, sunstroke and wicked natives were always in my mind. I adopted a formula which I repeated every time they went out. "Don't go into the grass! Don't go near the well! Boss-up for snakes and keep your hats on!" Even then I was always on the alert for an emergency which I felt I should be incompetent to meet and which would, therefore, prove fatal.

I spent hours writing to my mother. She loved my letters and thought I was a heroine. "My brave darling, how can you do such things?" I think this is the most wonderful thing about mothers, they believe in one so utterly. In her eyes I was brave and clever, and this belief helped me to be brave and to try to be clever. No one knows what our mothers have been to us, the home-makers of the colonies. As I said to the Pioneer, Godfrey King,

"One gets so tired of always being somebody's something, as somebody's mother, somebody's wife, somebody's mistress." I meant, of course, a native's mistress but he took it the wrong way and made me laugh. I meant that there was always a position to keep up, always a part to play, one could never be a separate individual.

The first year dragged on. I did not like the natives because I could not manage them properly. I did not like the sun because it made me sick. I did not enjoy my neighbours because we had few things in common. The bond of chickens and crops was yet to come.

Early in the new year Nkosi began harassing the Lands Department to find him a farm. The Government land available in those days was practically in the tsetse fly belt and Nkosi was taken out by an official to view what there was. He found it many miles from the railhead and the boring machine for supplying water was promised within the next three years. They bumped over rough, overgrown tracks and stopped at farmhouses where lived lonely, rather peculiar people. At one farm, a widower was making little attempt to bring up a family of fever-stricken children. Another farmhouse was black with flies and Nkosi was shown five lion-skins whose owners had been shot that week. The woman begged Nkosi to bring his wife and children out, because all her other female neighbours had died of fever.

Nkosi came back determined that nothing would make him accept any of the tracts of land offered. He said that even if he could grow maize it would not be worth the cost of getting it to the railhead. He decided to find a farm nearer Salisbury and civilisation. We were lucky enough to discover a tract of virgin land about fifteen miles away from where we were staying, and under a new scheme, we were to pay a fifth of the price in cash and the rest, with interest, over twenty years.

Towards the end of the year our employer who had been abroad returned, and as he had promised to reward Nkosi for having diagnosed a disease in his cattle and given the necessary injections, he had said we might live in his house rent free, with some of his staff, and all his produce until we were settled on our own farm. This was very generous of him.

We carefully packed everything into our crates and sewed our pieces of furniture in canvas and moved into the beautiful farm house. This time I had Myros, my still inefficient cook-boy, Samson my nice wash-boy and Dick; and as the only servant left in the house was the head house-boy, I was able to make a better stand.

Two days after we had settled in we received a letter from a stranger saying the house was let to him and would we please vacate it as soon as possible as he had an uncle waiting at the coast. The deal had been made by wire while our employer was travelling down to the Cape. I refused. For once in my life I was not amenable and told Nkosi to say we were not going. Major Y then came to visit us. The river was swollen and each party looked angrily over the intervening angry waters. Finally, he decided to wade over and we drove him back to the house. This is the only time in my life I have taken business out of Nkosi's hands. He would have agreed to move, but I had made up my mind that nothing would make me unpack again until I did so in my own house; threats, bribes, nothing would avail. I said I would leave when we had found a farm. It would not be long. Then he began offering a bribe, he would give us five pounds a month if we would go. I said I had no intention of going and felt quite sorry for him because I knew nothing would persuade me. I was not to be bribed. I would not unpack again. He talked on and on. After another half an hour he said "I will give you ten pounds a month if you will go." Then I found Nkosi looking at me sternly and before I knew what had happened I had given in gracefully. I was rather ashamed of myself at the time, but in later years have boasted of it as my one good business deal.

It was not a great deal of trouble unpacking and when I unpacked the large crate containing blankets and rugs I found we had packed a pregnant mouse.

Chapter 5 — How we moved.

People whose idea of a move is based on the English pantechnicon from which spring kindly men who pack everything as skilfully as possible, whisk it away, and unpack it in the new house, have no idea what A Move is like in Rhodesia. A native's idea of a move is to move things. It does not matter where or how as long as they are put in a different place.

Our move necessitated a trek through almost untouched veld. Our vehicles were a large heavy waggon drawn by 16 oxen, and our old car for the light things, livestock and breakables.

When we took up this piece of 2,500 acres of virgin land we found a faint track through the veld which the previous owner had used on his twice-yearly camping trips. There were no fences or visible boundaries for the land around belonged either to absentee landlords, or to farmers who left large tracts of land undeveloped. It seemed to us as if we were right in the heart of darkest Africa just as the books say. Two tall pointed kopjes, called by us the Twin Kopjes, and by the natives *lo Belli ka lo umfazi* (the woman's breasts), marked one of the beacons, but the others were only hearsay as the farm had not been surveyed.

The previous owner had built a *pole and dagga* hut in which the women of the party slept, while the men had a grass shelter. In preparation for the house they were going to build one day when they retired, they had planted a jacaranda drive. A native, Beza, was in charge and his job was to cut down the grass round the hut every year, so that when the veld fires swept through the country the hut would not be destroyed. Afterwards the neighbours told us that the yearly fires always came from our direction and this gave us reason to believe that Beza used to set fire to the grass from the hut outwards. In this way the jacaranda trees had been burned yearly, and we only discovered them when some of the six-foot grass had been cleared away.

For a week before the move, Nkosi had gone backwards and forwards taking the things he needed most, so the track had become quite clear. Like the Anglo-Saxons, Rhodesians take the line of least resistance, and when antbears make their sudden holes or trees fall in the way, they merely swerve into the veld to avoid them and return as soon as possible to the track. So Nkosi swerved and by the time the family was ready to move, the road Home was tortuous.

On the day of the move, I rose early and instead of cupping my small, delicate face in my hands and watching the dawn, as Frances did, I wrapped my head in a scarf and began to work. I rolled up my bedding, then turned Nkosi and the children out of their beds, and rolled them up (beds). Then after feeding hastily, we began loading the waggon.

This drew up to the house with great crackings of the whip and screams from James, our driver. There are no adequate words to describe a native driver addressing his span of oxen. It is a mixture of an hysterical woman in full cry and a pig being caught for weighing. James was one of the most soul-shattering drivers I have known. The waggon arrived, and he gave that peculiar shrill whistle which means "Stop!" Then pandemonium reigned, for our staff of newly engaged house-and-farm boys began to move. Foolish greenhorns, we had not known what would happen. Like a swarm of ants they attacked our household effects. Everything was seized by willing black hands. Our prized, now beautifully polished, round table was carried away on a woolly head, and by rushing after it, screaming, I saved it from being put top first on a batch of saucepans. Many hands, when black, do not make light work, though black fingers are certainly light. A Move is a grand opportunity for petty theft. With so many boys

about, nothing can be traced to any one boy. I did not know
that when a household moves in many stages from one place
to another, the hammer, the sharp kitchen knife and the bicycle
pump are always in the "other kaia" * and by the time you
have proved that they are in neither they have gone for ever.

While he moves, a native chatters, he also clowns, bumps
into his companions, pretends he is wounded to death and
laughs all the time. "Natives," wrote Nkosi when he preceded
me to Rhodesia, "are a good-humoured lot and are always
having jokes among themselves." They certainly are good-
humoured, but when you have a vital move on, it is difficult
to appreciate a flow of wit and buffoonery. They never
listen to what they are told; if they listen they do not understand what is said; if they both hear and understand, then they
do the exact opposite, not from illwill, but from a sudden
unexpected and unwanted stirring of an otherwise completely
dormant initiative. To tell one boy not to move a thing is
useless, you must tell each one, and some twice over. Even
then a zealous ignorant will understand his mistress to have
said that was the very thing she wanted him to move. As our
country architects (ourselves) are not clever with passages and
halls, the number of doors to a Rhodesian house, as I have
already said, is appalling and this house had more doors than
any I have known. Doors are maddening things because, as
the art of managing natives is to prevent them in all or most
of their ways, a superfluity of doors makes this impossible.
While I prevented one boy from taking down the kitchen
shelves, a fixture belonging to the house, another ran off with
my hat in the pastry bowl. I had put it there for only a
moment. While I raced after my hat, a third carried off my
Box of Cooked Food which was to be the mainstay of the
family for the next day or so. Then, hat on head for safety, I
had the Food Box brought back, and found the large trunk
had been spirited away. Rushing after it, I stopped its being
heaved on top of an open box of last-minute crockery which,
of course, was not to travel by waggon at all. When I got
back, another boy had taken the kitchen shelves right down.

At last the waggon was loaded and the kitchen shelves
refixed, and a further attempt to dislodge them was met with
a scornful "uh! Uh!" from the previous offender who registered
surprise and disgust that any boy could be as foolish as to
think of doing such a thing. Finally, I shoo'd them all out,

---

* "Kaia" means "house" or "room" or "hut".

and locked all the doors with a masterkey Nkosi had made.

I went outside and saw the waggon was fully packed. The mattresses were placed on the very top, ready it seemed to me to roll to the ground at the first lurch. To keep them in place were the bentwood chairs (now four only), which raised scandalised legs to the sky. Gardening implements, umbrellas and other ill-assorted companions were lashed together unhappily; very much, I thought, like some married couples. I mentioned this to Nkosi as he stood there, but he said, "I don't know why you brought out an umbrella, they are no use here, when it rains you get wet." I cannot forbear to say "Ah, little did he know!"

When it seemed that nothing more could be done. James cracked his whip over the oxen, "Bulawayo! England! Very nice! Whisky!" he shrieked, and the oxen thus addressed by name began to pull. The next moment there was terrible confusion. The picannin pulling the leaders had entangled them round a jacaranda tree and in trying to obey the shouted instructions of every boy in sight, had made matters worse, so now the oxen, reins, yokes and tree were all hopelessly mixed, the oxen were backing and butting at each other, and a complete deadlock had been reached. James, despairing of ever getting them unravelled, climbed on to the waggon to find the chopper in order to cut down the tree. He had started rummaging for it in the box that held our shoes when Nkosi, who had been getting the car ready, came up. As usual he took charge of the emergency and, giving the boys a short, pithy history of their immediate ancestry in which I believe baboons figured largely, he sorted out everything, freed the oxen and saved the tree. Once more the waggon lurched off, this time followed by a shouting Myros, waving the frying-pan which had been left behind. James' renewed shrieks to his oxen made him deaf to Myros' shouts, so it was not until every boy within a hundred yards had joined in the cry that he realised something was up and gave the long shrill whistle.

The waggon safely on its journey we then had to finish packing the car by catching the livestock. First there was Mrs. Mashona, a very old hen we had bought from the natives for eating, but who had been saved from the pot by having laid an egg. This was nearly a year ago and since then she had controlled her output, so that only when the pot loomed did she lay. A few weeks previously she had decided to go broody and pushing a sister from her legitimate nest, she had reared six healthy chickens. The other hens travelled on the waggon, but Mrs. Mashona was privileged.

Then Nkosi began to pack his family and the breakables into the car. The two children squashed in front, Bryan holding Fluff, the cat, and Peter with Biddie, the dog, held between his fat knees. At their feet was the sack of sugar, not breakable, but "breakinable", and therefore not to be out of sight. I was put in the back as a shock absorber. On my lap were the two baskets of week-old chicks we had hatched in our new incubator, and a box of setting eggs was at my side. On my other side were the large mirror we had bought at great expense and our large sea picture. Between my knees was a big enamel jug half-full of boiled milk. The incubator straddled the box of eggs, and Nkosi impressed on me how careful I must be that the bracket that held the lamp was not broken off. As this could only be done against my unwilling flesh I was as careful as possible.

The swerves in the road threw me off my balance and I had to wait in whatever position I found myself until a swerve the other way put me right. The bumps, too, were most disturbing. Every few minutes the breakables and I bounced into the air and never came down quite in the same position. Desperately and feebly I had to try to right these things, helped by Myros and Dick who were standing on the running-board on either side. How I wished they were in the car and I had the freedom and comfort of the running-board. Every muscle of my body ached. I think on these occasions the body tries to recover primitive powers of holding on, for the soles of my feet ached with trying to obtain purchase as my ancestors had on boughs, and the muscles of my seat were also strained as if some instinct remained in me to hold on with my long-lost tail. My shoes were soon full of milk, but I planned to use it for Fluff. Now and then after an extra bump or swerve Nkosi looked back and said, "All right?" taking the silence for consent instead of exhaustion.

We passed the waggon on the way. As they heard the car, the natives who were sprawling upon the bedding, slipped down and by the time we caught them up they were plodding beside the waggon. As I could not bear to think of their unwashed, verminous bodies on the bedding, I made Nkosi stop and tell them on no account were they to ride on the waggon. They replied that they would not dream of doing such a thing.

We arrived and I was dug out. Nkosi expressed his satisfaction that nothing had suffered hurt and congratulated himself on having driven so carefully. When my "pins and needles" were bearable, I limped into the hut. It was completely full. Nkosi had done this during his many journeys. Where were the things in the car to go? What about the waggon-load? There was no other shelter but a tiny broken-down hut which was to house the pots and pans. I demanded that all the farm implements and impediments should be removed at once and commented on the strong smell of cows. Nkosi said it must be the ox-reins, and reminded me how lucky we were to find a ready-built hut which, with a little patching up, was weather-tight.

While the hut was being cleared I told Myros to make tea, and I gave the children some sandwiches from the Food-Box. Oh, how we worked, while the sun began its descent! By dark, six o'clock, I had to have the four beds made up and all things that could be stolen, all creatures that could be molested by wild animals, sheltered in the hut. The floor sloped upwards and outwards like a saucer and the four beds met in the middle so that the slimmest body, even sideways, could not cross the room between them. We managed somehow. Mrs. Mashona, family and friends were barricaded in coops outside, the week-old chicks were in a box under the bed. The flour and the sugar sacks lolled against the chest of drawers. However, the children were clean and comfortable in their own beds, sharing our one mosquito net. Completely exhausted, I crept out.

The shiny round table had been placed as far under the eaves as it would go and it stood at an angle. Dick had laid it with the dinner mats and the brass candlesticks and placed a chair on either side. Dinner . . . . soup, fried eggs and bacon with fried potatoes, was served out of the darkness; how, I did not care. We levered up the congealed food from the cold plates in silence. When Dick had cleared away, I still sat at the table watching the guttering candles. Nkosi put on one of our two gramophone records, "In a Monastery Garden". It sounded very beautiful in the still dark night. Nkosi walked up and down, I could see the moving tip of his cigarette.

"When they had finished coffee Frances sat on with head on her arms while Hugh, lighting a cigarette, walked up and down in the darkness. The fierceness of the wind had died down again, and the veld was very still and silent and the dark velvety sky was studded with stars. A black sea of grass surrounded the hut, swishing and whispering very gently.

There was no glimmer of light to be seen anywhere. She stretched her arms across the glossy table. Home seemed very far away. She felt lonely, small and insignificant. Around her stretched wild, untouched country. She and Hugh were going to wrestle with this great dark land. She wondered what awaited them in the darkness. As the veld closed round them so did the future; unknown, impenetrable. What was it Rhodes had said, had quoted as he died? 'So much to do .... so little done.'"

PART II

THE CROWDED DAYS

Chapter 6 — Water!

AS the first streaks of dawn came through the curtain-less window, I woke stiff and tired but kept quite still pretending to be asleep. When Dick knocked at the door Nkosi got up and said,
"Blast it! My slippers have gone and this loose earth has got between my toes."

Our floor was supposed to be made of beaten earth but it was quite soft and already each of the sixteen iron bed legs had dug itself to a different level. Nkosi took the tray and looked round for somewhere to put it in the overcrowded hut. Knowing that my prostrate stomach was the only horizontal surface not cluttered up, I sat up quickly and took the tray on my knees.

Bryan and Peter by this time were wide awake and leaping about under the net.

"Can we get up?" they cried.

"No," I replied, "Daddy must dress first, there is only room for one at a time."

"If that," said Daddy removing Biddie from his shirt, which had slipped to the floor and shaking it indignantly. "To-morrow night that dog sleeps outside." Dressed in shorts, shirt and jersey he paused before opening the ill-fitting door to give final instructions. "I'm off now. See that the children don't get lost in the grass, there are heaps of snakes. Keep them away from the rocks, I saw another python yesterday. Don't let them climb the Kopje or they will fall down the precipice and be killed. Don't let them go anywhere near the spruit and see they keep their hats on."

Off he went and I added to myself, "Yes, and see that some-how without a stove in a high driving wind breakfast is cooked and served. Make the beds, unpack, set up housekeeping without a house and . . . . "Heavens!" I said aloud, "How this place smells of cows! Daddy should not have put ox-reims in here."

"It isn't that," said Bryan. "The boys mended the holes in

the wall with cattle-dung. They did it when I came here the other day with Daddy and he said I was not to tell you until after we had moved in."

"What on earth for!" I said indignantly, "Cattledung!"

"Yes," said Bryan, "They mix it with the *daga* because it makes it strong."

Once dressed — and this was quite easy as my clothes were in a basket — I helped the children dress and sent them outside with all the warnings Nkosi had given me plus a few I had thought out myself, such as meddling with the car or the things on the waggon. Bryan stood hesitatingly at the door.

"Well," I said, "what are you waiting for?"

"I was wondering what to do," he said, in his serious way. "You seem to have thought of everything." I gave him a hug and sent him off and . . . . here I see Frances, always ready for an effective pose, stood for a moment at the doorway, looking at the fresh veld around her. For me it was too darned cold and I shut the door turning with thankfulness to the fug of the hut, a thing no self-respecting heroine would dream of doing.

The first thing to do was to make the beds, but I was stumped at once. Although there seemed no floor space on which to stand the sheets had managed to find sufficient to become brown with dirt. When finished I felt as if I had done a bout of violent physical jerks. Though the beds looked odd shapes I left them, because I had a feeling Myros would be doing something wholly unnecessary.

The kitchen hut was old and dirty. It had no window and instead of a door it had an aperture four foot high and this meant doubling up when you entered for there was a sharp jutting-out stick in the thatch and if you were lucky it only spiked your hat off. When my eyes got used to the gloom, I saw Myros busily unpacking the china and kitchen utensils all over the dirty floor. "*Aikona*" (no) I said, with the inflection "not yet." "This *kaia* is very dirty, you must lime it before you put the things out."

Myros' face fell, his hope that cleanliness could not be maintained in a daga hut was dashed. His horselike face always lent itself more easily to indignation and exasperation than to smiles.

"First," I said, "you must make the porridge."

"Lo pollige," he said with restraint, "I have made already."

"Now, you will cook five eggs, *fife eggis*, and leave this for by and by."

Myros said nothing very strongly, a native's way of registering stern disapproval.

The next thing to do was to attack the drinking-water problem.

Above the tall grass a green bough was bobbing up and down, coming nearer and nearer. Dick was bringing water from the *vlei* (marshy ground with water holes). Gradually, a petrol-tin appeared under the bough, then Dick's head, then finally he himself stepped out of the grass and, putting the tin down, removed the green bough which had prevented the water from slopping over.

The water was neither clean nor clear. Bits of stick and leaves were floating on top, some animal life was paddling about in the middle and at the bottom was a muddy sediment. I strained it through muslin into the large kettle which I set between two stones, removing the small kettle in which the water for breakfast tea was boiling. Myros always liked it to boil at least an hour before making tea. All boys do this. They tilt up the lid so that the water may keep on the boil without spilling over. I fed the little fire with sticks taken from the porridge fire and explained to Myros, who was watching my interference gloomily, that the big kettle was for drinking water and was not to be removed under any consideration. As I left him I saw him preparing yet another little fire, presumably for the *fife eggis*.

By this time Dick was trying to lay the polished table for breakfast and the high wind was having a game with him. When he put the cloth down it blew up at the far corner. Slowly he walked to the other side of the table and pulled it down, whereupon the wind promptly lifted the corner he had left. Then he walked round and the same thing happened. I watched him fascinated, wondering how long he would proceed from side to side. Finally I suggested some stones and these placed at each corner solved the difficulty. Dick gave a beam of admiration. Whether he admired me or not — probably not — Dick was always an appreciative audience which was infinitely better than Myros' hurt disapproval.

Now the hut demanded attention. The little chickens were peeping shrilly to be let out but it was far too cold. They must just go on peeping, they had not half as much to put up with as I had. With great energy I put things inside each other and threw other things outside under the eaves. I had reclaimed several feet of floor space when Dick knocked at the door and said "Leady Skoff."

Leaving the hut I went first to the large kettle which I judged should be nearly boiling. It had gone. Myros, on his haunches, was squatting over the red embers making toast. He explained that he had poured the water off into the watersacks.

"But I wanted to see it boil!"

"It boiled!" said Myros sulkily.

"Stelek?" (Strongly).

"Stelek! Nyannis! (truth) *Trutugod!*" replied Myros, evidently of the opinion that a lie worth telling is worth telling well.

Unconvinced, I ran to the tree from which the sacks were still swinging. The water was certainly hot but it had never reached boiling point. It seemed unnatural that the kettle should boil just as Myros wanted the embers for toast. I know now that natives think it is a mad trick to heat water, then cool it before drinking it. If, as their masters tell them, there are *skellums* (animals) in the water, why not take them out? If, on the other hand, these *skellums* are too small to be seen, why worry about drinking them? When Nkosi came up I explained the situation, and he said we must not risk it and the water must be reboiled. Myros was called and made to refill the kettle which he did with a very bad grace. Telling him not to move it from the fire whatever happened, I followed Nkosi to the table. The cloth had shaken itself free from a stone and dabbled itself in the milk and the marmalade. We sat down at uncomfortable angles and ate our porridge in a biting wind.

"We must look like a futurist family," I said brightly as I propped a stone under Peter's chair. Nkosi gave an exclamation of annoyance as he tried to find resting places for all four legs of his chair at once.

"Couldn't you have found a better place than this?" he asked.

I did not answer but with purposeful brightness continued buttering the children's bread. "I wonder," I said as I dug out an entombed ant, "what would be the best way to keep ants from the bread? Can you think of anything?"

"No," replied Nkosi, "I've too many other things to think about. You have no idea what I have on hand. Boys stumping, clearing grounds, burning, ploughing, brick-making. You must think out some way yourself."

"I know," said Bryan, "couldn't you get four balloons and fill them with gas and have the breadbox hanging from them?" Bryan always had the mind of a great inventor.

"That is a very good idea," I said, "and the only way in the world one could be sure of stopping ants."

Bryan beamed. "I have two balloons," he began; but his father said, "Don't talk nonsense, the way as you know, is to put each leg in a small tin of paraffin and see that the box does not lean against the wall."

"The bread-box," I replied "has no legs. It is a petrol-box holding two petrol-tins and it used to hang from the kitchen rafters."

"Well, sling it from a tree."

Here in my novel, I described Hugh leaving the breakfast-table and striding through the grass away to the lands which he had cleared in the veld, thinking of all the work ahead. To alienate my readers' sympathy from him and fix it on Frances, I referred to Hugh's stooping and short-sightedness.

Nkosi's thoughts would be the same as Hugh's anyhow. How the rains would break in four months' time and by then he had to mould the bricks, sun-dry them, burn them, cool them and build his house, none of which things he had done before. Also before that time he had to find fairly level stretches of suitable land, stump them clear and prepare them for a crop. He knew that many settlers do not build a brick house at first, but put up a collection of *daga* huts; but he was determined to put up a permanent house of some sort for our sakes, mainly on account of Bryan's continuous bouts of bronchitis. The crop would have to be maize because tobacco had just slumped.

Some years after the 1914—18 war, tobacco had boomed and an official had come to Rhodesia from England and with great enthusiasm had told the Rhodesian planters to put in all the tobacco they could as Britain could take all that was grown. The planters were only too glad to do this. Money was spent lavishly, credit given for the asking, and then, of course, when the crop was grown and cured, Britain could not buy it and the planters went broke. This was the end of the Tobacco Planters Period, of Gertrude Page's Rhodesia. Most of those planters packed up and went Home. This was not really bad for the country in the long run, because those who remained were those who loved the land, who were farmers at heart, and from them has been built up the real farming community we have to-day.

Nkosi, after his four gruelling years of war, eight equally gruelling years of unrewarded work on our Kentish farm, and one year of workless boredom, was ready for the fray. Maize was easy and it made eleven or more shillings a bag. One hundred and fifty acres of maize yielding even eight bags per acre, and sold for even ten shillings per bag, would bring in six hundred pounds. He would make good if he could get through the next hard months. A failure to a man like Nkosi can never be forgotten until it is wiped out by success, he was therefore weighed down by work and responsibility.

While Nkosi was striding over the veld, his wife was trying to find places for the things she had ejected from the hut. Anyhow I was very busy, when I suddenly remembered the drinking water. I knew Myros was not going to remind me. I ran over to the fire and there was the kettle rattling with impatience and gushing water on to the fire which hissed in loud protest. Myros informed me plaintively that the fire would soon be dead, but I ignored him and told him to begin liming the kitchen. He was not at all pleased about this. He told me he had not seen the lime. I led him to it. He told me the brush was dead. I found a new one. He told me he had no water but I showed him he had enough in a tin. Giving a sigh which was almost a groan he started on the lumpy walls. Leaving him I poured the well-boiled water in the drinking sack and hung it from a tree.

The water question settled I turned to my poultry, and after much nervous disturbance we had them all settled. I then attacked the question of Food. When I opened the Box of Cooked Foods I found it was colonised with black ants. There was a plain cake with clusters of ants like currants. The joint of beef was also swarming and the paper of butter was an ant mortuary. The opened tin of marmalade was filled with another variety, the sugar-ant which to the ignorant always looks as if it were walking backwards. It took some time to get rid of these visitors, and when the food was at last fairly free I had to find some place to put it inaccessible to ants.

As there remained but one loaf in the bread-box, Dick and I decided to use this box for cake and biscuits, and sling it from a tree. First of all we had to persuade the ants to leave their newly discovered home in which they had settled down very happily. Shakings, beatings and bangings had no result at all and we had to heat the box by the fire before the ants decided to evacuate. Dick, delighted to leave his usual work, helped me gladly and Bryan and Peter took the part of audience.

"There," I said with pride, "Unless they crawl right along the branch they won't be able to get inside."

"They wouldn't mind doing that," said Bryan wisely.

Then much ingenuity had to be used to plan how the rest of the food might be kept from attack. We slung the little safe from another tree, and the meat inside it was placed on an upturned bowl so that the invaders would have difficulty in climbing. The marmalade tin, remains of the milk, and the butter were placed on dishes of water.

Full of pride I left the scene of triumph and turned to the kitchen *kaia*. To my surprise Myros just finished it but looking inside I saw why. Too lazy to get more lime, he had made the mixture very thin so that ugly brown streaks showed everywhere. I told him it would not do and ordered him to get the bag of lime, which he did in stoney silence. He then said he had no more water and taking up the empty petrol tin he went off to the *vlei* and I could see that it would be a long while before he returned. It was annoying that he should prove so difficult, but I cheered myself with the triumphs over the ants and went to look at my handiwork. The safe was immune. Africa was an awkward customer to deal with but perseverence and determination did it!

I went to the bread-box and to my horror found a long black trail of ants was streaming up the tree trunk and out along the branch and I was only just in time to stop the triumphant entry of the pioneers. I called loudly for Dick who came running up. He suggested binding the branch with a rag soaked with paraffin. I routed out an old piece of rag and he bandaged the limb most expertly, but he said the rag must be kept very wet with paraffin or the ants would walk over it. We took the same precautions with the safe and left a jam tin of paraffin ready so that we could keep the bandage sprinkled. As I finished this bit of foresight Dick with broom and dustpan went to the hut, opened the door and stood undecided.

How was it, he said, that he could sweep the floor when there was no floor to sweep? Looking in, I saw my few feet of floor space would not be enough, I must do some more weeding out. The next hour was spent carting out things we had the night before carted in. We sorted out clothes and linen we would not be needing immediately, and locked them in a large trunk which we put as flat against the outside wall as we could.

After we had cleared the hut as much as possible I fixed up the little curtains I had made for the window, and to see them flowing in the gentle breeze which had followed the early morning blast gave the first touch of home. Coming out of the hut I looked for the children and could only see Bryan who was making a miniature garden in the sand with wild flowers, little stones and sticks. He was utterly engrossed.

"Where is Peepy?" I asked. He said he did not know. Peter had kept walking over his garden so he had hit him and he had gone away angry. Peter seldom cried unless he felt it was a good move. He adored Bryan but their ideas of amusement were poles apart. Peter was always for the broad, large, perhaps violent, things in life, and he joyed in companionship of many people. Bryan liked to be by himself and play by himself, and his delight was always in tiny things. I called Peter but there was no answer. I asked Myros who was just returning from the vlei but he had not seen him. I made Dick go and look and I myself climbed up the kopje and scanned the horizon but there was no Peter; just a world of thick waving grass spreading out as far as I could see with a granite kopje rearing here and there. Peter had evidently wandered away and got lost in the grass, which, twice as tall as he, would be like a forest to him. But surely he would cry, would call for help: he had a fine pair of lungs. But no, my own shouts could not penetrate the huge space. Then I thought of snakes biting his fat little legs and of the python Nkosi had seen at the foot of the kopje among the trees and rocks. I thought how it would fix itself round a tree and then crush my fat darling, dirty, little Peepy. Here my feelings were for once far more intense than those of Frances over her step-children. However much you love other children, I do not believe they can hurt you as much as your own. Their sufferings can never bring that physical anguish which imagination of some hurt to her child can bring to a mother. As they grew older both Bryan and Peter would enjoy bringing me a bleeding wound so that they could see the green sick look which spreads over my face, outcome of the terrible sinking feeling only their hurts could give me. As usual I prayed furiously, recanting all my wickedness, and promising superhuman behaviour in the future and then....
along the jacaranda drive I saw Nkosi striding dragging a small khaki figure by the hand.

I rushed to them but Nkosi was frowning, "What have you been doing? I found this child...." How many times since has an indignant father used these words.... "I found this child.... I found these children?" "I found this child up by the Fort kopje killing a snake with a stone." Peter was four then and this was only one of his many exploits. His fearlessness frightened me, but he had a surprising streak of acute caution while Bryan, who was naturally timid, always hid his fear with a sudden wild recklessness which was far more dangerous. I was near tears with thankfulness. Nkosi turned to Bryan saying he should look after his little brother. Bryan was very upset at his father's words, for I could see he had been very worried over Peter's absence and I expect he remembered the smack he gave Peter and Peter's dignified retreat. However, there were hugs all round and when Nkosi demanded a drink, I was able to show him the sack of cool, clear water hanging from the tree. He drank it as if it had come from a tap, instead of being the results of Determined Effort.

To cheer up the little boys he told them to come and help him mark out the dining-hut. This he did in the sand just as we mark out sand castles on the beach. Then came natives carrying bundles of thick sticks on their heads. With bits of iron they pierced holes in the ground and the sticks were put in as near to each other as possible, making the framework of the hut. The children were very interested. Then suddenly Nkosi turned his head and saw clouds belching out of the bed hut. He rushed up just as his wife dashed out choking and spluttering, followed by Dick in the last stages of asphyxiation.

"What the hell's the matter?" cried Nkosi, while I ran round in circles gasping for air. "Have you set the place on fire?"

It was not smoke, however, but dust. Dick explained the situation. "I swept!" His face was quite grey. Nkosi took a deep breath and entered the hut but came out very quickly.

"What do you mean by letting him sweep the floor when it is all loose earth?" he said. I said I did not know that this would happen, and Nkosi showed surprising domestic knowledge by saying that no one swept a dirty carpet without first sprinkling it with tea-leaves. I was very impressed but as I felt guilty of two flagrant offences in one hardworking morning I said nothing but fetched another cup of water, feeling like a martyr. Little did he know what battles I had already waged that morning, the effort behind the water he was drinking, the effort behind the bed in which he would be sleeping, the effort behind the lunch he would soon be eating . . . . but here I realised that unless I saw to it immediately there would be no lunch at all.

While Myros was finishing liming I prepared the vegetables, and then we carried into the hut two rickety old tables, and placed them one on either side with an eighteen-inch aisle down the middle. The borer-dust from the rafters was pouring down in a regular stream, and it was no use placing the many utensils on the table until this was remedied. I took an old sheet and tied it to the rafters to act like a bulging ceiling and collect all the borer-dust. Over the other table, which was not so bad, I fixed a very old mosquito net to cover the entire surface, being careful that it did not hang against the walls and so encourage black ants or lie on the floor and encourage white ants, and that each leg of the table was placed in a tin of paraffin, so as not to encourage sugar-ants. As the net was very badly holed I tied knots in the holes so as not to encourage bluebottles (always females and pregnant, I wonder why?).

As I emerged, ripping my scalp on the pointed eave, I saw Dick running in and out of the bed hut carrying small logs and stones, and by this I realised that Nkosi was levelling the incubator. I kept well inside my kitchen-hut sorting things until I saw him emerge and go to the tree where he had fixed a stand for jug and basin (at a height the children could not reach, a height which made the water run up my sleeve when I washed my hands.)

"A nice time I've had with the incubator," he said.

With wifely tact fairly oozing I said, "Yes, I am sure you have, the floor is not very level."

"Level?" he said and I turned away to escape the explosion. The idea of giving a soft soothing answer to a husband when he is vexed is all wrong. Swearing is the natural outlet for a man, especially a husband and even more so a farmer and settler .... I have learned this, but then I was feeling mar-tyrish. "I suppose," he continued addressing my suffering back "now I have levelled it you can put in the eggs?" Then he was sorry for me. I always know when this happens though he will never tell me. But he now made up for his crossness by telling me about the plough. It seemed the boy using our new plough felt he would like to be clever and adjust it. He did this wrongly and when he started ploughing again, broke the whole thing. Nkosi had come upon the scene and had tried to remonstrate, but the boy had run away. In a fury of indignation Nkosi had seized the heavy plough chain and given chase to the boy. Again and again he swung the chain at the flying figure but every time he was a foot out, the boy had altogether escaped, and now the plough was out of action until new parts could be brought from town. It was after this that he had found Peter, had come back and found the hut belching smoke, had struggled to level the incubator on the sloping hut floor in semi-darkness, had come back, and found me being inefficient. I joined him in rage and horror at the criminal carelessness of the ploughboy, but said it must have looked awfully funny seeing him try to catch the nippy nigger waving a heavy plough chain, and he laughed and thus the tragedy became one of our "stories." Then I went to see about lunch, cold meat again, and could have cried aloud for the safe was full of ants. I could not see how they managed, but Bryan showed me where a spider had conveniently thrown a web from the tree and the ants were crossing with the greatest facility.

When dusk had fallen and the children were in bed, I went into the hut, washed, changed my smock and breeches, and put on an old evening dress (someone had given me.) Over this I wore a jersey and thick coat. I came out of the hut to find Nkosi burning a fire guard round the hut, he said he was going to burn a little every night. When the last tufts of smouldering grass had been beaten out Nkosi went into the hut to bathe in the basin. On his return it was a pitch black night and dinner was served on mats on the polished table. As we sat down a biting wind arose, and the candles in the brass candlesticks guttered and went out one by one. We tried to drink our soup in the dark but it was surprising what parts of our face we mistook for our mouths. Nkosi could bear it no longer. He jumped up and with Dick's help rigged up a blanket to hang from the eaves. The curve of the table made it bulge into the night but we were able to see the way to our mouths, though the candles wept tallowy tears on the polished table.

When dinner was over Nkosi, greatly refreshed, walked up and down as he had done the night before. I was too tired to do anything, but sat with my head on my arms.

Chapter 7 — Food!

The following morning I awoke to the realisation that Food Supply was the next problem to be tackled. The milk we had brought with us was finished and we should have to live on

condensed milk until the two cows we had bought calved.
We had counted on getting our milk meanwhile from neighbours, but mounting the kopje we could see no sign of farmhouses, only one small *daga* house which the boys told us
belonged to some Afrikaans people. Nkosi walked over and
asked if they could supply us with milk, but they were very
short themselves because it was the dry season, though they
very kindly gave us a bottle. This, of course, was not what
we wanted, so we decided that when the gift was finished we
would return to condensed. Our meat was also finished, but
as it happened to be Friday we had to send over to the Store
with which we had been dealing for our mail and could buy
some meat there. Bread was the real problem. During the last
year I had made yeast in a screw-topped bottle, put it by the
fire at night, and in the morning it was all alive and bubbling
and bread could be made easily. I had told Myros to set the
yeast the night before, so this morning I walked over to the
kitchen hut to see how the bread was progressing. Myros met
me with a long face.

"The medicine is dead."

"Oh Myros!" I cried, "How was that?"

He explained that he had made the yeast as usual, wrapped
it up in its old blanket but in the morning when he had
arrived he had "seen that it was dead." He picked up the
bottle and showed it to me, the yeast was lifeless and cold.
"No good," he said, and he was right. I wondered what to
do, there was only a crust left, hardly enough for breakfast.
I decided to make a baking-powder loaf and told Myros to
dig a hole in the ground, light a fire and let it burn out. I
would then put the loaf in the cookpot, stand it in the ashes
and place red embers on the lid. In this way the loaf would
soon be cooked.

While he was doing this I went into the kitchen hut, but
drew back in alarm for there was a peculiar sound. The next
moment Biddie was licking my hand assuring me that there
was nothing to fear, as all her family had arrived safely during
the night. I bent down. There in a wooden box under the
table were seven wriggling puppies. For a moment I felt like
crying at this addition to my burdens, but Biddie grovelled at
my feet begging for congratulations and I had not the heart
to withhold them. I told her she was a clever dog, and a good
dog, for after all it would have been worse if she had had
them on Nkosi's shirt the night before. Relieved and thrilled
Biddie cuddled down with her puppies and at that moment

Myros came into the hut. When he saw the puppies he said, "Uh! Uh! Very Good!"

"*Aikona,*" I replied, with the intonation "not in the least!" "Not good! Seven puppies! We shall have to kill half of them!"

Myros looked shocked, he could not understand the mentality of the white man who, rather than rear a tribe of starving flea-bitten mongrels, as the native does, prefers to destroy all but the best of the litter. Bending down over the happy family Myros suddenly seized the cloth on which they were lying. It was a glass cloth. Horrified I watched him draw out three more and gather them up for washing, hairy and stained.

"No, you dirty creature!" I cried snatching them from him. I told you to wash these towels yesterday afternoon. Why didn't you do it?"

"I forgot!" he replied sulkily. "I will wash them now." He made to take them from me but I drew hastily away.

"*Aikona!*" I cried, with the intonation "Not on your life!" and running outside I threw them all on the open fire and held them down with a stick and watched them burn. Myros stood by watching, how was it, he asked, that he could dry the plates when there were no cloths? I fetched him some old flour sacks, and said he would now have to manage with them as many other boys had to do. As my anger cooled down I rather wondered if I had done right to burn all the glass cloths; they might not all have been stained and after a good boiling.... also they could have been used as dusters.

Then I made the baking-powder loaf and put it in the bake-pot. That done, and finding the children were feeling cold, we all three ran up the kopje and came back warm and breathless. Though this kopje was easy and safe to climb from the hut, we had discovered that on another side there was a sheer granite precipice over which any careless little boy could fall to his death. We took the children to the brink and showed what waited for them below, hoping we had cowed them into being careful. Many years afterwards they told us they used to slide down that precipice on their seats regularly. I never found out, but I do remember now that their khaki shorts seemed to wear in holes continually.

When we came down they were allowed one peep at the puppies, and afterwards we had breakfast in a hurricane. The fried eggs were glued to our plates and I could see that Nkosi was very miserable and worried. He said everything took twice as long to do as he had thought. I agreed with him heartily, citing drinking-water and bread, but he dismissed these things as of no moment.

The bread cooked to perfection, I went off to the hut which still remained a battle-ground. I brought with me tea-leaves so that the mistake of yesterday would not be repeated. Now I secretly wished the floor had been made of cow dung because Nkosi had told me that it can after some time be highly polished. Had the bed legs dived into the loose earth evenly it would have been all right, we should have lain horizontal even at a lower level, but the earth gave unequal resistance so that each bed was a cripple and the floor was churned up. To make things worse the splashes from too vigorous or too careless washing turned the loose soil into mudpies. The sheets were all dirty and Bryan's covered with mud. Though the linen trunk had its own floor space there was no room for my body when opening it and I had to lie across the children's beds to reach it and get a clean sheet out. As I burrowed for a sheet I was aware of a damp smell. This was ridiculous for how could anything be damp when it had not rained for three months? When I reached down to the bottom of the trunk I found that white ants had already worked through and fastened on to a pillow slip. Wriggling to the door, I called for Dick. While he carried everything out into the sunlight, I assessed the damage. The white ants had come through the floor and worked their way in.

Another contingent had made tunnels of gravelly stuff all up the side of the trunk in order to travel in darkness to the blankets which were on the top. We brushed away the excavations, poured paraffin on them, then set the trunk back but this time standing on four stones. The pillow slip smelt like graveyards, and when I rubbed the gravelly stuff off I found it was full of holes. I wrote to my mother that night, "Give me a worm. A cheerful earthy worm that enjoys rain and sun, rather than these termites that are nothing but a living death." The rest of the morning was spent in safe-guarding the other things in the hut. I had also to inspect and continue to inspect the hanging safe and bread box, and see that the kitchen tables were also free from invasion. It was hard work but I did not mind because it was mail-day and I knew that before sundown the boy would come back with the home letters. He would also be bringing meat, potatoes and tinned food.

The children were very happy helping the boys to *daga* the dining-room hut. In those days the boys mixed the mud with their feet and Bryan and Peter joined in joyfully. The extra work of washing and cleaning them, I rated as worth the relief of knowing that they were not being drowned or suffering some other violent death.

Nkosi said at lunch time that he had cleared away some ground near the spruit for a garden and vegetable seed would be put in the next day and that he was going to try to dig a well, because carrying water took too much time. The baking powder bread was so delicious that the loaf was finished at one meal and that meant that directly after lunch I had to make another. The bake-pot unfortunately was only large enough to hold one at a time. Though Geography was never my strong point, I always imagined that the sun rising in the east and setting in the west could only shine on half or at most three-quarters of any circular object. But no, the Rhodesian sun managed to spread its smile completely round our hut. I therefore spent a very busy afternoon protecting the pieces of furniture huddled under the eaves from the sun by covering them with sacks. There was only one square yard where the sun did not penetrate and that was because the kopje intervened. This should have been reserved for the round table but I felt the Store containing our food was even more important.

Houseboys always go off after lunch, but this afternoon I bribed Dick to come back early. I needed his help and moral support in making the Store. Taking one of the large packing cases, we put it on its end, and fixed two shelves and many death traps. Dick held the hammer and offered nails and gave "Uh! Uh!'s" of admiration at my prowess. While I worked, hit my thumb, and spiked my fingers, Dick draped himself about in useful attitudes and held firmly on to things that needed no holding. The shelves in, I fashioned a door out of the lid. When hanging it I very cleverly put a wedge under so that it would not droop from the hinges. I had seen Nkosi do this. Then we realised that unless the thing had legs which could stand in paraffin tins it would be useless. We therefore turned it upside down and nailed on four stout legs. I did not attempt to make them equal because the hard mud outside the hut was completely uneven. I just put the shortest legs on the highest ground and then either used wedges or scraped away the soil to make all of them even. There were many nails sticking out, but as I knew where they were and I was the only person who might legitimately open the store I felt it did not matter, was in fact a good thing, as a burglar could not fail to tear his hand and I should find the blood marks. We then put each leg in a fish-tin of paraffin. I had to open a new tin to make a fourth. Finally I had the great joy of putting on the staple and hasp, inserted the padlock and put the key on my bunch.

When Nkosi came in to tea, which we had under a shady tree attended by flies, I asked him to come and see my store. He said without enthusiasm he supposed he must but instead of rhapsodising he said why did I have to take that particular crate? Urged to look at the shelves he said why use such long nails? He wanted those two-and-a-half's. But did he like it? He smiled, there was not much one could *like*, but he supposed it would do. Oblivious of the rising storm he continued that it was not very safe as the boys could easily steal the groceries. The padlock? No, they could not open that, but who would want to when they could pull out the nails from the hasp quite easily? Men like Nkosi have a wonderful sense of danger; they are aware of snakes for instance and can foretell thunder storms; yet they are peculiarly unaware when they are in mortal danger from their loving spouses. Nkosi never knew how near death he was. I was thinking of Jael.

That evening as we sat shivering over our tinned herrings, I told Nkosi that I could not go on baking individual loaves, a batch of real bread must be achieved somehow.

"Where can you bake it?" he asked, peering for bones by the flickering candle-light.

"In an ant-hill" I replied. "I have all the instructions here in this little South African magazine. South African women on trek always bake bread in anthills."

"How are you going to keep the yeast alive during this perishing night?"

"I'm taking it to bed with me," I said.

"That doesn't sound very nice."

I replied that it was our yeast and our bed and we ate the bread, so what was wrong? And off I went wrapping the bottle in my eiderdown and placing it at the foot of my bed.

It was so terribly cold that we could not sit outside after dinner, and we did not like to go for a walk in case the children woke up in a fright. Besides, we had seen the spoor of a leopard, and on the two previous nights we had heard the cries of jackals and hyaenas. We had been told by a "Very Efficient Woman" that though lions were not common they occasionally passed through, so that while one might not actually expect to see a lion one would not be surprised if one did.

"Surprised?" I had said, "I'd be terrified."

"No need to be terrified," she had replied. "Should you meet a lion you take no notice of it at all and it takes no notice of you."

"But," I said "wouldn't it be very difficult to take no notice of it, trying to look unconcerned?"

"No," she replied, "Lions are only dangerous when they are hungry," but she did not tell me how one knew whether a lion had dined or not.

There was nothing for us to do after dinner but to go to bed. We went in about 7.30 and should have liked to have read but the candle attracted all the insect-life of the veld. They queued up to commit suicide in the candle and those that could not get near buzzed in my hair, flapped in my face and dived down the front of my nightgown, so I was forced to put the candle out and lie in the darkness until sleep came to me.

I dreamt that night that the incubator had hatched out sixty young ducks and that the "Very Efficient Woman" had been so jealous she had taken a gun and shot them. Waking up with a start I realised there had been a loud report.

"What is it?" I cried to Nkosi, "What have you shot?"

"I haven't shot anything," he replied waking up and fumbling for the matches, (he had mislaid his torch). As the flame flickered up I saw the eiderdown at my feet from which a white fluid was trickling. I investigated.

"The yeast," I said, "hasn't died: it has committed suicide!"

"I told you so," said Nkosi untruthfully.

"No," I said, "You only told me it wouldn't be nice."

I unwound the eiderdown. It resembled a swiss roll. The yeast and broken glass had managed to spread themselves like the cream filling.

We gathered the eiderdown together and threw it out into the night. "Thank Heaven for natives," I said as I crept back to bed, "Dick will soon get it clean."

Chapter 8 — Daily Bread.

The next morning I arose full of determination. I would make sufficient baking-powder loaves for the day and at night I would make the yeast and be very careful to give it as much warmth as it needed and no more.

When this was done I had to prepare for my first turkey. The usual way to start turkey-raising is to buy some hens and set the eggs but I was in too much of a hurry and accepted the offer of the Very Efficient Woman to sell me a hen and her hatched brood.

The children were very interested watching the boys put up a grass garage. A very old native was combing dried grass on a board studded with nails, ready for when the framework of the building was finished. For this the boys had sharpened slim young saplings and were setting them side by side in the hard earth and were tying them firmly together with long strips of young green bark.

Nkosi was having a bad time with stumping. The small stunted trees which covered the veld promised little opposition to the stumper, but he found that the roots were enormous, showing that the trees had been cut down years before and allowed to grow again. We found out later that this part of the country had been the headquarters of a tribe of Mashonas who, when the white man came, were given ground in a nearby Native Reserve. On the next farm to us there had been fourteen hundred huts and not only was all the wood second, maybe third, growth but traces of their occupation were to be found on many of our kopjes, mostly broken pottery.

On the top of one we found traces of a fort or lookout, probably used by the Mashonas who lived in dread of the Matabele raids. This kopje is of ironstone formation and later, when we ploughed the valley below, we came upon half-melted iron and pipes made of baked clay. In one tree root very far down we found an old iron *badza* (hoe), the shape of a shield and another which had been mended with a crude sort of rivet.

In what we called the Monkey Kopje we came across a cave which had partially fallen in, and climbing down we crept through a rocky place a couple of feet high and found the spruit running through. By the water was a perfect native pot, but unfortunately as we tried to drag it out we broke it. Once we tried to grow maize by the Monkey Kopje but the monkeys were too destructive. One day Nkosi took his gun. On his approach the wicked band ran off but one female was left behind. Nkosi saw her tearing after the others dragging a little monkey child by its hand. It looked so very human that he could not shoot her.

Nkosi had found soil suitable for brick-making near the spruit, and it was fascinating watching the boys making bricks. Two holes were dug next to each other. In one stood a native using the level ground as a table, in the other was water in which the boy dipped the brick moulds before he filled them with the *daga* piled by his side. When filled the moulds were carried away and turned out on a level stretch of land, like blancmanges, covered with straw and left to dry in the sun. Nkosi had started brickmaking some time before we moved and so now he was able to build a kiln and put the firing in.

Our Afrikaans neighbour had walked over to see us and when he found wc were drinking vlei water, he promised to come and divine a well for us.

He did this by holding a small forked stick in his hands and walking over the ground round the hut. When the stick dipped of its own accord near a fig tree and an anthill, he marked the site for a well.

Now for the lady, called by Bryan Mrs. Turkey Tops. She arrived completely upset by her journey, and when we put her in her coop with her children, instead of greeting them with squawks of delight, as Mrs. Mashona would at such a happy reunion, she looked at them with complete indifference and when they tried to nestle under the maternal feathers she remained standing while they cheeped plaintively. I tried to remind her of her duties by putting her children near her, but she immediately pinned down one little striped body and then looked round wondering where the noise came from. Bryan rescued the poor little thing and the mother immediately upset her tin of water and in this the little turkeys, anxious to be out of this terrifying world as soon as possible, paddled.

"They must not get their feet wet!" I cried in agony of mind and Bryan carefully picked up each one and wiped its feet with his handkerchief. Knowing of the coming of Mrs. Turkey-Tops I had cherished a tin of shallots for her family. The tops of these I had cut and chopped, mixing them with bran, mealie-meal, pollard, bone-lucerne-and-meat-meal with a sprinkling of ground monkey nuts.

Having been warned how difficult turkey poults are to rear, I was determined they should have every vitamin they could possibly require. Did they appreciate it? No. They shrunk away from the tin of food as from poison, but their mother stretched forth her long neck from the coop and in a trice had disposed of half the valuable mixture before I could stop her. The little turkeys still sought warmth and comfort from their parent but she denied it and stamped upon them relentlessly. Bryan stood by rescuing them one by one as they were flattened.

"Do you know what they say Mummie?" he asked. "They say 'Peek, Peek! I am so weak, weak!'"

So I began turkey rearing and lost all affection for those most unlovable birds. A turkey hen is the most unmaternal of all creatures. She does not care if her children starve or perish of cold. She takes them for five mile walks and never notices if she comes back a few short. Most mornings the turkey owner has to remove flattened corpses.

Just before the sun set a car came up the drive and out of it stepped our next door neighbours, Jim and Effie. Effie was very enthusiastic about everything and surprised that I had even brought my birthday cake with me. She asked what she could do to help, and I arranged with her to supply the milk. We were to send a boy every morning. It was sold in whisky bottles, the standard measure. Effie told me she would fill the bottles and tie the cork with a double bow. I asked why, and she told me that, as natives could only tie a single bow, we should know if the boy carrying it had drunk from the bottle. She said it was the usual thing, and that he would fill the bottle with *spruit* water as he passed. She also told me that another branch of the railway ran some five miles away on another road, and that we should do better to order our meat and groceries from town to be delivered (thrown out of the train) at the siding. She told me to have a private post-bag which would also be thrown out and collected by our native. She made her bread herself, she said, but then she had a brick house and a proper stove. She was very nice to the children and went away in her new Model A Ford van leaving me feeling uplifted. I looked round and saw that in a few days we had accomplished quite a lot. The milk question was settled and the bread problem as good as solved. All would be well.

That night I made the yeast and wrapped the bottle in Nkosi's dressing gown. He didn't like the idea, but I said that the gown would provide just the right amount of warmth and anyway I would put it on the trunk so that if the bottle should burst it would do little harm. In the middle of the night I crept out of bed and unrolled it. It was bubbling happily and I went back to bed content with the thought that though Africa was a tough customer I was her match and I was winning. In spite of the insect-life I kept the candle on while I re-read the article on how to make bread in the veld. It was very simple. I could hardly wait for the morning to begin this delightful experiment.

At last tormented by the *hor-hors I blew out the candle and lay still. Then in the darkness I heard the padding of feet round the hut and the breathing of a large animal. It sniffed under the door. Biddie, I told myself, and then remembered that Biddie and her surviving puppies were barricaded in the kitchen-hut in case of leopards. I realised that Biddie could never have given that sniff .... it must be a leopard, or remembering the Very Efficient Woman perhaps a lion .... a hungry lion. As we race through the veld in cars under protection of large husbands we scorn the dangers of the veld .... but at night .... it is very different. In England the night means sleep and one can almost hear the country-side snoring, but in Africa the night is extraordinarily alive and alert. The moon shining full suggests active life. You may think the night is silent, but if you lie awake and listen you will hear it is full of sound; and when you are alone it seems full of menace. By this time I felt it might be a lion but it was most certainly a leopard .... pad pad sniff .... pad pad .... and then .... the door burst open and almost on my bed sprang a huge tawny animal. I shrieked. Nkosi was up and had his torch shining on the lion who promptly bounded back into the night.

"Stop making that noise" said Nkosi in a quiet assuring voice. "You will frighten the children! It is only a dog!"

"It's a lion! I know it is a lion," I sobbed.

Nkosi standing out in the moonlight said "Yes, a dog, a huge brown dog .... Oh, if I only had a brick!" Putting his hand down he found a stone left over from my store activities and he threw it at the invader and a yelp told that the shot had got home.

"Now is it a lion?" he said, "Did you ever hear a lion yelp?" He laughed.

"No," I said with dignity, "but it frightened me just as much as if it had been a lion." Frances would have traded on that fright. I can see Hugh comforting the trembling little figure with the large frightened eyes. I should have realised that all nice men like being protective, but at the

---

* A Dutch word goggas pronounced hor-hor — meaning insects.

moment I was "the courageous woman grappling with the Dark Continent" and I felt angry that my real fright and terror were only laughable.

Because, in those first years, we were not mauled by lions, attacked by natives, drowned in floods, burnt in fires, or killed by snakes, one may say that those early days could not have been at all frightening; but they were. In imagination the children, Nkosi and I suffered every ill and death, not once but a hundred times over, and to meet these tragedies, spurious as they were, courage and endurance were needed.

I was up before the boy brought tea, eager for my next tussle with Africa and anxious to wipe out the shame of having cried because a large dog jumped on my bed. Unfortunately, it was too cold to move the yeast from its warm nest. Looking at Nkosi's watch I found that instead of my being early the boys were late, for Africa had decided on a *Makaza, A Makaza* is a day that slips in between the never failing sunny days. Instead of popping up behind the hills and flooding the veld with glorious sunshine, it rises secretly behind a cloud and persuades the boys that it is not time to leave their huts. Naturally they are only too glad to be thus fooled. When it is well up in the sky, the sun pops out just to show how late everything is, and then hides itself for the rest of the day, leaving the veld to cold winds or drizzle or anything but the lovely sunny day which we Rhodesians look upon as our Right.

Early tea was so late that Nkosi could not wait for it, and the children when dressed and sent out came back to the hut because it was so cold. Mrs. Mashona excellent mother that she was, took her children along for a vigorous scratch in the veld. I was getting a little sorry for Mrs. Mashona because her children were growing up and instead of rushing eagerly to her not always reliable "Hor-Hor-Ho!", you could see them telling each other it was most likely a false alarm and anyway they preferred to find their own breakfast. Mrs. Turkey-Tops greeted the Makaza more mournfully than ever. Without the sun her children could not live. The idea of brooding them did not enter her stupid narrow head. She looked for the sun, first with one eye then with the other, while her children gave that piercing peek of a young turkey welcoming death.

We had a miserable breakfast and then, suggesting the children went for a short walk with Daddy, I decided to attack the bread. It was a cruel trick that Africa had played

on me to send a *Makaza* the very day I was baking bread
out-of-doors but I should carry on regardless in the true
Pioneer Spirit.

I took my bottle of bubbling yeast, wrapped it carefully
in a blanket as a mother would her new-born child, and
took it to the open fire which I had persuaded Myros must
be good. I made it into dough and putting in on a box as near
the fire as possible I told him to keep moving the bowl
round so that it did not get too hot or too cold in any one
part. Then I turned to the article: —

"To make bread without a stove, cut a hole in an anthill
and scoop out the centre. With a pointed stick make a hole
in the top."

"That won't take a minute," I thought, remembering how
easily a dog makes a rat hole, and in my new breeches I
sent off with swinging stride to the anthill in sight, the one
near the place where the boys were digging the well. It was
about eight foot high and covered with grass. Rather larger than
I needed but I had to take what was at hand. Arriving there
attended by Bryan and Peter who had come back warm and
rosy, I knelt down and proceeded to "cut a hole." The crust
was like granite and the badza gave an unpromising clang.
I could see I should never make any impression on it so I
called Dick and said,

"Make a hole." He took the badza and began clearing
away with difficulty the tufts of grass. Impatient for results
I walked away to the bread and found it was rising nicely.
Triumph! Africa beaten! Even if she did send a *Makaza* on
the very day I needed the sun. When I returned on the
scene of activity I found Dick had made no impression at
all and the sweat was pouring down his face. I think for
once in his life he would have preferred his own work.

"That's funny!" I said. "I thought it would be easy to
make a hole! Biddie just throws the soil away. Here Biddie!
Good dog! Rats, Biddie!" Biddie turned away, the mother
of a family has no time for levity. Then Nkosi came up to
see how the well was getting on and I called him.

"I see the bread is rising," he said kindly.

"Yes, darling, but we do not seem able to scoop this
anthill out." To illustrate this Dick lifted the badza and let
it down with a mighty blow which split the handle in two.

"You want a pick for that," said Nkosi sent Dick for one
the well boys were using. "What does the book of words
say?" he asked.

I took the magazine from the branch of the tree where it was resting and read, "Make a hole in an anthill and scoop out the centre."

"We ought to be able to do that," he said, taking the pick from the perspiring Dick. He swung it high and broke off a square inch of the anthill. This he repeated until he was red in the face. Then Dick carried on and was soon exhausted, so Nkosi took over again.

"It ought not be so difficult," I said apologetically.

Nkosi snorted, "Perhaps not but I assure you it is!"

Followed an hour of effort which absorbed Nkosi, Dick, Myros and the boys digging the well, a hole of sorts had been excavated.

"Talk of Rock of Ages," said Nkosi wiping his brow, "What does it say next?"

"With a pointed stick make a hole in the top."

"Pointed grandmother! No pointed bit of iron would go in that!" He knelt down at the base of the hole and a party of ants came out to assess the damage. "Look at it, it's like reinforced concrete. You couldn't put a pointed anything through that."

"No," I said in the most soothing manner, "This is not going quite as we hoped."

"It certainly isn't," said Nkosi as he removed a soldier ant from his knee.

"I think you have done very well, darling," I said. "And we shall just have to do without the hole with a stick."

"Can you manage?" he asked hopefully, for I could see his heart was in the well or perhaps the brick kiln.

"Yes," I said, soothing, capable, courageous. He went off with relief and Dick ran for some firing while I read the directions. "Set and light a good big fire in the hole. Then close up with a sheet of tin and a little *daga*."

Dick came along carrying a glowing red wood ember on a piece of bark, put it in the hole with a handful of dry grass, blew it until it burst into flame. However it did not like the atmosphere of the hole and went out at once. Dick began again and fed it with choice little bits of stick, but having eaten them up with avidity, the fire refused the larger timber and went out.

"It wants its hole with a stick," said Bryan.

"Oh, be quiet!" I said crossly and began to blow at the one remaining spark which died immediately. Peter squatting almost in the hole so that he could get a good view began to shout that the ants were biting him. I pulled the tenacious little insects off his fat legs, and Dick began fire-making all over again. He took great care and slowly, slowly the wood took light. In revenge it blew out clouds of smoke in our faces so that, black and white alike, we all became grey.

"Close up the hole," was like attacking under gas. In agony Dick and I pressed the flattened petrol tin over the gap.

"Quick, Bryan, quick! Put on the *daga!*" Bryan who was detailed for this job, picked up a lump of liquid mud and sloshed it over the joins. "More! More! Again! Again!" I gasped. Both little boys worked hard and Dick helped them while with streaming eyes I clung to the tin. It was done. Four derelict human beings sat on the ground gasping in great draughts of fresh air. I reached for the instructions and read:

"When this is done allow the fire to burn out."

"Willingly," I muttered and collecting my family we went to wash off the smoke, soot and perspiration.

Clean, I made up the sweetly rising dough into loaves and set them to prove. I then remembered I had not made my daily inspection for invaders so the next hour was easily filled in. The bread proven, I covered it with a blanket and approached the Oven. With great excitement the tin and hardened *daga* was peeled off. What was left of the fire inside was scraped out and my beautiful loaves placed inside. Quickly and easily this time the tin was replaced and smothered with *daga.*

"Will it cook without a fire?" asked Bryan. Then I proceeded to tell him how in his great-grandfather's house there was a huge old bake-oven made of brick in which all the week's baking was done after the fire had been taken out.

"How long will you leave it?" asked Bryan.

"It does not matter," I replied, the Africa Tamer very much in evidence. "We will leave them in an hour and a half to make sure."

I then sat down to mend the seats of my children's shorts and practised to myself what I should say to the Very Efficient Woman. "How do you like my bread? Made it in an anthill. Oh, it's quite easy when you get into it." Well, that would be the truth, it was only the first time that it had been so difficult. Next time it would be perfectly straight-forward. It had needed a bit of determination certainly, but it was done now and there would be no need for the ever-lasting baking-powder loaves. I thought I would give the rest of the loaf to Biddie, but remembering that new, spongey yeast bread is not good for children I decided to keep it.

Time passed quickly and at the appointed hour we went joyfully to the Oven. I carried the tray on which the loaves were to be stacked. We pulled down the barricade with great excitement. The loaves looking pale as death were lying there uncooked and covered with a slight layer of soot.

"We've opened it too soon!" I cried, "Shut!! Shut" Frantically we replaced the tin and slopped on *daga*.

Nkosi came in to lunch and enquired about the bread.

"It isn't quite cooked," I said. "These bake-ovens take time."

An hour later we all went to the Opening of the Oven. The loaves ware exactly the same but on top of the soot was a layer of *daga*. All had gone flat but one. This one I carried off and put in the cook-pot, the rest I threw into the veld. As I left the anthill forever, I saw the termites had already sent a relief party to the scene. Little workers were each bringing its grain of sand while others placed their drops of fluid which make these cement-like fortresses. Wonderful civilisation, typical of Africa who carries on her plans regardless of anything we humans can do. I put the children to rest, took out the real loaf which was small and heavy and made a baking-powder one. I was defeated.

That afternoon the Afrikaans neighbour from next door called. She had no car but had taken the opportunity of coming with a guest who was staying with them, and had offered to drive her over.

I told her my troubles and she laughed and said the mistake was that the article was meant for South Africa not Rhodesia. The anthills in that part of the world were small mounds nothing like our rocky fortresses. She said we must make a dutch-oven and tried to explain how to do it. Finally, seeing I was not too bright, she picked up her stick and walked over to Myros. Then she began speaking to him, not in halting Kitchen Kaffir but in fluent Zulu. Myros understood for the first time in his life. She came back.

"I have told him what to do," she said, "But he already knows quite well how to make a dutch-oven."

"But why didn't he make one before?" I asked.

"He says you wanted to make bread in an anthill so it wasn't his place to stop you." I felt like murdering the wretched boy. She said natives often pretended they did not know how to do a job, because it meant less work.

She said that though she didn't let a native touch her bread, in my case she would advise me to give the yeast to Myros, and say "Make bread."

That night I made yeast again and in the morning I found Myros had made a dutch-oven, a petrol tin was laid in some old bits of scrap iron and covered with *daga*. I don't know how it worked, but from that time we were provided with our Daily Bread.

Chapter 9 — Fire!

It was Sunday, the day of rest. Inez, my sister, used to say when we battled on our Kentish farm. "In it thou shalt do all manner of work, thou, thy son, thy daughter, but not thy manservant nor maid-servant because they go out for the day."

I think that why one accepts Monday morning so cheerfully is because there is not the constant strain of trying not to work. On a Rhodesian farm, everything happens on a Sunday; fires, floods, births, deaths. All natives fall sick on a Sunday if they happen to be house-chicken-herd-boys who should be working. Those who do not work on Sunday are, of course, sick on Monday. On Sunday they have their quarrels, their beer drinks, fights and disputes. The reason why veld fires always come on a Sunday, is because on Saturday night or early Sunday morning the natives go hunting with their dogs and burn the grass for rats and game. That the fires do thousands of pounds worth of damage does not matter at all to them. This is their way of hunting. They spread the fire by dropping smouldering pieces of dried dung along a certain line. Once Nkosi came upon this and was able to put out each piece before it burst into flame, but he was not able to catch the boy.

This particular Sunday I had decided that we should have the luxury of a sit-down bath as bathing in a basin on a loose earth floor was very unsatisfactory. At breakfast, the Africa Conqueror announced that this morning we were going to have a real bath. On Nkosi's enquiry, I explained that I was having the large zinc bath brought into the hut and while I was enjoying myself he would look after the children. Then I would do the same for him.

"The zinc bath," said Nkosi, "is too small. You might be able to sit in it, but I couldn't."

"I've thought of that," for eight years of married life had taught me to see and provide against Nkosi's natural objections to any of my ideas, a study of which I have now brought to perfection. "I have thought of that. I am using the zinc bath for sitting accommodation and we shall use the large flat enamel bowl for foot-work."

"It will make an awful mess."

"That can't be helped," I returned, "Standing in the basin is just as bad, the floor is always liquid mud afterwards, and you have no idea how much I long to SIT in a bath."

Nkosi grunted his unwilling consent and as he always enforces conditions when he surrenders he said I must draw the curtains over the little window which would of course exclude every scrap of light left in the dimness of the hut. I had to agree. Then he said he thought a cow was going to calve and he must go to her. He would come back in a few minutes. While he was away I cleared the hut for action and Dick brought in the bath of hot water and a petrol tin of cold water which he put on the floor. I brought out clean towels and a new piece of soap and waited for Nkosi. He returned worried about the cow who seemed unable to get on with her job, but he said he would look after the children if I would be quick.

I went inside the hut quite excited, and longing for the glorious feeling of hot water lapping my body. I undressed in the pitch dark, hoping my eyes would soon get used to the gloom. As the tin was too heavy to lift I had to scoop the water out with my tooth-brush-holder and when this was done there was a good-sized puddle on the floor.

I sat down in the bath and immediately the water in one great tidal-wave slopped over on to the floor. I had not reckoned on displacement. I made a mental note that Nkosi must be careful for there would not be room for much water when he began displacing. I rose hurriedly, forgetting that the foot-basin was light, and it shot away from me so that I fell between the two receptacles. I got back into the bath very muddy. However it came off easily and having used the soap I flung it carelessly on to its dish from which it bounded and skidded under the bed. As I still had a good bit of surface to soap I had to retrieve it and in my cramped quarters this could only be done by lying flat on the muddy floor and reaching for it.

In the bath again I tried to wash off the fresh mud, but the water was now nearly chocolate colour and I realised that as I should never be really clean I might as well dry myself and then wipe off the visible smears. I was gritty and very uncomfortable. Just then Nkosi thumped on the door.

"Hurry up, for goodness sake! I'm hanged if I'll wait while you steep yourself. Be quick, I want to get back to the cow!"

I dressed myself, my clothes hiding most of the brown smudges. I wiped the dirt from my face and went outside, blinking in the sunlight. I called Dick to change the water. As he came staggering out with the zinc bath Nkosi said jocularly,

"Heavens how filthy you were!"

I was in no mood for a joke. The fact that I had used enormous effort to come out smudged and gritty did not appear funny.

Then Nkosi went in and shut the door but he had the advantage of the curtain being drawn back. I waited outside until he had settled.

"My God!" he muttered "you've spilled the water everywhere. There isn't room to stand."

"Good Heavens! Why did you put this thing on a tilt? I might as well be in a boat at sea. Hell! Give me another towel. This one is wet through."

I went inside. Nkosi looking the picture of misery was crouching in the zinc bath his boney knees under his chin. The displacement had been very great.

"Call this a bath?" he said gloomily.

Silently and efficiently I collected all the used towels and made them into a little island on which he could land when finished. Then placing two clean ones within reach I took the children up the Kopje so that we could hear no more of his troubles.

On top of the kopje we saw that there was a veld fire on the horizon. I had warned Nkosi so many times of an approaching fire which had turned out to be "fifty miles away and not even coming in our direction" that I did not want to give another false alarm when he had the bath and the cow to finish.

I consulted Bryan who said that the wind was blowing it away from us. Anxious to show off my veld craft I licked my index finger and held it up in the "Hark, Hark the Lark!" position and found that it was the back of my finger that was chilly. Bryan pointed out that my dress was blowing away from the kopje, but I preferred to do things the right way. Just then Myros panted up the kopje to say that Nkosi wanted us immediately.

We ran down and I opened the hut door to find a very disgruntled Nkosi trying to wipe off brown smears.

He said, "the herd-boy says the cow is in a bad way. Get me hot water, vaseline and the piece of rope we used for the waggon." I hastened to get ready the requirements for the accouchement and Nkosi went off.

There were several things I had to do before I could attack the terrible disorder of the hut and I had barely started when a boy came to say that there was a great fire coming towards us and Nkosi said I was to put all the animals in or around the hut, fill the car with petrol and water and have it ready; he would come directly he could leave the cow.

The wind had now changed and the air was full of floating specks and in the distance was a pall of grey smoke and sudden bursts of flame.

I did what I was told and left the car facing the right way on a slope as so often it refused to start without pushing. I packed oranges and a bottle of water in a basket and put it in the car. A highly indignant Mrs. Mashona was caught and locked up and Mrs. Turkey Tops, of course, had hysterics and trampled a child to death. We then sat, all three of us in the car waiting for Nkosi. The fire was still quite a distance away and we had a good-sized fire guard round the but, but I could see that with the gusts of wind that were blowing, if the fire was allowed to reach the guard a burning strand might easily be tossed over the fire guard on to the roof of the hut. I knew the safest thing to do was light a fire from the hut to meet the oncoming fury, but then the cow and the cattle kraal would be between the two fires.

Nkosi had an anxious time. He was torn between the cow and the fire, but was going to try and save the animal first and then light a back fire from the narrow road that passed at the end of our avenue of trees linking the Afrikaans neighbours' farm with Effie's farm and the siding five miles away.

It seemed a long while before he came up. The cow had been delivered of a dead bull calf, and the herd-boys were rounding up the cattle and taking them to a safe spot.

When we reached the road Nkosi cut green branches for us, lighted the far edge to the roadway, and made us stand behind it beating out any flame that tried to burn back into the grassy road. As he had had some experience in firefighting the previous year, and before that had known the great forest fires of Brazil, he told us we must always have in mind a place of retreat in case the fire got beyond control.

A back-fire is a feeble unwilling thing. The wind is against it and it goes slowly and shrinkingly towards the great enemy. As our little string of fire crept along it seemed that it would never go far enough to keep the great advancing flames at bay.

The main fire was approaching at a terrific rate .... a great, long line of red. We could feel the hot air from the high flames. By the time our fire was going and Nkosi had burned enough grass on which to park the car and to which we could retreat in an emergency, the natives had arrived from the compound. Some were sent to light a trail down to the spruit where the fire would be automatically halted and others to the left where the road passed the compound, and beyond that to another spruit. We three were left to follow the fiery trail beating out any intrusions and we thoroughly enjoyed the thrill of protecting our home.

As the fire drew nearer it was not so good. The air was thick with burnt grass and so hot that our faces became red and scorched. Peter went back to the car and ate an orange, but Bryan and I stayed where we were. Out in front of us leapt rabbits and frightened buck, all racing before the red terror. Our wretched little backfire crept slowly forward and the main fire roaring like a train in a station rushed towards it.

Standing waiting for the two fires to meet, it is difficult not to be afraid. You know that if the guard is wide enough the huge hungry flames cannot harm you, yet it seems as if they must.

We stood together watching them come. A tremendous roar and crackle, immense searing heat and then suddenly it was all over. The back-fire had done its work and there was nothing left but black ashes and shrivelled trees.

To our right the boys had things in hand, so we followed the road Nkosi had taken. The fire, balked in its straight course for our hut, was now bearing in that direction and we soon saw that the compound was threatened.

Ever since we had arrived Nkosi had told the boys to make a fire-guard round their compound but they had not troubled. Now as we drew near we saw great activity as they tried to set light to the all dry grass before the fire arrived. The boys shouted as they darted about with lighted torches and the women screamed as they rushed through smoke dragging their children to safety. Suddenly, with a roar the fire pounced on an outlying hut and it went up like a torch.

Luckily the other huts were saved and the wind shifted and the main fire turned and raced to the spruit. A few moments of tense beating and the compound was saved except for the one hut lying in a little black heap.

We now realised that we were very tired and walked back to the car where I gave my menfolk water and oranges.

We drove up and down the road to make sure that no smouldering tuft might ignite the dry grass on the hut side of the road, and then went home.

On arrival I found Myros in charge, his reason for not joining the fray was that he had to protect his own hut which was under the kopje. Nkosi went to see how the cow was getting on while I released the animals.

When Nkosi came back I called for hot water for we were all black with smoke and dust. We went into the hut, and, among the puddles and mud, each had a bath.... in the basin.

PART III.

THE BUSY WEEKS.

Chapter 10 — Visitors.

TIME is measured for us and we are given calendars with which to divide it, yet as we look back we find that the days and weeks are not equal at all. Some of them are long-drawn out and hold all sorts of events and experiences, and others are crowded together until they lose all identity.

So it was with us. The first days in the hut were each like a lifetime, every minute holding its own problem, but as the problems were solved and routine crept in, the days shortened in a remarkable way.

The next week things were easier. Bread made its appearance without any fuss. The ants and other skellums were resting, waiting for the inevitable weakening of my vigilance. Effie sent the milk over, and I inspected the knot carefully while the boy watched. Perhaps that is why I found no tampering.

It was a great disappointment losing our first calf, but soon afterwards the second cow calved, so that later on, we were able to have our own milk. As we had no separator I steamed the milk in a double saucepan, and poured it into a shallow enamel basin to set. From this Devonshire Cream I made butter with an egg whisk. The skimmed milk was quite creamy enough for use.

Meat came by rail once a week and gave much trouble to keep it fresh, although it was winter-time. The butcheries of Rhodesia had been a great shock to me. Compared with them, English butchers are surgeons. I found meat was hacked into lumps, not joints, and all oddments were sold as boys' meat. I used to cut my weekly slab into three portions and rub salt in one. The first was used for frying steak and stewing steak. The second began as roast, and when it had gone through the stages of cold, rissoles and curry, we started on the salted bit. It was a nightmare trying to obtain fresh vegetables. We used to buy huge cabbages when we went to town, and for

the rest we had to rely on the generosity of neighbours. Fruit
was the greatest disappointment. I found the oranges pressed
on me were not grown under irrigation, so they had very
thick skins and were sour; but naartjes, which I recognised
as tangerines, were delicious.

The seeds in the vegetable garden came through nicely,
and looked very trim in their neat, raised beds. Beyond a
few excavations by large animals the garden remained
untouched. We did not realise that this was because the
denizens of the veld were waiting for the seedlings to grow
to an edible size.

We built a grass fence to keep out straying oxen, wild pig
and porcupine, and the garden thrived. Then the insects
attacked, and the birds, instead of eating them, pounced on
the peas and cleared them up. Sometimes white ants would
take the trouble to build passageways so they might eat the
tender little plants, when they had the whole wide veld as
their larder. Then the moles would pop up just to see what
was going on. We were told not to worry but just go on
sowing seeds; the idea being to have such an enormous garden
that when everything with a mouth had taken its fill, there
would still be enough for us.

Mrs. Mashona realised at last that her elderly family had
no use for her not even at night so, hearing the cry of the
incubator chicks who were now several weeks old and had
no wish for a mother, she ingratiated herself with them and
in a short while had the whole troop running after her. I was
very glad, because shut up they were a nuisance and an
expense, and Mrs. Mashona relieved me of a great responsibility. She was very watchful for eagles, and when she
located one would gather her chicks under and round her.
Hens, unlike turkeys, seem able to count their chicks, but
twelve or fourteen must be their limit. I am sure Mrs.
Mashona's little brain must have ached counting her huge
family. She lost only one the whole time she brooded them,
and I am sure it was the chick's fault.

Mrs. Turkey-Tops unwillingly raised her family. There
were three little weak ones with large heads and long beaks.
They carried their wings like badly-rolled umbrellas. I dosed
these little wretches and coddled them, but from morning to
night they stood feet apart swaying and crying, "Peek! Peek!"
refusing to thrive and refusing to die. They invited their
mother's feet, but when in the morning I pulled out a
flattened chick it was always a healthy one, and the three

miseries continued their painful existence and their maddening "Peek! Peek!" Finally, the mother finished off all three one night and the rest of the family decided to live for the present, for after all, they knew there were so many other ways for a turkey to die, and that I should feel it more keenly if they waited a few more weeks before rending the veil.

We bought four more turkey hens and a gobbler. Instead of laying in safety near the huts these creatures took the greatest pains to find the most dangerous spot they could for their nests and when rescued would sit nowhere else. We had therefore to barricade them on the chosen site and take them off every day for exercise.

Effie called again, and when she got home she sent over a note saying she had dropped her keys while walking round our domain. As the domain was nearly all grass or loose sand, the children, the staff and I had a difficult job hunting for them. Finally, I had to write over and say they could not be found. The next morning she sent over again, this time to say she had found the keys under a broody hen.

Effie had a nice house, a good piano, and a lovely voice, which was a great joy to me through the years, so much so that I borrowed it for Frances. It is the easiest accomplishment to give a heroine as you only have to describe the effect on the audience.

Soon after the fire we moved into the dining-hut although it was not ready. The red mud walls were still damp and the loose soil of the floor unbeaten. In it we put our home-made furniture and when the brass candle-sticks were brought out and the sea picture hung from the rafters it looked very pretty. Nkosi made some mistakes in this his first building. The single window had to be put in sideways because of the overhanging thatch, and for the same reason we had to manage without a door and make do with a heavy kaffir blanket hung from a rod over the aperture. This was better than nothing, but the wind used to blow the curtain suddenly, where it would either billow round my head or sweep all my needle-work or papers off the table and bundle them out into the veld. To prevent this I weighted the bottom down with heavy stones. Then, of course, the children, Nkosi and the natives would come bursting in, tearing the curtain off its rings, and tripping over the stones. I was furious with them for this, so removed the rings, nailed the curtain at the top and on one side and used a heavy rock as a door stop.

As things began to get easier I was able to make more

experiments. Very carefully I mixed a ginger cake and put it in the heated cook-pot, laid red-hot ashes on the top and it came out perfectly, light, moist with a glorious gloss on its top. I longed for someone to see it and for I think the only time in my life, the wish was granted. That afternoon a car came bringing a family of neighbours who lived some five miles away. Nettie, the mother of the family greatly admired my cake and gave me very helpful advice, for she too, many years before had started farm life in very much the same way. She warned me about having a lightning conductor on our hut. Some friends of hers had been killed while sitting in a hut like ours during a thunder storm. When I told him, Nkosi said it did not matter as we should be out of the hut before the storms came along. It could not rain in August.

In August, although the winter is still with us, either with its purple dry grass or its stretch of burnt-out ruin, the m'sasa trees burst out in shining glory. There is a wistful sadness in the red leaves of an English autumn but in the red leaves of a Rhodesian spring there is no sadness but the great joy of renewed life.

Seen from the top of the kopje, the flat tops of the trees look like wonderful carpets of red and gold and all the many tints that lie between these two colours. Early one morning in the veld or garden we feel a soft tremor in the air, a sort of sweetness, a caress of the wind, and then we know that spring is coming. The next day there may be howling wind or biting cold, but we know that it is only the last grumble of Winter who knows he must soon be off.

I worked tirelessly on a strict routine and felt that I was as near domestic perfection as a mortal woman could be. I wonder Nkosi did not murder me. I have now learned that perfection is not for me; it is rather a thing to be avoided as the reaction is so great. I know that as sure as night follows day, my fit of energy and efficiency is followed by one of laziness and muddle, and that if my spirit does not rebel at Strict Routine, then my flesh will, and I go down with some ailment and Routine is no longer my grim master. The success in defeating Africa, spurred me on to greater effort, I increased my activities, and took no afternoon rest. This was breaking one of the rules for white women living and working in a tropical country. If a woman wants to keep her complexion and steer clear of a nervous breakdown, she should have a short rest every afternoon.

The weather changed suddenly and now, instead of joy

between cold morning and evening, mid-day was a torment. It was a relief not having the icy blast but there are more pleasant things than a hot, dry wind.

Whirlwinds are surely possessed of an evil spirit which delights in finding the most irritating thing to do. Over the veld they come, careering madly, collecting all sorts of rubbish, mealie sheafs, dried grass, black embers, dust, sand and whirl them round and round like an insane waltzer. Sometimes these whirlwinds made direct for the dining-hut, increasing in volume as they came, and when I saw one from the little window or heard it coming, I would fling my head and arms on the table clutching everything movable and wait for it to pass over me. This it would do, blowing in the blanket and covering me with debris. Sometimes, seeing I was fully prepared, it would change its mind at the last moment and turn aside and I would see it whirling round the bed-hut, snatching limbos and light articles, bowling over tins and chasing last week's paper.

One day in my efficient busy week, it was beautifully warm and I had the blanket hitched up while I darned and taught Bryan. We heard the rushing and saw the whirlwind pass us by and gambol up to the kitchen hut. "What have we here?" it seemed to cry contemptuously and the next minute, to my horror, I saw it had run careless fingers through the thatch and then the entire roof was lifted off as if it were a lid and deposited on the table nearby where Myros should have been working. I ran to the hut and of course found all my ceiling arrangements were broken and everything covered with dirt, including the milk setting in its tin. There was nothing to be done for Nkosi had gone to the siding with Peter. I returned to the hut, lowered the blanket, fixed it with stones and Bryan and I resumed work. Bryan had no great love of learning but he had a fine brain. He grasped slowly but perfectly and permanently, yet had a maddening inability to learn anything by heart. He seemed to have no sense of rhythm but grasped the full meaning. All through his childhood he was sick more often than he was well, but when he returned to his lessons he always picked up the thread just where he had dropped it.

As we were settling down again Dick burst into the hut, falling over the stones and dragging the blanket from its nails. He cried, "Babbijaan! Babbijaan!"

"Where?" I asked, the hardened colonial ready for any emergency.

"On top of the Kopje," he replied and running out of the hut we saw the baboon, just as he had said, sitting on a high rock and gazing around at the landscape. I was wearing out some court slippers which slipped at the heels, but I could not wait to change them. Seizing a gun, a .22, and amunition which might have killed a guinea fowl if shot through the heart, I climbed the kopje as quickly as I could followed by Bryan and Dick. Bryan suggested I should change my shoes and take the big gun, but I ignored him. I climbed up as quickly and as quietly as I could, and as I neared the top I saw the baboon looking out and away from us. I suppose the wind must have been against us or otherwise he would have noticed our approach. Within about twelve yards he heard me and looked round. I levelled my gun though Bryan said, "Please don't shoot, Mummie! The .22 is not strong enough."

"Don't be a little coward!" I said. Then I took aim and fired. Only a shot as bad as I am could have missed the huge bulk of him, but luckily for me, the pellet did not touch him or he would have sprung at me and torn my throat to bits. In my novel, dear little Frances wounded the baboon because she could not be such a bad shot as to miss, and then as the baboon sprang at her, a neighbour, handsome but unhappily married, managed to be on the spot with a loaded rifle in his hands and shot the animal in mid-air. No wonder the publishers were not impressed. In actuality, the baboon turned round and glared at me with his little, fierce eyes and then barked furiously, and while I waited for the fatal spring he leapt off the rock and ambled away down the other side of the kopje, voicing his strong disapproval. I turned round to find Dick was nowhere to be seen, but Bryan was standing by me as white as death. Was ever a mother such a blind, conceited, melodramatic fool? As we walked down the kopje we met Dick who explained his absence by saying he had gone to find a stick, in order to hit the baboon when it attacked me, but unfortunately had not been able to find one.

Bryan was very quiet for the rest of the morning, but I was thrilled, planning how I should tell Nkosi of my adventure. I wished I had shot the animal. It would have been so lovely to have met Nkosi with,

"Come and see," and then have led him up to the huge, brown body of the dead babbijaan.

Anyway, it would be interesting writing up the story for my

mother who would of course, reply "Oh, my brave darling!"

Nkosi came home and of course the decapitated hut was the first news, and then I told him of the baboon. To my intense disappointment he was furious. First of all, the baboon sitting high above as he was, was no danger at all. He was only an old male baboon expelled from the pack and making his journey across country. Many times since we have seen just such another; they spend the night in the cave under the balancing rock on which they sit. Secondly, I was mad to climb the kopje in highheeled court shoes and a complete fool to think a .22 would kill a baboon. If I wounded it.... here he told me in great detail how a baboon attacks his foe. Finally, I was a criminal to take Bryan up with me. When he had delivered himself of these sentiments he left me, to arrange about the re-roofing of the kitchen-hut, and I went away alone, and instead of realising what a poor sort of creature I was, I felt furious. Nkosi was a brute!

We had lunch in silence and afterwards I put the children to rest and set out to look for trouble. I soon found it. Chicken water-tins were empty, hens were discovered eating their eggs, turkeys were unattended. The two house-boys were of course, taking their siesta and I found the contents of the kitchen spread out in the revealing sunshine. The saucepans were filthy, the china smeary, and the kitchen towels unwashed. In the safe was a blue-bottle. The bread box smelt stale. Hot and cross I went from discovery to discovery, my temper rising as I went. What had made me so pleased with myself? What had made me think I was a success? Not one of my triumphs had been lasting. On every side were instances of neglect.

When the longed-for mail bag arrived, there was no English mail. This only happened occasionally but when it did it was a tragedy. Besides bills there had been a letter from an acquaintance of Nkosi's saying he was bringing his wife for a long week-end the next day. I was not to worry for they would bring all their food, a tent, camp beds and an efficient servant who would help to prepare food. I felt at least I ought to make a cake, so I set to on a ginger one exactly like the one that had been so admired. I felt the success of the cake would wipe out a little of the awful sense of failure that rankled with me.

When I got the children up, I found that Dick had burned the front of Peter's shirt while ironing it. The type of iron we used held red-hot cinders and when the boys blew at these, sparks often flew out and burned the article being ironed. Dick had folded the shirt so that I should not see the burn.

When he came back there were more fireworks about this, and Myros had a display regarding the kitchen's state of filth. Just as tea was made and I was going to sit down and cool off, a boy came to say that Nkosi would like to have his tea sent out to the lands and that meant cutting sandwiches. When he saw them, of course, Peter wanted some too. When Dick brought the thermos I found it had been put away dirty and had "*very much smell.*" Why hadn't Dick washed it? He replied he had not heard the smell.

When the tea was ready and sent off I found Bryan and Peter wanted more sandwiches and, having been cross I felt I must do this to make up to them. When Peter asked for even more I got angry. I wished I had never come to Africa. I was not a heroine, I was not even capable. I did damn-fool things and could not even housekeep properly. Then remembering the cake which by now should be cooked I went to the hole and found Myros in the act of putting on the lid. I screamed at him and he explained that he was only looking, but I knew the worst had happened. The lid of the cook-pot must never be taken off though I had intended having the tiniest peep myself. I saw that the cake had sunk down in the middle, never to rise again. I took it out. It was absolutely uneatable and with a cry of rage I threw it into the veld and passionately set to, to make another, telling Myros that he would be responsible for the cooking of it, and if it went *panzi* (down) he would give me two and sixpence (an idle threat as Myros knew very well).

I went back to my darning. Woollen socks covered with black-jacks and grass-seeds like hedgehogs. The sand inside went down my finger-nails and I had been the washer. I would never trust woollen socks to the boys. My temper raged. I was inefficient, foolish, criminally careless. I was no good. I wished I were dead, and when Peter upset my darning basket and everything rolled into the sand I smacked him. He opened his mouth into a square and gave way to the tears to which I also longed to indulge. It was not pain, but surprise and loss of dignity with him. Bryan was very kind to him and lured him away with the promise of a game, and I thought the two of them were ranged together against me. Everybody was against me! Oh, for my mother, who alone appreciated me! But I would not cry; I was too angry.

Then Myros came up with a snapshot I had taken of him

before we moved. He had begged me to do it and offered me
sixpence towards expenses. He had arrived for the picture
dressed up. He wore shrunken white trousers over which
were drawn brightly coloured bicycling stockings, showing
up his bandy legs cruelly, a gent's evening tail-coat, a yellow
striped tie and a gawdy bead decoration on his lapel like a
foreign order: an old straw hat and a walking stick completed
the ensemble. I had begged him not to be taken like that, but
he insisted that his mother in Nyasaland, who had asked for
the photograph would prefer it. Now Myros — evidently not
aware of my state of mind — came up and taking the
dilapidated snap from his pocket-book handed it to me. He
said his mother had written that it was not pretty enough, so
could he have his sixpence back? That was the last straw! My
sense of humour was dead! I seized the stocking basket and
threw it at him and, realising that his request would not be
granted, he walked away muttering dark things about
"skellum missises."

I left everything then and ran up the kopje and over to the
far side. Here I found what I have since called my "Misery
Seat," a place I have always retired to so as to be able to
indulge in a good cry without worrying Nkosi or harrowing
the children.

When I came down I realised that I was aching all over,
and must have been aching all over all day, and now there
was a pricking in my throat. I put the children to bed,
trying to make up to them for my beastliness. My fat Peepy
hugged me tight, and it seemed he still loved his nasty
mother. I knelt down by Bryan's bed and told him how
horrible I was. He said I was not, that I was very brave to
try and shoot the baboon. I put my head on his chest and he
stroked my hair and told me I was his own Mummie-goat.
When people say that all children are little animals, selfish
and aggressive, I disagree. To me there is nothing more
wonderful than the way a child accepts punishment from an
angry and often unjust parent, and bears no malice at all.

I did not feel hungry that night and Nkosi, seeing my
swollen eyes and blotchy face, tried to make up for his
censure, which had been perfectly justified. He talked of the
people who were coming the next day. I said that I had
made a nice ginger cake, I had the weekly raw meat and as
the guests were bringing bread, cooked meat and a cooked
ham, there was no need for me to do any more cooking.

We went to bed, but I could not sleep because my legs

ached so, and I lay and thought of the baboon and how it might have torn me to bits before Bryan's eyes. I had not thought of that, and how he had stood by me. I thought of my happy little Peeps and the smack I had given him for no real fault, and how he had hugged me when I put him to bed. I felt slight resentment against Nkosi. I felt that my stupidity about the baboon should not have wiped from his memory all my many courageous and successful activities. It seemed that when things went right he gave no praise, but when they went wrong he never hesitated to allot blame. I told myself that to make him proud of me again, I would manage the week-end before us perfectly, however achey I felt. I went to sleep planning . . . .

When I woke up the next morning my throat was sore. It might have only been borer-dust. Borer-dust fell from the rafters in a continuous stream, and once I had found a little pile on Nkosi's forehead. Since then I had wrapped my face up in butter muslin until we could afford another mosquito net. I got up and found my legs were aching badly, and having gargled, that my throat was only slightly better. I dressed and dragged myself around. My throat became worse and I could feel the pain of ulcers from the outside. I felt hot and shivery and knew it to be my old enemy, tonsillitis. As there was no way of getting in touch with the visitors to put them off and I wanted to show Nkosi what I could do, I wrapped my throat up in a scarf and went slowly from duty to duty.

I had prepared tea for my visitors but they did not arrive until darkness had fallen and there was a scramble to put up the tents. To my acute disappointment I found that the "efficient servant" was sick and had been left behind. In his place were two extra guests. To my catering eye, they appeared large hungry-looking men.

We sat down to dinner, the five of us crowding the little hut on four chairs and a petrol-box, the lady guest had gone straight to bed as she was not feeling well.

After we had finished, I walked across in the pitch dark to the kitchen-hut where, by flickering candle light I found Myros trying to sort out vast quantities of raw meat brought by my guests. The ham was also raw. Besides this, one of the extra men had shot a buck on the way out and now its dripping carcass was added to the shambles. I told Myros to sling it from the rafters, but as the roof was too low to allow it to hang over one of the two tables and drip decently in a basin, it had to hang over the narrow aisle which was already occupied by Myros and myself. As we stacked meat on dishes, balanced them on bowls of water, and covered them with old curtains, the buck gently buffetted me on the back and dripped blood into my shoes.

It was too dark to see if we had made the meat really ant-and-fly-proof but I did not care. I told Myros to barricade the door as the last time we had killed a buck a leopard had tracked and taken it. Then promising myself I would be up before the flies got busy, I made my way to the sleeping hut. As I went I saw the four men sitting smoking and yarning in a pool of light; the guest had fixed his car spot-light on a tree. The darkness around them seemed more intense.

The next morning I was up before the sun. The ham had to be cooked before it was time to put the joint in for dinner, mid-day. I only possessed two saucepans.

Meals had to be served in two sittings and it was only when Myros asked for bread to make toast for myself and the children that I found that my visitors had forgotten to bring loaves as they had promised. Had I known the night before I could have set the dough but now the only thing to do was to take the ham out of the pot and make a baking-powder loaf immediately. My guests and family so enjoyed the hot, new loaf that nothing remained after the second sitting had been served. It was the same with dinner, with tea and supper; the hot loaves were greatly enjoyed and as I made loaf after loaf my thoughts were not hospitable.

In between roasting, boiling and baking, I battled with the raw meat and the bleeding buck. The second extra guest, not to be outdone by his friend, had been out early and shot a koorhaan. It was not only illegal but unnecessary and I felt like reporting him to the police. As the day grew warmer the meat began to smell. I sent a joint each to my neighbours but that made little impression and everything that was not a recognised joint and might be called for by name, I gave to the boys. I rubbed salt into what seemed like acres of flesh and packed it in petrol-tins which leaked blood. All day long I had to keep pulling the lumps out to see where flies had laid their eggs, remove the eggs and rub in more salt where necessary. There was blood on the old curtains, blood in every bowl and basin and pools of it on the floor. All that week-end I battled in a red world and wished that my sore throat would ascend to my nose and so mercifully deaden my sense of smell.

Nkosi enjoyed the visitors. One of the extra men surveyed the farm which was a great help. The children were very good, but I remember Peter rather shocked our lady guest. He showed her the puppies now crawling about.

"These puppies" he said, "came out of Biddie's tummy."

She passed this over by saying kindly, "Oh, did they?"

"Yes" said Peter, hoping to convince her, "You may not believe it but that is what happened."

She countered this by saying how nice it was to have some dear little puppies, but Peter replied.

"It wasn't really very nice because she had them on the dish-cloths."

The two extra men went off on Monday morning but the original guests stayed the week, during which I went on fighting a losing battle with the law of decomposition, and the habits of ants and flies.

My throat was clearing up when we saw our guests off. By this time we were eating salted buck and on Sunday evening to celebrate our freedom we went over to Effie's.

After tea she played all the old tunes way back to "Egypt, my Cleopatra," "Navaho" and "Goodbye my Bluebell." We sang until we were hoarse and ended with "We are but little children weak."

On our return we found a boy with a tale of woe. Our herd-boy had lost one of the oxen and had visited the Mashona squatters to look for it. These natives, evidently with a bad conscience and full of beer had attacked our boy with a chopper and cut his head open. His friend had brought him back to the compound and would like Nkosikas please go to him and see the wound.

For once I refused and told Nkosi he must go because I could face no more bleeding meat.

Chapter 11 — Wild Weather.

It had been a very hot day, most unseasonable for September. Even before breakfast it was hot and by ten o'clock it had settled down to what Nkosi called a stinker.

Walking out into the sun was like entering an oven. There was not a breath of wind and the flies were entertaining all their relations for miles around to sup on the sweat of suffering humanity. It was a day when the milk would curdle, the meat smell, the butter melt and the bread rasp the throat that tried to swallow it and when the housekeeper, if she is wise, does not look to see what has gone wrong because she has no intention of doing anything about it.

Hotter and hotter and from twelve to two the sun just stood still and stared. The children and I lay on our beds in the hut, panting, and hoping poor Nkosi had had the sense to lie under a shady tree.

At four we washed and emerged for tea and found that though the sun was no longer flaming, it had settled down to a steady glow and had no intention of leaving us until it had to. As the children were so cross and tired, I gave them a cold sponge and put them to bed early for it was cooler in the hut. They lay tossing on their beds. When I came out of the hut I noticed that the air was unnaturally still, and as I gave my baby ducks a last feed I saw the sinking sun was lighting up a huge black cloud in the east. It was almost dark when I had finished feeding the ducks, and I wanted to see if the newly-hatched chickens were all right so I took a candle to look in the box which stood under a tree. As I carried it, the flame did not flicker and I left the candle burning there.

The failing light had a peculiar tinge, and the veld seemed to be holding its breath as though it were waiting for something momentous to happen. As the sun disappeared so darkness fell and up sprang a hot fierce wind, knocking down the candle and sweeping everything before it. The bread-box fell with a crash from its tree and Nkosi's basin and oddments clattered to the ground.

"What is it?" I cried, but Nkosi was rushing about saving things from the hurricane, and I joined in.

The wind became bitingly cold as the great black cloud raced menacingly towards us. Distant lightnings lit up the sky beyond the swiftly approaching cloud, bush-fires raged. A wind carrying anything it could pick up whirled past us so that we could scarcely move against it. We fought our way about shutting things up, saving things in this weird half-light. The wind moaning eerily increased every moment. We struggled to shut Biddie up in the dining-hut but we were buffeted about and had to cling to each other. The trees bent to the ground and we were blinded with twigs and husks and sand. There was a sudden silence and stillness and then . . . . with a roar the rain came down like an overturned bucket. We dashed to the hut as a huge clap of thunder rolled overhead. We shut the door and lit the candles, but they were immediately blown out for the wind came over the rough walls under the thatch and played havoc inside. Our little window which had been half open was blown outward and wrenched back and the rain beat over the boxes stacked outside, into the room. It was some time before we could force it shut again. When this was done it became a frame to a wild picture which every few seconds was lit by the vivid flashes of lightning.

"It looks as if the evil spirits are out to-night!" I said but Nkosi did not answer: he was attending to Bryan who complained that the rain was coming through the roof on to his bed. Then we saw that the old grass roof could not stand up to the fury of the rain and was not only leaking in many places, but here and there the water was coming through like a tap. Quickly we set to work on Bryan's bed which was soaking. I collected the wet sheets and blankets and found that the rain had not penetrated the mattress. We moved the bed as much as we could in the crowded space, and covered the others with mackintoshes on which we set any utensil we could lay hands on which would hold water. We used the wet sheets and blankets to protect the other things. The floor was soon a river of mud and the flour and other perishables had to be lifted on to the beds. The storm was furious, but we were so busy that we had no time to be frightened. Peter did not share in the excitement. He said in a momentary lull:

"I don't like that nasty noise!" As the thunder rolled and rolled against almost incessantly, I left Nkosi and Bryan to carry on with the salvaging, took Peepy on to my lap, and sat on a bed holding the umbrella over us both. I held him tight because I remembered my neighbour telling me of her friends who were struck by lightning in their *daga* hut. She had said,

"They died instantly."

We had no lightning conductor on the hut because we had been told that it could not rain in August. We knew now that there was a great deal of banded ironstone about. In another lull Peter asked

"Is it God making that noise?"

"No, darling. God would not frighten us."

"Oh, well, it must be Jesus and I wish he wouldn't." The lull was now at an end, the storm gathered force as if annoyed at having expressed itself inadequately. It had meant MUCH More. Crash after crash and the wind shrieked round our little hut. "Away with it!" it seemed to cry and forced itself through fresh places. Bryan came and sat next to me and

Nkosi left his basins and toothbrush holder to ask if we were all right.

"Put the gramophone on," I said, "and then we shan't hear the noise so much." Nkosi put it on the bed in the middle of his family and slowly wound it up. He put on our second record, "Hear my Prayer" and came and sat next to me. There was a lull while the organ introduction was played. Then 'Hear my Prayer, Oh Lord incline thine ear', the boy's voice rang out clear between the thunder peals. I thought of our village church, snug and warm, with the organ pealing out while a thunderstorm raged outside. Nkosi turned it to the other side.

"Oh, for the wings, the wings of a dove...." and the thunder rolled away and the torrent of rain became a steady downpour. Further away went the storm, now only just audible, and the rain came down in a decorous way: then silence, save for the drip, drip of the thatch. Peter fast asleep was put rosy and warm into his bed. Bryan's bed was made up with fresh sheets and blankets from the trunk. Nkosi opened the door, the night was quite clear. Came a scamper of wet splashing feet and Dick arrived carrying a tray. He explained that, seeing the storm, he and Myros had taken a burning log into the kitchen hut and what wood they could lay hand on and had been sitting round the fire happily, not minding the smoke and quite water-tight because of the new roof. Dick brought coffee, damp bread and butter and cheese.

"Good Boy! Good Boy!" I cried and told him to make himself some coffee which I am sure he had already done. We sat on the bed and ate happily.

The next morning: lovely, beautiful, rainwashed world!

Chapter 12 — The House.

For over a year Nkosi and I had been drawing beautiful plans for The House. He, being practical, went strangely ornate and I, being imaginative, went extremely practical; so while he designed arches I designed built-in cupboards. When it came to the actual building however, all designs and plans were scrapped for we found we could only afford to build three rooms in a row, the middle one fronted with mosquito-netting wire, behind it one closed-in room with a fireplace, and behind one of the bedrooms an open veranda where we would have breakfast.

We engaged a native builder who said he had built many

large and beautiful houses, and we chose for a site a stretch of level granite on which we decided to cement the foundations. Our builder seemed rather hazy about angles, and I leapt into the limelight by remembering that three square plus four square equals five square and a hypotenuse came into it somehow, I was not quite sure where; but Nkosi seized on it with joy and knotted pieces of string and so the foundations were true.

Instead of being right out in the blue, I found we had several neighbours, all kindly and anxious to help with advice about building. The only difficulty was that each one had a different theory on roofing, and scorned the ideas of everyone else. Nkosi practised brick-laying after the boys had gone home in the evening. At first he had to pull his work down before the Master Builder saw it, but he soon became proficient.

When the walls were several feet up, we noticed that there were no doors. What would have happened had we not noticed it I do not know, though perhaps when the Master Builder found he had to use a ladder to climb inside, it might have dawned upon him. This mistake, added to the lack of right angling, made Nkosi lose his faith in the Master Builder, and so saved us much trouble in the future.

We started building in September and it was late October, suicide month, before we got the roof on. I have often wondered which month should be given the laurel for beastliness; February, when everything is so wet that no more moisture can be absorbed so it just hangs about; or October, when everything is so dry that one feels that one's life stream is being sucked out of one's body. I think October wins and that first October was the worst I have ever known, because I had to paint all the windows and doors three coats each in the glaring sun. If I suffered, Nkosi suffered more, because he had to make the huge wooden frames for the roof. These structures were to straddle the roof, and it was only when they were hoisted up into place that we found that, in spite of the hypotenuse, the walls were not straight and each structure had to be individual.

Then came the nailing of the iron. This was in the peak of October when the sky was cloudless and brazen, the air thick with smoke of distant veld fires, and searing hot winds blew fiercely. Luckily for us a nephew of the Afrikaans neighbour was out on holiday, and he very kindly helped Nkosi put on the roof. The two men found the iron so hot they had to sit

on sacks and how they swore; Jan in Afrikaans, Zulu and
English and Nkosi in English, Portuguese and Arabic. They
had a couple of natives to hand them things but the nails
slithered down the iron, hammers clanged to the ground, and
fingers were torn and bruised. I gave them dark glasses for
their red eyes, and cooling drinks for their parched throats;
and for the rest I left them alone, for though they had to
suffer there was no need to do so in silence.

When the roof was on we thought the worst was over, but
found our next step, guttering, was far worse. It seems that
putting up gutters is a peculiar form of torture. In all my
brilliant ideas of alterations, additions and improvements
through the years, I have learnt to steer clear of gutters
because Nkosi's patience may survive new roofs, but never
gutters. That first guttering made a deep impression on him.

After this the house seemed to stand still for the Master
Builder had to plaster the walls and later on cement the
floors. The *daga* he used for the walls was pure mud and
ever since we have been patching them. Week after scorching
week I continued painting, for though I rose at dawn it was
mid-morning before I had finished my daily rounds, and no
one who has not painted one, knows how many surfaces a
window has, or the vast acreage of a door on a hot day when
the painter cannot decide which way the brush strokes should
go. I could not endure the sun, and after repeated bilious
attacks I found I must wear a heavy felt hat and something
thick down my spine as well.

The veld had become purple in its dryness, and the young
tufts of grass which had sprung up after the early fires had
now shrivelled. The veld spread black around us, and the
road-tracks stretched across it like twin hair partings. The
cattle wandered about unable to fill themselves, for we had
no reserve silage to feed to them. Several of our precious
beasts died; and when we made the herd-boy take them to
the vleis where a few green tufts remained by the shrunken
waterholes, the hungry oxen waded in the water to drink and
stuck. With no energy to pull themselves out there they
stayed, lay down and died. We began to dread the sight of
the herd-boy.

Our capital was now finished and the crop which was to
bring in cash for us to carry on was not yet planted. Everything
was in its infancy. The hens, turkeys and ducks were still
liabilities. Everything demanded money to be spent on it and
gave nothing in return. The huts, instead of a refuge became

an abomination because flies invaded them, and I found it impossible to keep the food from going bad. The Very Efficient Woman had told me how to make a water-safe. You put a bowl of water on top of your safe and from it drags a bit of soaked sacking. The water percolates through this into tins below so that it is always wet and therefore always cool. Instead, it is always dry and warm, the only thing that is wet is the food inside the safe, and that helps decomposition. The ants, too, loved this way of easy access into the safe. I quite realise that it was my fault that the safe did not work, but the boys· never did anything unless I watched them, the house was at least a hundred yards away, and I was busy painting every moment when I was not cooking or teaching Bryan, and I did not give it the constant attention it needed.

October heat extended into November. Our well dried up and had to be deepened, and that meant all the fixings had to be removed and replaced. We found several petrol tins had been dropped inside. This explained the constant bickerings between Myros, Dick, the odd-job boy, and the builder's assistants over the ownership of petrol tins. Each boy had his allotted number to work with and I learned later that, when a carelessly tied bucket fell into the well, the owner went off and sneaked the bucket of another boy.

The oxen were too weak to work much, and as there were still journeys to be made to the siding for building material and farm needs, the ploughing was not going on as fast as we had hoped. The driver was always coming to say the waggon had died on the road. Nkosi would take out the old car to go and succour the waggon and that, too, died on the road and had to be resuscitated before it could go and resuscitate the waggon. Meanwhile, the waggon boys and attendants sat on the roadside doing nothing.

The heat became more and more intense and we longed for a House, somewhere to get away from the sun and the flies. At night the veld was trimmed with red rims of flames. We could see the outline of the hills and wondered how there could still be veld unburned.

November dragged on. Occasionally it rained miles away and the air cooled a little, but the next day it began "working up," for the heat has to reach a certain height before the rains can break. At first we had been glad that the rains held off because early rains would have found us shelterless: but now we were divided between our longing to begin planting and our need for a roof over our heads and cement under our feet. The Master Builder handicapped us daily with his lack of knowledge and experience. In cementing the floors he always managed to walk over a wet, soft floor to get to the next.

One day, I think it was November 25th, dark clouds gathered and thunder threatened, so although the house was in no way fit to receive us, we moved in putting our belongings on the floors not yet cemented. That night the rains broke. The noise of the violent rain on the roof woke us up and we soon stopped congratulating ourselves when we found the new roof leaked like a sieve. We began moving things about, catching leaks where they could do harm, and leaving them where they would help the cement. New daga walls not yet distempered were washed away in channels, but our beds were dry and it was a joy to have a real roof over our heads. Strangely enough, for years afterwards, when-ever there was a big storm, Peter insisted on going to bed, saying he liked lying there and feeling the rain could not get to him. I suppose it was the result of the storm in the hut.

While we were pottering about diverting the floods I said "Just in time! Isn't it lucky?"

Nkosi said, "Must have a bit of luck considering I have lost five oxen." (That was counting the one the Mashonas stole).

"This will help the grass," I said, ever the encouraging wife.

"It will if it keeps on," he said and, as if it had heard him the rain stopped and, going outside, we saw the night was clear and cloudless though a few optimistic frogs were croaking.

The next morning there was not a vestige of rain. The parched earth had sucked it all up and when the sun came it squeezed out any drops of moisture not already absorbed. So followed days of work and heat. We could see it raining in far away places but it would not come to our private Sahara, and every week was a week lost for all maize should be in by Christmas.

My surviving ducks were sold to the butcher to pacify him, but my turkeys, a flock of forty youngsters who had escaped death and only suffered casualties from hawks, eagles and snakes, looked well. At least they had been looking so well that I had relaxed from giving the unstinted attention they had had when younger. Then I became aware that they were looking miserable and when I caught one I found that its head was covered with wart-like spots. The Very Efficient

Woman diagnosed this as Chicken-Pox and showed that each little wretch had it. The treatment was loathsome; the spots had to be dabbed with raw kerol and the dried-up scabs had to be removed and burnt, or chicken-pox would spread to every other feathered inhabitant on the farm. Some of them bubbled at the nose and these had to be wiped. If not wiped, the noses swelled up into great red shiney lumps and the disease went to their throats and choked them. About ten died immediately, another ten could not make up their minds, but after a fortnight's nursing, decided life was not worth it, and gave up. The others survived to live a stunted life. These were my first dealings with turkeys and long years of misery followed. It is only now, when I can have any sick fowl killed immediately, that they thrive.

PART IV.

THE ANXIOUS MONTHS.

Chapter 13 — The Rains came.

THE rains began at last and there was great activity on all the farms. The men shook off their troubles and worries and seemed years younger. We were all sure that now the season had started with such good rains we should have bumper crops.

Harrows followed by planters were creeping up and down the lands, and it was lovely to know that under the soil, little maize seeds were swelling and green shoots were bursting.

The convalescent turkeys shook off their lethargy and jumped at the first flying ants as they broke from their sealed prisons, lifting crumpled wings and joying in their moment's freedom. Parrots squawked with delight and at sundown came the *brbrbrbr* of the night-jars as they swooped round the house. At night the deep croaking of the bull-frogs sounded like hundreds of old men talking in their London Clubs. In the mornings, white mist clung to the valleys, making them look like inland lakes among the mountains.

As the days passed, green shoots of maize began to appear in long lines and the grass became luxuriant. The famished cattle took on new life and the cows gave richer milk. The rivers, for so long dried up or stagnant, now flowed along happily if muddily, and later on the mimosa trees were a joy to see.

Although my days were spent in cooking, teaching, distempering and painting, yet in the evenings I found myself making flower beds. At this time of the year we women always ache to put our fingers in the moist, sweet-smelling earth. The brazen sky that had tormented us for so long was now bright blue, and lovely little clouds lingered about like blobs of cotton wool.

Nkosi though very busy, was really happy at this time. He put in two hundred and fifty acres of maize and calculated that at only ten shillings a bag, and only ten bags to the acre, we should rake in a thousand pounds or more, which would meet the mounting debts and carry us on to the next year.

He now fancied himself as a bricklayer and put up a garage with a deep inspection pit which was so pitchy black that it was quite useless for any inspection and which collected hammers, spanners and an occasional snake. When the heavy rains poured through the thatch it became flooded.

The first great storm washed my vegetable garden completely away. Since then hardly one year has passed when it has not been carried away sooner or later. This is inevitable since garden boys are annuals. They arrive say in August full of energy and prepare many beds, nearer and nearer the spruit. When told that the rains will wash the beds away the garden boys will not listen. When rains come and the garden goes the mistress says, "Now you see!" and he replies yes, he sees, and he will never do such a foolish thing again; which is the truth because when the rains are over his brother will be sick, his wife unfaithful, or his father will die, and he will be called away and a new garden-boy comes and has to learn the same lesson.

At first it rained only at night so that the sunny days were cool and fresh. Then it began to rain in the mornings also, and when Nkosi cultivated his maize and the weeds were smitten, a healing shower revived them. Finally great storms broke one after the other until the lands were too wet to touch and the weeds reigned supreme.

The house leaked badly, but we knew now where to place the bowls. Driving rains came slanting through the wired front of the house, and the open-room at the back was soon under water. Rain pushed its way through the window frames and in the evening our only escape was the inner room which, having no ceiling, received from the open veranda not only rain and wind but myriads of insects which were attracted by the lamp. On cold, wet nights we lit our fire which smoked foully and sat before it in coats.

In our English farmhouse we had suffered a chimney with a straight draught and remembering this, Nkosi had designed a nice curving chimney stack, the top of which was cemented. From the beginning it smoked badly. The smoke was willing enough to go up the chimney but the tortuous course discouraged it, and after fruitless attempts to find a way out, it gave up and came back. After a miserable evening when we had had to choose between either warmth and suffocation

or being able to breathe and shiver, Nkosi mounted the roof
next morning, and found that the Master Builder has dropped
down the opening a large lump of cement which had completely blocked it.

The rains set in solidly and the roads soon became
impassable. As visiting ceased every farmer said that when it
cleared he would mend the roads. Nkosi spent his time
standing on the doorstep scanning the skies for a break in the
grey clouds. I spent my time trying to keep things dry in a
wet house. It is not usual in Rhodesia to get days of unbroken
rain, so that when they do come they are very depressing,
for we live with the sun streaming through our windows; we
walk in it; or sit on our verandas warming our feet in it. We
air our clothes in it, and expose cockroach-infested boxes to
its kindly rays. After a week or more of the wet weather I
felt like a fish in an aquarium and could almost feel my eyes
goggling and my mouth agape.

Our dreams of a bumper crop were shattered, for the maize
turned yellow and stopped growing while the weeds towered
above them. When we had sunk into utter depression the
weather suddenly cleared, and a thick crust soon formed on
the soil. We attacked the lusty weeds, but realised that virgin
sandveld was unsuitable for maize. For tobacco it would have
been excellent.

At the end of January, Bryan started going to the next-
door farm for lessons. The daughter there had just left school
and took him and another little boy, who lived two miles
away in another direction, and was brought to school every
day by a native on a bicycle. Later on two other children
came as boarders. The Government paid the teacher's salary
and provided books and stationery.

For the first few weeks Peter and I, the dogs and cats
walked with Bryan to school. Peter used to run before us
turning head-over-heels like a catherine-wheel. I must have
passed some of my fears of the veld to the children, for
though they were quite happy together, neither now liked
to go out alone. I knew it would not be long before Bryan
suggested going on his own, so I did not hurry him.

I used to take the .22 with me and the dogs got very
excited and tried to retrieve my kill. So as not to disappoint
them I used to shoot when they were not looking. Peter once
told a neighbour:

"My mother doesn't shoot birds, she shoots trees."

When we first came to the country Nkosi had bought me

a revolver. He put up a target and shutting the children in the house for safety, had given me my first lesson. I did not do so badly and thrilled with my prowess, I suddenly decided to draw and fire as they do in the wild-west films, but the revolver went off during the backward fling and narrowly missed Nkosi, who insisted that the shot passed under his feet and refused to teach me any more. He said that any native seeing my firing would have more respect for me than if I were a crack shot. But my mother was very impressed, she thought me very brave and called me her "wonderful girl."

My kitchen proved a great disappointment. By the time the house was finished the Master Builder had been sacked, and Nkosi had to tackle the kitchen on his own. He was so tired of building that when the walls cleared his head, he put the roof on; not a roof with king and queen posts but just iron nailed on top of the bricks. In consequence, through all the long years I have had to wear a hat when I cooked in hot weather or else suffer a bilious attack. There was only one reason I had been glad to leave my English kitchen, and that was to get away from the huge and clumsy built-in dresser which had covered one wall and held nothing if one did not have a step-ladder handy.

One Sunday Nkosi, as a surprise for me, carried in an enormous dresser he had been making for me secretly. This was worse than the home atrocity because it bulged from the wall. The top shelf touched the roof and the others were so narrow and widely spaced that they were quite useless. It had no drawers as the other one had, and no lower shelves at all, but it was a labour of love, and I had to endure it smilingly for many years before I could manage to dispose of it without hurting his feelings. He was in great need of planks I believe and I said I would sacrifice my dresser to help him.

I knew that Myros was not looking after the kitchen as he should but I was so very busy that I had not time to pin him down. There was always something more urgent to do. The eye attached to a body that is always running from one job to another does not see clearly, it does not want to, and the cluttered brain is only too glad to accept any excuse.

One afternoon I went into the kitchen instead of taking my short rest and found it full of smoke. Myros, too lazy to chop wood the right size, had rammed large logs into the stove which were now dropping out on to the floor. Gasping for breath I made my way to the closed window, which was warped with rain and thick with fly spots. When the smoke cleared, I noticed that the limed walls were grey and the inside of the iron roof was blackened with smoke. On the rickety saucepan-shelf was a layer of soot and dust and pots and pans were dull and greasy. Then I examined the petrol-boxes which held china. Every cup and plate was fly marked and as I moved a pile of plates, two fat cockroaches ran out. Cockroaches in a new kitchen! Myros must have imported them in the petrol boxes!

As I had no sink I had nailed a piece of zinc on to the old table and this was now red with rust and the corners black with grease. A pair of very soiled shorts was hanging on the same nail as the glass cloth.

Good housekeepers will protest, "SURELY the woman must have noticed some of these things!"

But the kitchen was low and dark, with soft daga walls which refused to hold a shelf. All my bright hopes had died at birth and there was little I could do about it. In the house itself there were hunderds of jobs that I must and could cope with, so I rather avoided the kitchen and acquiesced when Myros assured me that it was clean. I tolerated much from him because I dreaded having to do without him. He was a cunning boy. He was always "about to do" the thing I mentioned and made me understand that it was only overwork that had prevented him from doing it before. When I traced a crime to his door he always traced it back again to some fault of mine. The flies were abundant because my home-made spray was useless. The pots were not as clean as he would like to see them, because. he had not been provided with pot-cleaners. The cloths were dirty because I had been mean about soap. He longed to scrub the table, but how could he with a scrubbing brush that was quite bald? Check-mated, I would hurriedly leave the unappetising kitchen and do my cooking on the back veranda in the bright light thus avoiding the dark little hovel called the kitchen.

This afternoon the sunlight was streaming in and my eyes were opened. When Myros returned he received the full blast of my anger which was all the more furious because I knew that I was to blame. It was unfortunate for Myros that he was always in a state of indignation, because now he had no way of expressing his hurt surprise and outraged dignity. Luckily for me, Nkosi came in and Myros left hurriedly, never to darken my kitchen again.

I managed without Myros but it meant leaving other jobs, so I was delighted when a neighbour, hearing of my plight, sent me a boy with a briefie.

He arrived small, bright and in spotless white.

"What is your name?" I asked, trying not to appear too eager.

"Lice," he replied.

"Lice?"

"Ya, Nkosikas, me name Lice."

"Haven't you another name?"

"*Aikona*," with the intonation of "No Honestly," "me, Lice."

"I couldn't call you that," I said wondering who had given the boy such a name. I had heard of "Bicycle," "Just now," "Towel" and "Coffee". To my relief Nkosi came up and continued the interview.

"It's all right," he said, "the boys' name is Rice."

I explained to Rice what a dirty boy Myros had been and he seemed suitably aghast. "And," I said as I left him, "Remember your name is R R R ICE."

He smiles, "Ya Nkosikas, me name Lice."

Chapter 14 — The Army Came.

One evening when we were walking round the farm, Nkosi was for once quite talkative and, instead of striding on ahead of his panting family, sat down on a fallen log and said "This place is very beautiful. We are having to work far harder than I thought, but I think it will be worth while." I was absolutely thrilled and, answering suitably, I made him talk of the future, a thing I loved doing. I remember this evening because he said I was doing well, and, as always when I was young, a word of praise made me feel I would face untold dangers and work myself to my last quiver of energy to justify his praise. Always the desire of appreciation! How it keeps coming out! I was quite annoyed when Bryan ran up and said, "Daddy, look at this caterpillar!" We told him to run away but he persisted, determined that his father should look at the little striped insect in his hand. Nkosi said "Run away. It's nothing particular, I've seen hundreds prettier than that."

"But it's a new one Daddy. I've never seen it before." — Bryan, with his eye for detail.

"There are thousands of insects you have never seen before," said his father. "Every day I find a new one. Run away." Our delightful conversation came to an end; we started to go home. Bryan said, "I wish you would look at them Daddy. There are millions and they are eating all the mealies. Oughtn't we to pull them off?"

Nkosi said bitterly, "There is always something eating the mealies. Don't loiter."

"But, Daddy, there aren't hardly any mealies left. Look!"

"A bad patch. Come along."

Bryan hesitated and then ran after us as we passed into the bush. As we walked in single file along the white path, green trees brushed down on us and peculiar fruits fell at our feet, while the sunshine glinted through the branches. When we emerged into a clearing we could see the dark green of tree-covered hills, and the bright green of the younger maize. Beyond the hills rose others of mottled brown, and behind them the mountains, dull blue, peak after peak.

On that evening we were at peace and found for once in our busy lives that we had time to look about.

There are so many tiny wonders in the veld, but anxious and worried, we pass them by. There are many strange insects, and coloured butterflies, and the tiny bird-like butterflies themselves, darting about so quickly that only sharp eyes can follow them.

The dread and repulsion I had first felt for insect-life in its rightful habilitation was now being replaced by wonder and amazement. Nkosi had shown me the leaf-insect, more like a leaf than many leaves, the stick-insect with joints like knots in a stick. Then the busy white ants making their tunnels, and the black ants pushing a beetle into their underground homes. It was some time before I actually saw the female beetle laboriously pushing its ball of dung containing the precious eggs. It is interesting to watch how every few minutes she mounts the ball to take her bearings, and then reassured of her direction, jumps down and goes on pushing, the lazy husband hanging on to the side taking a free ride.

This evening as we wandered over the veld we disturbed dove pairs who suddenly sprang from the thickets on the tall anthills. Occasionally a koorhaan flew up, and Biddie darted after it barking loudly and jumping in an absurd effort to catch it.

As the sun dipped, we saw our little homestead looking small and comfortable among the trees, a thin spiral of smoke telling of the waiting fire, unnecessary but delightful. Once again we walked into the darkening bush and when we emerged, we saw the house nearer, bigger. The sun seemed to sigh gently as it left the sky and the darkness hurried on, and as we came up we saw the night-jars circling round the house with their long, black tail-feathers. Home! Those evening walks in the wet season are always a joy.

The next morning I was making biscuits on the veranda when Nkosi came back from the siding with bad news. The country was attacked by Army Worm. He had heard it from the Guard. In some parts the Army was so great that the train skidded on the lines. These creatures came like a sea, and when they had passed everything was stripped bare.

Nkosi, having broken the news went out into the lands and came back with a caterpillar like those Bryan had found the night before. It was green with long yellow stripes. The Army Worm had attacked our maize.

As it was Saterday Bryan was at home so we all turned out to go from land to land to find out the damage. It was very great. On some of the plantings each maize stalk was covered with the nasty crawling things and the leaves were mere skeletons. The ground and the grass verges were smothered with the little striped bodies.

For two long days we worked picking off the caterpillars from the stricken plants. In bad places we knocked them off with sticks, trampling them into the ground with fierce joy. We had trenches dug in front of the untouched lands in the hope of checking their ruthless advance. On the veld between the lands we tied branches to harrows and dragged them up and down, but still the Army Worm advanced and the mealies held up their stripped midribs pathetically or, weighted down with the numbers of fat, full caterpillars, lay broken on the ground. At night when I shut my eyes to sleep, I could only see the striped bodies crawling, crawling, crawling.

After three days the Army had passed, leaving in most of our lands complete destruction. One large land was past all hope, so that we allowed the oxen to graze there. The others, though they looked very bad, might, Nkosi said, revive if we had rain.

We were very anxious. A soft rain would help the maize, but the sun so earnestly prayed for seemed to have come to stay, and day after day dawned cloudless and brilliant and the mealies gave up the fight and died. The crop so anxiously waited for would be less than half of what we had expected. We should have to save enough bags to feed our natives, our stock and poultry. How many bags would there be to sell to meet the bills steadily mounting up? Besides this we had to finance another year.

No rain fell, and every day the ground became drier and harder. February, usually the wettest month of the year, had brought only half an inch. Nkosi dug his stick into the ground a hundred times a day fo find moisture. He kicked it with his heel, but it was bone dry. The eaten mealies turned blue and came off in his hand when he touched them. Each evening we went for our agonising walk, until one day Bryan burst out crying and said he was not coming.

I tried to cheer poor Nkosi, but he refused to be cheered and kicked clods and swore. I tried to explain to him how often I find that I have been concentrating on the little things for weeks, nasty things like cockroaches and fish-moths and stains on mats, and I said,

"It really is silly when there is all that space over the mountains and up into the sky."

He said, "I wish there were some decent looking clouds."

I stood and watched the blue fading now. Golden clouds hid the sinking sun, but there was one strange patch of rainbow colour among a grey bank of clouds, as if the silver lining were hanging out. There was an amazing assortment of clouds. Surely there must be one that would suit Nkosi. Some of the clouds were like young carrots, some like little black mats, and others like lumps of swansdown. Then there were banking clouds, clouds of every shade and texture, as if Nature had a table full of beautiful remnants. In the North far over the mountain range, clouds were banking up in a grey line but we could still see the golden rim of the earth below it.

"Aren't they rain clouds?" I asked Nkosi but he was squashing insects. He now had a complex that way. "Do look!" I said. He raised his head, and we saw that from the dark a thin line was spilling, a little dark column .... it was raining far away. As we watched the line it thickened.

"Rain on about half a farm," said Nkosi.

"Look, it's splitting further up," I said, and we saw that another streak was falling from the dark cloud. Fascinated, we watched the two streaks broaden and approach, the lightning flashed again and again, and the thunder became louder, the growls now deep rumblings.

Zig-zag came the forked lightning and the mountains were lost in a thunder cloud. Still the sky was clear grey above us.

"Will it come?" I asked.

"There is a chance," Nkosi replied. The sun having dipped,

we walked back to the house. Together we stood at the door facing the oncoming storm. Would it come or would it leave us at the last moment as it had so often done? There was a solemn stillness as if the thirsty earth were waiting, longing for relief. Flash again and now a heavy roar, forked lightning over the hills, then the black spreading cloud hid the hills and a cold wind blew heavy with the glorious scent of fallen rain.

Now ribbon lightning pierced the blackness and the cloud spread and spread. We could not move. To the left, sheet lightning, to the right prolonged flashes, and in the centre crackling lightning, and still no rain.

I said, "Why doesn't it rain? I could tear my hair and shriek and roll in the dust! It must rain!"

Nkosi said, "My God, if it did rain it would put hundreds of pounds into my pocket."

A lull again and then came the wonderful scent, parched earth gasping new life. The wind dropped and the thunder rolled away into the distance. Darkness. Silence. The storm had gone.

We turned from the door disconsolate.

Suddenly, there was a great roar and flash after flash of lightning. We rushed out. The mountains were visible again, for the great canopy was overhead. Roars; louder roars. Oh, God! let it rain! A spatter on the roof, gentle rain, hardly more than a sighing of the wind. "It's raining!" "It isn't! Don't say that or it will go away!" "Now it's gone."

A strong patter which quickly died to nothing. It was wonderfully bright towards the mountains. It was not going to rain after all! Listen! Soft again, a swift rattle, and a frog croaked. Then a steadier rain on the iron roof, and the thunder and lightning stopped. Only the fringe of the blasted storm, the blasted fringe, someone else is getting it! Hell! Listen! Listen! The steady rattle is stronger and louder. It IS raining. Don't speak yet! Louder, stronger, gutters are getting busy, are overflowing. At last, down comes glorious rain so loudly now that no one can be heard. Through the windows a black world. Occasionally a flash shows up the wet, running paths and the grey sheet of rain over the land. Oh the relief of it! The earth drinking in greedily .... new life, new hopes.

Chapter 15 — Disappointments came.

After the drought in February, the continued heavy rains in March surprised nobody, and the mealies having turned blue with drought now turned yellow with rain, as they had done in January. The chameleon-like behaviour boded no good. I learned that the old joke that a farmer is never pleased with the weather is stark truth. I have known Nkosi the most reasonable of men, to want sunshine and rain at the same time; and I have felt that if the Creator were to take an intelligent interest in the prayers of farmers He would go insane.

Our maize crop was a depressing sight and our estimate of possible yield, grew less and less.

My hens were laying fairly well, but the eggs had to go towards the grocery bill and, as other farmers' wives have found out, just as a hen is in the right mood for laying, the food gives out, and by the time money has been found to buy fresh supplies the hen won't play. Some of my turkeys were now ready for sale, but nobody wanted them. If it had been Christmas, yes, or Show Week, but not during other months. They might be accepted at a cheaper rate of course, so, as the butcher was in arrears, we gave them to him at his own price.

March went out with a few violent storms to finish up the destruction of the maize crop. What mealie stalks were left were dashed to the ground and immediately set upon by white ants. April, loveliest of months, came in with the grass still green and an occasional harmless shower keeping the flowers bright and the air cool and sweet.

I had not started another garden after ours was swept away, but tried to grow a few lettuces near the house. This was just possible in the wet weather, if one could prevent the hens from straying. During the February drought I used the bath-and-washing-up water. A refuse garden like this is never inspiring; the ground becomes white with grease and suds, and the lettuce lacks appeal when you find an old bacon rind twining itself round its heart. Nearly everything had been eaten by insects and hens in February; the remainder had been drowned and flattened in March; and now in April it was no use starting again because drought would begin any moment. A new garden had to be made near the river whenever Nkosi had time.

Although finances were low I decided that Bryan should

have a bicycle. All the other boys of his age had had bicycles for years, and were now riding horses and learning to shoot. Constant illness was having a bad effect on him and I felt something must be done to give him self-confidence. The grandparents and Kitty, his very generous godmother, always gave the children good presents, and any money gift was put in their Post Office Savings Bank because however hard up we were I was not going to take their few pennies for living expenses. I used a little of his money, added thirty shillings of my own and bought a second-hand bicycle. It was too big for him and therefore he took some time to learn, but as I panted after him I felt it was the right thing to do. When he had learned to ride he used to go backwards and forwards to school, and all over the farm. All trace of fear went.

This, when we had not enough money for food, may seem wrong, but I knew his need for independence was greater than his need for better food; and thirty shillings was only a flash in the pan or, rather, a figure subtracted from an "account rendered." Besides our hopes of a crop, though diminished, still existed. No doubt Frances and Hugh would have denied themselves and their children all pleasures and have grown thin and wan with mournful eyes. But in reality, when one is young hope keeps bubbling up and one cannot be depressed for long, because one knows that better times are coming.

Lice's reign was short-lived. He was clean but dishonest. Dick who had been so good in the huts, deteriorated in the house. Once we had settled down he found he had to do his own work, and he became impossible. After he had borrowed Bryan's bicycle without permission and had had it taken in lieu of a gambling debt, we decided he would have to go. Fortunately, we got the bicycle back. Fate having taken Lice and Dick gave me Charlie, who was a native from Portuguese territory. He was light-coloured, with a tattoo mark on each cheek bone and had a wonderful sense of humor, even if it was caused sometimes by my ignorance of the language. He had a great love of children and strangely enough in a native, a love of dogs.

In England one tries to save labour which is the most expensive item, but in Rhodesia one can only economise on ingredients, as labour is cheap. The Very Efficient Woman always made things and looked askance when I bought groceries and cleaning materials.

"Oh, but you can make them at home!"

Some of the economies the Very Efficient Woman gave me I found out later she had never tried herself. I have still my recipe book and on the recipe for making boot-polish I have written "Rotten!" That was mild to what Nkosi said when he found the sticky mess on his shoes. I was also given a recipe for floor polish. It contained beeswax and the house was immediately attacked by bees which as we had no ceilings, could not be kept out.

Rhodesian bees are one of our trials, decidedly nasty and most vicious. I used to think fondly of the dear old brown bumbly bee buzzing in our garden on summer afternoons in England. No one could raise any affection for a Rhodesian bee. I know houses which have been taken over by bees and at least two dining-rooms which every year pour honey on to the carpet. Rhodesian bees love motor-cars. Often ours has been invaded, and once, when Nkosi was in a hurry to get to town, he found at the last minute that bees had swarmed under the front seat of the car. There was no time to clear them out so he put a sack over the hole of egress and I had to sit on it.

It kept the bees in, but all the way into town I was wondering how long is a bee's sting.

I once made soap. Soap-making is very exciting because the caustic soda foams madly over the tin. I bought some rancid fat from the butcher and mixed it with mealie meal, which has great cleansing powers, and sifted ashes. When it was ready I poured it out into petrol tins cut lengthwise and lined with damp rags and allowed it to set. The great joy was cutting it up with a piece of wire. When this was done it had to be piled up and dried for some weeks.

My boys hated it, they said it was like a stone.

Through our long friendship, Effie and I have had our great moments of organization, enterprise, discovery and invention. If the credit for new ideas was a little in my favour, then Effie had far more to show for her efforts, for she is practical and thorough, so when I have "had an Idea" Effie has followed suit with improvements.

In the matter of soap, Effie was fascinated when she called to find me cutting some up and went home determined to go a step better. A week later, she sent me a piece of toilet soap. I was not feeling very well at the time with a cold in the head so I did not try it out at once.

The next days Nkosi said "The cat has been sick in the bathroom!" I said the cat had not been in the bathroom. "It must be Biddie, then," but as I could find no evidence of either of these accusations, I thought no more about it.

Having finished my work and washed my hands I sat down to do some mending and it was soon borne in on me that Nkosi was right, some creature had been sick. I asked Peeps, but he was very indignant and, though I was frequently sick when I had been out in the sun, I knew I was not the culprit. I searched the rooms diligently but could find nothing.

At lunch time Nkosi came stamping out of the bathroom "Someone *has* been sick!" he said angrily, "and not only in the bathroom!" He then walked all over the house sniffing violently, I followed joining my lady-like sniffs to his. "Damn it!" he said, "It's everywhere!" After more hunting accompanied by accusations and great indignation we traced the smell to the bathroom . . . . to Effie's soap.

Effie had found a recipe for toilet soap which needed eggs as well as fat. Not wishing to waste new-laid, she had used up some eggs she had put down in water-glass. Some of these had gone bad. When the soap was mixing she had noticed the smell was not very good, so had emptied into it a bottle of expensive eau-de-cologne her husband had given her for a birthday present. Alas! though the soap lathered and was lovely to took at, the eggs were too much for it.

When Nkosi found the cause of the trouble he picked it up and went to the old anthill that had defied my bread making. He came back smiling.

"Do you know that an ant's sense of smell is several thousand times as keen as a human's?"

Gradually the green of the country faded to a dull brown and the mealies, purple in their dryness, stood waiting to be reaped. It was a time of great nervous strain for, while other crops can be reaped and sold, maize has to stand for many weeks in the field before it is dry enough to be shelled.

During this time the natives steal the cobs wholesale, and as the lands are scattered about the owner cannot guard them. He has to learn that stealing is a sort of overhead if underhand expense; he must either grow no maize at all or grow enough to cover the plunder.

Money was very short and the farm was crying out everyday for more to be spent. The only way we could raise enough for current expense was to put up permanent brick-and-iron buildings and then ask the Government for a small loan on them. Nkosi built a cattle-dip by cutting it out of decom-

posed granite. He saved a great many bricks in this way and
the advance was nearly all profit.

The Jewish storekeeper near our first home, insisted on
continuing to supply us with goods, though we told him we
could not pay. Years afterwards, when we cleared up his
account, we asked him why he had gone on trusting us, and
he said he used to see us going past in our old dilapidated
car, and he knew that as long as we managed with that, his
money was safe.

The big agricultural dealers, however, were not so trusting.
They had lost large sums of money in the tobacco slump. They
were to blame for pressing credit on the growers, but now
that tobacco was worthless and the debtors had gone bankrupt, these dealers put up the prices and demanded cash
payment of monthly interest. With our crop about to be sold,
they all clamoured for "Stop Orders" and this we had to
accept. Meanwhile, Nkosi would prowl round his shrinking
crop every evening and see where precious cobs had been
pulled off by thieving hands.

At this time, the mail-bag, instead of being a joy, was a
thing of horror because it contained nothing but bills. Not
the friendly tucked-in envelopes with pleasant green half-
penny stamps but solid, sealed things, plumped up with a
covering letter to the account rendered and bearing a red
penny stamp.

One day when Bryan had opened the bag and found nothing
but typewritten envelopes bearing penny stamps he sighed
and said,

"Only raspberries to-day."

When our mealies were shelled we found that after sufficient
maize had been set aside to carry us through the next year,
for seed, native rations and food for the poultry and animals,
we had only four hundred and fifty bags to sell. Even at ten
shillings per bag this would not go far in paying our debts
and then there was the next year to be financed. It was a
great disappointment, but worse was to come.

Nkosi, on going to Salisbury to sell the crop, found no one
wanted it. Maize had slumped to 6/9d. per bag and the
recognised price of production was then seven shillings. We
thought ourselves very lucky to sell at seven shillings. Most of
this went in "Stop-Orders" and little or nothing was left to
meet the accumulation of bills.

Determined to make money somehow I sat every turkey-hen
that showed any inclination to sit. The Very Efficient

Woman said that when a turkey-hen does not seem to be able to make up her mind, a drink of port will influence her. As port was very cheap (2/6d. a bottle) we had a little left, I dosed one of my hens. However instead of making her feel drowsy it made her riotously drunk and she broke all her eggs. In the morning I found her sleeping it off with the result of her debauch scattered around her.

As the creature hatched I became pressed for coops and asked Nkosi for help, but he could not afford to buy wood and had not time to build brick so I wasted many hours trying to make the small boxes I had collected into large hocks, but it meant that every upright plank was in two shaky parts and when a roof was attempted, these collapsed and sank to the ground.

In desperation I started brick-laying. I had often helped Nkosi and it looked easy. Now I found that the size of a brick is definitely set to the span of a man's hand, and that a woman's hand can only stretch across it with much straining of muscles.

It was in the hot sun of a September afternoon that I started my single-brick wall. When it had risen to four feet and I was thinking of starting the second one, Peter, who had joyfully relinquished his afternoon's rest to help me leant heavily against the erection and it fell to the ground. Nkosi came up and asked what I thought I was doing with his bricks. I explained with heat that turkeyhens were sitting on nests of live (and dying) chicks, because I had nowhere to put them. He said I knew that he was going to make hocks when he had time, which he tried to make me believe was that very afternoon. Most husbands tell these little falsehoods but their unhappy wives know that to bring a husband to the point, some blood-sacrifice must be made by the wife.

Peter was now five and a half and I felt that he should have regular lessons. When one has a crowd of things waiting to be done, one has little patience to spare while a child dawdles over lessons. Peter seemed unable to think unless he was standing on his head. I used to show him the large cardboard letters I had brought from England and say, "What is this?"

He would say "Half a tic," rush to the home-made couch, stand on his head, throw his legs in the air, come back and say, "D". Now he was learning short words I found this method exasperating, but is was the only way that gave results. His heart was entirely in the farm, and numbers meant nothing to him. Directly I started talking of spans of oxen and half spans he would grasp the point immediately.

Everything seemed to take so long to do and it was not a question of management; no management can cope with lack of tools, leaky tins, insufficient brushes and the great shortage of everything. Nkosi would come in and demand "something shaped like this" or "something that will do for" a "something else". Then his eye would light on a most valuable part of my house equipment and I would spend the rest of the morning moving things round to try to make good my loss. I also found that a man must not be disturbed while he is doing a job, but a woman is essentially disturbable.

The time of the year between the selling of one year's crop and the planting of the next, sometimes three months, is always very trying. There is of course, plenty of work to do, brick-making, mending of implements and building, but nothing at all that brings in money. To our great shame we had to write home for help. Nkosi's father sent us £ 200 but pointed out that it must be a loan and repaid as soon as possible.

Earlier in the year we had invested in a pig. It was the runt of a neighbour's litter which we bought for a few shillings and she, Mary, was being fed on old scraps and broken mealies.

As farming seemed to be a "mug's game," everyone was trying to find gold. Our farm is on the contact, where the diorite rock intrudes into the older granite, and is a likely place for gold. We searched everywhere and chipped every reef we could find. Every evening I would hear the clank! clank! of the pounding and would go outside and watch Nkosi washing the crushed quartz, swirling the tail round and sometimes finding the tiniest trace of gold, but more often pyrites and a great deal of iron. Subsequent panning never brought a trace.

November came along and we were like "greyhounds on the leash, straining upon the start" and full of hope. After all, we told ourselves, we could not expect much the first year from virgin soil. This year there would be no Army Worm to ruin it and the price would have to go up, the Government would have to do something about it. Nkosi realised now that if he had to grow maize on the sand veld he would have to green crop it. Sunnhemp, the only available green crop, was at that time 30/- a bag. This was more than we could afford. Nkosi therefore bought one bag to sow. This precious stuff was to be reaped and the next year it would plant several acres which would be ploughed in. This land when planted with maize would yield a good crop. We also put in a bag of potatoes, though we were told they were usually unsaleable.

The rains broke early that year and we were soon up to our eyes in work and simply bursting with hope.

At the end of the year the School Inspector came out to examine the pupils of the little school. He praised the two boarders for their work and said they would be ready for Standard 2 when they went to school in the new year, but Bryan's work was disgraceful and he would not be promoted. I looked through his books and saw that Bryan's work was not as good as it had been when I handed him over. It was not the fault of the teacher, she was a kind, gentle girl; Bryan had just done as he liked. He had played about and allowed the other two to catch him up and beat him. I was furious and gave him the biggest scolding of his life. When we made it up he said he was ashamed of himself, but he had enjoyed playing about. He agreed to do lessons with me during the holidays; so that he might after all get into Standard 2 in January. The little school was now shut down as all the children were going to boarding-school. The boarding fees were £ 16 per term plus tuition fees, but through a friend we managed to get a small Government grant to help with this. Bryan had to go to school and the fees would just have to wait until we could pay them.

So the first year closed, bills mounting up, debt to the Government accumulating interest, but the lands green with maize and the treasured sunhemp sprouting up as it ought to. All our faith and hope lay in Next Year.

PART V

THE HARD YEARS.

Chapter 16 — No hope for us.

IT was difficult finding the many clothes demanded on Bryan's school list. To save buying a blazer, I accepted an old one given me by a friend whose son had just left the same school. It was, of course, twice his size but with an enormous amount of work, little skill and endless fittings, I made some sort of a job of it.

I had been advised to get Bryan to school early, so that he would have time to look around before the hundreds of strange boys arrived. As the heavy rains had made the roads impassable, we arranged that I should take the child to town by train on the Saturday, stay with an elderly friend and take Bryan to school on the Monday morning. I would then stay one more night so that I might visit him before returning to the farm.

Things went wrong. Rain fell in inches and the road to the siding was a sea of mud over which no car could pass. We should have to travel by waggon.

It rained all night and when the morning dawned bright and clear, the boy told us the river was still in spate, and it was very unlikely that the waggon would be able to cross in time for the train.

Undeterred by this, we started off on the waggon, Bryan and I sitting on his trunk, Peter leaping about as usual and Nkosi walking behind. When we had offloaded Peter at Effie's, we took the road again and immediately heard the roaring of the river some half-a-mile away. It began to rain heavily and Nkosi covered us with sacks.

With the waggon brakes clamped on we slid and slithered down the steep hill which led to the river. Sometimes the great wheels were axle-deep in the mud and at other times, when the waggon lurched over a bare rock which the rain had swept clean, we were thrown off the trunk. The river was so swollen that it came into sight long before we expected it. It was flowing at great speed and dashing over the small falls at the left side of the ford, heavy and thick with mud and broken branches. When the oxen sensed the rushing water they became restless and refused to go forward. Instead of a picannin we had chosen the tallest boy in our employ to act as leader, who was now pulling at the reins trying to force the oxen forward. James goaded them on with screams and whip crackings and Nkosi directed operations.

Gradually the leading oxen were pulled into the water and the others, still fighting, followed. A span of sixteen oxen is so long that the waggon was still on the land when the leaders were plunging about in deep water. They were still struggling when the waggon took off and Nkosi jumped on to the tail-board.

The next moments were frightening. The leaders were off their feet and water came lapping through the floor-boards of the waggon. Bryan and I sat on the trunk and I told him to cling on to me whatever happened. I looked towards the place where the water was dashing over a hidden fall and chose the branch of a drowned tree at which I could grasp if we were upset. In the middle of a flood it is very noisy, very cold, and very remote.

After what seemed an age of indecision, the leading oxen found their feet and gradually drew into shallow water, the others floundered after them followed by the waggon bouncing from rock to rock. There was a sickening moment when the oxen were straining up the muddy bank and the waggon seemed left alone to float over the falls, and then as the water began to lap our feet, Nkosi said,

"It's all right now. Heavens! How green your face is!"

The rest of the journey was sheer happiness because the danger was over and now Bryan would get to school in time. At the siding we climbed into an empty truck for shelter and waited only half-an-hour for the train because it happened to be punctual: it was Saturday and the driver was anxious to attend the races in Salisbury that afternoon.

Nkosi promised he would not recross the river until it had gone down. Though it was still raining, we could see the brightness in the direction of the river's source.

We arrived in Salisbury soon after one o'clock and took a rickshaw to the bounds of the town, where our friend met us in his old car. Possessing no driving licence and being Civil Commissioner, he could come no further. We went back to his beautiful home, where the old Persian carpets, antique furniture, fine pictures and silver were a delight after our primitive conditions.

That afternoon I had toothache, which increased in violence during the night. I spent Sunday lying down with a hotwater bottle. Bryan was very happy in the beautiful garden. It was a great treat for him, but, unfortunately, he was attacked by a swarm of bees. He was not stung very badly, but the stings he suffered, added to all he had gone through in the waggon had unnerved him. In my determination that he should not suffer shyness and loneliness I had exposed him to greater dangers.

After a sleepless night my friend 'phoned the dentist saying that his daughter was bringing me in to have the tooth out.

Before we went to the dentist, we took Bryan to the school boarding-house. The matron was not at all pleased, but my friend said it could not be helped as I had to go for the extraction. So Bryan was left alone with a fixed smile on his face.

The dentist gave me gas. I generally took it like a lamb but this time I woke up with my head on the floor against the cabinet, and my legs pointing to the ceiling against the chair, but my skirt defying all laws of gravity, was drawn over my knees.

My friend would not let me go back to see Bryan. She had told him that she could not allow me to come and he must be brave, and I would come the next day.

I was given a lift to town the next afternoon, and walked the mile and a half to the school in the heat. The boys were resting and, looking through the long windows of the ground floor dormitory, I saw one little boy lying on the bed crying quietly. It was Bryan. I made noises and signs and he looked up and saw me. I then sat outside where he could see me and waited until he was released.

I soon had him laughing, and he said that he had only cried that afternoon because he was afraid I might be too ill to come. I went home promising that I would come again the following week.

His first letter ran:

"Dear Darling Mummie and Daddy. I only cryed once when you went and once when a boy hit me. I had a sore throte but now it is better. I like school very much I hope Daddy's mealies are growing nicely and I hope Peter's are. With lots of love, Bryan."

The next week when Nkosi and I floated over another river to visit him we found he was in bed with bronchitis but we did not worry for we knew he was in good hands. Nkosi and

I were so busy working for our lives that we had to ask our children to bear their own troubles as far as they could.

On the farm Mary, our pig, was fattening nicely and inspired by this we bought two better bred piglets from which we intended to breed later on. They would go to the boar in August and present us with families, say, ten apiece, for Christmas. These families would pacify the butcher at Easter.

The maize situation was very worrying. The price had fallen even lower and the crop grown would be far in excess of local demands. Export price was a dead loss. A Maize Enquiry Committee had been formed, but the farmers saw ruin and were in a panic. The storekeepers, who had once forced credit on account of interest payable, now withheld it, and without credit no farmer could live. It was made very clear that farmers were unnecessary and a nuisance, and that the country could manage quite well by buying its food requirements with the capital brought in by settlers who had come to Rhodesia to retire. Finally, a Maize Control Board was formed and all the maize was pooled and the price offered even then was only six shillings a bag. The sandveld farmers packed up and those on rich soil had to rob their lands to live. It is only of late years that this has been put right and the farms nursed back into better production. A good farmer hates to starve his land, but he must do that rather than starve his children.

Our crop was slightly more promising this year, our few potatoes looked well and our patch of sunnhemp was guarded jealously. Another small blow was the news that the main potato crop would be larger than could possibly be consumed, and our only hope of selling was to try to dig them early before the rest were on the market.

In early March a chance came to sell if we could get them up and off in twenty-four hours. As we were now completely penniless, we accepted. The land we had grown them on was a small valley of heavy red soil. Nkosi was not happy because he said the skins were not tough enough for anything but immediate use. However, he said, if it kept fine it might be all right.

We started to dig, Peter and I picking up. The sun was scorching up the moisture from the ground and it was so hot that I covered my back with a heavy coat to keep off the rays. We worked all the morning but found we had not dug nearly enough. Charlie had gone off on a visit to his kraal and though I had Lupenga, my efficient houseboy, we had no cook, so ate a very scrappy lunch.

About three o'clock when we were straining every nerve to get done before dark, the rain came on heavily and turned the land into a quagmire. Peter, tired out, sat in the car and Nkosi and I and our few boys went on. Every potato now had a thick coat of red mud and when we tried to rub it off we rubbed off the skin.

My back was now aching so much that I kept in a bent position and must have looked like a canopied elephant. So we worked in the muddy wet world until it was dark. Then we loaded the waggon and every potato and every sack was soaking.

About half-past seven we crept home, found a hot bath but no food, only a crust of bread. Lupenga had forgotten to make bread. There was no meat left and only one egg. We cooked the egg for Peter, who ate it while we were having our baths and Nkosi said we would go off to a neighbour's to supper, for they were the kind of people who liked friends dropping in and they never started their evening meal until after half-past eight.

We arrived well in time and found them sitting by the fire. We put Peter on a bed and joined them, hoping every moment to see the boy come in and set the table. At nine o'clock we realised that they had had dinner early that evening and our hearts sank. Our stomachs had already sunk but we were too proud to tell them we had deliberately come to beg a meal.

We went off early, reclaiming the sleeping Peter, and on reaching home I routed out the crust and opened an emergency tin.

The next morning in brilliant sunshine the potatoes were taken to the siding.

Some time later the enraged dealer demanded his money back because the potatoes had all gone rotten. Nkosi went into town to see him and promised that the money would be returned as soon as possible.

Just before the end of the term I had a letter from Bryan displaying one of his few bouts of conceit. I welcomed this because he had a distressing way of hating and trying to punish his body when it did not accomplish the tasks he set it.

"We break up on Thursday. How am I comeing out? I am

one of the cleverest boys in our class. Don't tell anyone except Kitty, Grannie and Grampas and Daddy and Peter if you like. It has been raining regerlary every day for three days."

I went into town by train because friends had promised to lift Bryan and me to their farm from where Nkosi would fetch us with Peter. I have an account I wrote to my mother.

"When I arrived (walked) at the school I saw my friend's lorry piled high with sacks, groceries, and school trunks and the three little boys, one of which was my own. Handing them each a packet of sweets I squeezed into the front seat and off we went through the grounds dodging other cars with much the same load. As we left the town the children burst into song.

'Cheer, boys, cheer,
The holidays are here.'

in loud rasping voices which trailed off towards the end of the verses when the tune and the words became a little vague. Then came an interval apparently for refreshment and with the last gulp more cheers.

On the main road we whizzed past older, humbler cars, like our own, simply bulging with children, and in our turn were passed by beautiful limousines with perhaps one or two quiet children and neat trunks.

'Cheer, boys, cheer.'

We arrived at the farm and unloaded our excited freight. We three mothers embraced our little darlings, but unfortunately their faces were sticky and they had been eating onions.

The three heroes were joined by Peter and another younger brother and, after a huge tea, the schoolboys pulled off their shoes, stockings, ties and jerseys and rushed off to see the animals and pets. We mothers picked up the discarded garments and went off to look at the hens; the men went off to look at the pigs, and the dogs to look for bones."

The next term I decided that the time had come when Peter must be civilised. He was a dirty, attractive little creature. He loved the farm and grew his own crops and of late had taken to mining and dug deep holes in awkward places, and was always showing visitors his samples. He got on well with the natives but kept his dignity. He attracted a retinue of tiny picannins and I have seen him walking to the house with an egg in either hand, and a trail of picannins each carrying carefully, one egg. He used to steal biscuits for his retainers.

The Government had started a Correspondence School for country children and this term I enrolled Peter, for at six years old he had to learn seriously.

Whereas Bryan loved detail, Peter hated it and the more I tried to make him concentrate and make his letters carefully, the more his hand wobbled and the worse it became. In despair I wrote to his teacher, asking her whether she wished him to continue in this way or to write boldly and badly. She replied, "Boldly and badly by all means," and from that moment I liked her. I invited her to come out and stay at half-term, she agreed, and we thus formed a lasting friendship.

We called for Chris in our terrible old hoodless car with the doors wired together. She sat in front while the rest of us and the luggage and groceries were packed in the back. I noticed she was very well dressed and I feared for her clothes.

We had two punctures going home, they were now becoming a routine and she tells me she always remembers how on each occasion Nkosi jumped out and put things right without grumbling.

One morning she called me in early. She was under the mosquito net and asked me politely if the rats she could see were all right. I looked up and there on the top of the brick wall were little rats' tails hanging down. Yes, I assured her, they were quite all right, they just ran in and out of the house along the top of the walls and did no harm. She appeared satisfied, though she tells me now that she was very nervous of them, hence the net. When she got up and took a frock from the hanging cupboard (a plank and a curtain), she found that a rat had bitten through all her dresses on one shoulder. I shall never forget how I felt. Our wretched poverty prevented me from offering to pay for the damage. She was very good about it.

Chris was very amused at the way Bryan and Peter escorted her everywhere. From the beginning the children knew that women must be protected from natives and Chris told me that whenever they went for a walk, Bryan was in front to break the trail and fat Peter behind to protect the rear.

Earlier in the year I had heard from my elder brother in Australia. He had lost all his money when Australia had gone off the Gold Standard and I wrote suggesting that he married his fiancée and came out to Rhodesia, as it was the only country where Wireless — his profession — had not been established. Nkosi, though troubled by the maize reports, had consented, as we both felt sure that my brother would find some sort of work with electricity.

It was well we gave the guarantee when we still possessed a few sickly hopes, for as the season advanced, our crop seemed to shrink and we feared that the prices fixed would bring us nothing after the Stop Orders had been taken.

Nkosi, among his many other activities, built a guest hut. We had made the bricks, so it only meant buying one window and the cement for the floor. It was square with a tiny verandah under the thatch. For a second window we used the glass frame from an old chicken-box that had been given to us.

The furnishing department was mine. With a pound sent by my mother for the purpose, I bought some inexpensive orange-coloured cretonne for curtains and hangings to the wardrobe and a chest of drawers which I had made of petrol-boxes. On the home-made washstand I put the children's coloured enamel jug and basin, a relic of better days. I bought an old bentwood chair for five shillings and painted it white. For bedside mats I used sugar sacks embroidered very crudely with orange wool. For the sum of eighteen shillings we bought a secondhand iron bedstead and mattress. I painted the ironwork white and with the help of a boy, amid a frenzy of sneezing, teased out the flock interior of the mattress; when it was repacked it was so lumpy that I had to sleep on it for many weeks to get it level. As we could not afford another bed, Nkosi cut down a hardwood tree and made one with ox-reims. When called to admire it I sat down to test the spring of the reims. Immediately the bed split in half. Nkosi was naturally annoyed and said it could not be mended nor could he make another. It took years for me to live down this shame. As Bryan was at school we took his bed, planning that the children could take turns in sleeping on the camp-bed. I bought a cheap looking-glass which did strange things to one's face. When the room was furnished it looked, to my eyes, lovely. These preparations took many months.

Bryan was finding it hard to stand up for himself at school and when I found that the boys were teasing him about the blazer I had altered so inexpertly, I raced into town and bought him a new one: where the money came from I do not know.

He wrote,

"The boys do not heurt me now. Please take sixpence from my money and give it to Peter. I saw Mrs. Wite on Friday and she gave me a packet of sweets. I put them in my locker, and eat some of them and I found two masepan pears. I saved them up for you but when I came to get them I found a boy had eaton them all up so I could not send them to you. I went to another biceope last Friday and it was lovale. I plaid crikek on Friday afternoon, I am getting so fat. Wen I had your letter it made me larf whot you said about my nickers I made such a noise that a prefect hit me with a roller. I am so happy you would think I had been there all the year before."

As the cold weather came on things looked even worse. Maize had definitely slumped and there was no other crop we could grow. I wrote a cheerful letter to the grocer saying I had to make payments to two others before him but directly this was done he would receive something. This was a bad mistake. He immediately took offence and closed our account, saying we evidently considered his claim last. This was a blow because he had had every egg we could raise, in fact, two-thirds of his account had been paid in this way.

Things had to be cut down. The most blighting thing was that the car was eating up every penny. The garage man said it was not an asset but a liability, but as it was our only means of transport, it had to be suffered. I wondered if we ought to put off my brother, but Nkosi said we were in such a bad state that nothing could make it worse and it would not be fair when they had made their preparations. They were welcome to share what little we had.

There is a glow of pathos when we read of the mother giving her last crust to her child, but to the experienced, there is only ugliness. Poverty does not make a sudden swoop, it creeps slowly, taking with it one by one all the things that make life bearable. Even then there is a long, stark road before the stage when poverty makes life impossible.

If we were so poor, why did I have two servants? Because I could not draw and carry water from the well two hundred yards away, nor chop logs as well as my other work, and because the natives' food and wages went in with those of the farm boys and were hardly noticeable. I tried to make Lupenga cook, because the oven-like kitchen made me sick, and I took on the washing. Somehow it was different from England; the lifting up of the heavy tins of water, the heat at midday, and my total inability to wash heavy khaki clean. After a few weeks' trial I had to change over again and cook, wearing a thick felt hat.

We were a long way from real poverty but it was very depressing, because when things were broken they could not be replaced, could not even be mended, and the few treasured possessions had to be taken into every day use and broken by careless natives. The loss of the egg-whisk meant that eggs had to be beaten with a fork, the breakage of the cheap oil lamp meant cooking by a dripping candle.

Food went on a sliding scale. First of all went bacon. Meat, although cheap, we could now afford only once a fortnight. Then we had to economise with tea. I bought some unpleasant, cheap stuff like kindling sticks, mixed it with like quantities of good tea and half a pound of this mixture had to last a week counting the amount that is always stolen by the Staff. I then mixed chicory with the coffee and finally browned some breadcrumbs and mixed them with chicory. One breakfast time I served this to Nkosi.

He said, "Let coffee be a fragrant dream."

We could not afford to buy butter, but made enough for the children from our scanty milk supply, using the skim for tea. Sauces had to go at last. They had only remained because they disguised thrice-cooked meat.

Since the river had swept our garden away for the second time we had had no vegetables. Nkosi had not the time or labour to start another garden. Perhaps I should have insisted, but when a man is depressed and exhausted, you cannot force him to do more than he is already forcing himself to do.

Bryan was fairly well nourished at school. I remember how other mothers complained of the school fare, but compared with our home diet at that time, Bryan thought it was good. It was Peter who suffered. I gave him all the butter and eggs I could spare, but he would not eat the cabbages given me and I could not afford to buy fruit. He started veld sores and then picked up from the natives the harmless sort of ringworm we get in Rhodesia. This upset me very much and I tried every cure.

My Afrikaans neighbour suggested hornet's nest and spittle. I told Nkosi I would provide the latter if he would produce the former and there was a nice clay nest on the roof boards; but he said, No. Eventually I think blobs of ink cured it.

At the end of June a neighbour asked me if I would coach her little girl who was to go to school the last term of the

year and had lost the middle term's work. I was to cram the
work into six weeks, for which I was to receive five pounds
a month for keep and tuition and be supplied with vegetables.
I managed quite well with the help of the Correspondence
Classes. The extra money went on better food. During this
time we killed Mary, as Nkosi said he was tired of giving the
creditors everything, and I took on the job of curing her. My
Afrikaans neighbour came over to show me how to scrape
guts. This was a perfectly foul operation. We sat outside and
scraped them on petrol boxes. My groanings and squirmings
seemed to amuse her. The next morning we left lessons and
had a lovely time cutting up the pig. Pigs are so refined in
death, no blood, only nice, cool, white flesh. We borrowed a
sausage funnel and had the happiest time making sausages.
The hams took about six weeks to cure, but they lasted us
many months. We felt happier with these joints hanging from
the rafters in the open verandah room, though every half-hour
a spot of grease would drop on our heads. However, we soon
learned to dodge them. Peter wrote an essay:

"We cilt a pig.
It was a black one.
She was wite wen we tuck her scin off.
She is in our tummis now."

Chapter 17 — New Hopes Spring.

One afternoon I was washing my hair when the herdboy
came up to say that a veld fire was advancing towards the
slab of granite on which the precious sunnhemp was drying.
Nkosi had gone to the siding to fetch a bale of sacks, and
all the boys were working on the far end of the farm. I told
him to go back to the cattle and then called Peter and the
little girl who were resting, to come at once. My head was
white with lather but I could not wait to rinse it. Hastily I
wrapped it in a towel and then, fearing sunstroke, I popped
a large straw hat on top and taking the children by the hand
I set off to save the sunnhemp.
We ran down the jacaranda drive and saw that the fire
was coming as it had the first year, and it would be of no
use to light a backfire from the road because the sunnhemp
was in between. I pulled down three green branches and then,
seizing the opportunity of a lull, I ran the children through

a sparse piece of grass to the other side of the fire, where on blackened ground we were quite safe. I soon saw that the sunnhemp was in the direct line of fire and that the only way of saving it would be to beat the fire from a ploughed field in a diagonal direction so that it just passed the rock where the sunnhemp lay. I kept the children behind me to beat out any smouldering or obstinate embers and put every ounce of energy into my work. My feet were scorched on the smouldering grass, and in one flare-up I lost my eyebrows and eyelashes, but gradually the diagonal line was made and I knew that if only the wind did not change the sunnhemp could be saved.

Meanwhile, Nkosi having loaded up the bale of sacks, was creeping home, wondering if this time he had asked too much of the poor old car. Just as he started to climb Effie's steep hill he saw the smoke and realised that the sunnhemp would be caught. It was too far to get out and run and his only hope was to nurse the old contraption up the hill and then speed home as fast as he could. He was very worried because he expected me to be in the house, and was afraid the boys might not see the fire in time. I was working furiously and frantically, the result still in the balance, when he came up simultaneously with the boys and in a few seconds had finished my work. I saw him coming towards me and turned ready to receive the admiration and congratulations I knew were my right. Instead, he burst out laughing. I think this was the bitterest moment of my life. I had saved his sunnhemp at the cost of violent energy, brain-work, eyebrows and eyelashes, and scorched feet, and there he was laughing! It was too much. I told him what I thought of him and his sunnhemp and limped off in offended dignity.

In the bathroom I saw myself in the mirror. My face was, of course, brick-red. It was also black with smoke and the lack of eyebrows made it look a little bare. The soapsuds had made little rivulets down my face and I looked like a tiger. On the top of my towel still perched my sunhat. No one could have helped laughing.

Oh, Life! Why turn our most heroic moments into funny incidents? For it is as a funny incident the story of the saving of the sunnhemp is now remembered.

Incidentally, when it was over, Nkosi told me that, though he appreciated my efforts, the Right Thing to have done was to have lit a back fire *from* the sunnhemp, which would have met the oncoming flames.

The term ended, the maize was shelled, and the number of bags fell far lower than our estimate. It always does. In farm mathematics, the second half of the crop is never as large as the first half. We found to our distress that the first pay-out would be completely swallowed up in Stop Orders, leaving not one penny for the bills and, worse than that, nothing with which to pay the boys' wages. Most of them had willingly let their tickets mount up in order that they might go home to Nyasaland with a good sum, and now we could not pay them and to owe money to natives is a criminal offence.

Day by day passed and we were at our wits' end to know what to do. We could not ask for more money from home.

There was no need to be actually hungry because there was always plenty of mealie meal porridge, pumpkin, rice and sweet-potato, but one has to be really hungry to enjoy foods that do not please. I can remember smelling the well-cooked supper at Nettie's one evening and feeling quite swoony. To my delight she asked us to stay to supper, and it was difficult not to gobble up the delicious meal. When we got home we found that the native in charge had drugged himself, the water was cold, the fire was out, the little chickens left outside and everything neglected. Something snapped in Nkosi and he took hold of the boy saying he was going to kill him. I managed to prevent this and the wretched boy ran into the veld crying, "Thank you!"

Poor Nkosi! It was the climax. We had worked solidly for two years and were now in a far worse position than we had ever been. We could not expect another pay-out before Christmas, even if it could be kept from hungry creditors. Meanwhile, we had these boys to pay off, and my brother and his wife, with only a minimum of the capital required, getting nearer and nearer.

The next morning I spoke to a neighbour who happened to call, and he said there were always ways of fixing things up. If the creditors were nasty, you could threaten them and say, "Very well then, I'll go bankrupt and you will get nothing."

We had not thought of this. Nkosi went into town and told the owners of the Stop-Orders that if they took every penny, it would be the last they got and the other creditors would probably turn nasty. They saw reason and took only part of their just dues, and Nkosi came back with enough money to pay off the waiting boys.

We were then offered a contract to supply wood for a mine and though Nkosi hated cutting down the trees, he had to accept. Unfortunately, the first cheque went towards buying another waggon in order to fulfil the contract, so we were no better off. My brother cabled that they would arrive in October. However, before they arrived an aunt died and left Nkosi £70, which gave us new hope.

Immediately, the old car took the opportunity, when we were many miles from home one evening, of bowling one wheel off into the veld and leaving us to walk six miles across country in the dark. It could not be mended, so we bought another car for £17. The old car fetched five pounds, for the engine was still running as sweetly as ever. The "new" car was of quite a different disposition. It was a crusty, disagreeable car, and when some years later we got rid of it, Nkosi said he would love to be able to run it over the kopje.

Another stroke of luck was when my first poem was accepted by the weekly paper. It was called "Ladies Last," and was an account of how Nkosi says I read the paper. I followed this with another and then the Editor said I might go on writing every week. I signed the first poem "T," standing for " 'Tilda Price," the Dickens part I had played so long ago.

Heartened by the turn of our luck and the wood cheques to come, and reading that the prospects of tobacco-growing were slightly less gloomy, Nkosi determined to try to grow a crop of tobacco. He knew our soil was suitable for this, but we had no money with which to build barns. He approached a neighbour who had given up growing and asked if he would go into partnership and cure the tobacco if we grew it, but he refused. Then Willie, Nettie's husband, said he would take the risk, and Nkosi prepared the tobacco beds with unremitting care.

It was a great thrill going to meet my brother and his wife. We had parked Peter with a neighbour and had arranged that we would call at the school on our way out to introduce Bryan. Bryan now had most of his new teeth, and was still quite good-looking with his pretty hair. Imagine my horror when a hideous-headed boy came up to the car; he had had his head shaven because he said it saved drying it when he went to the swimming baths.

We took our guests home and proudly showed them the hut. I felt at the time they did not fully appreciate its beauties and the scheming and hard work behind it, but now I realise that it was all very rough for a city-bred girl. The inside of the thatched roof, the rough cement floor and the splintery petrol boxes in which the bride was expected to put her pretty trousseau. The scarcity of windows subdued the light, which, of course, increased her fear of snakes and spiders, and when they walked over the bathroom at night, they had to carry flickering candles. Our old tin bath had lost most of its paint. It had come off on Nkosi who had insisted on using it before the paint was dry. It was clean but unappetising. The lack of water-borne sanitation was always a shock to newcomers. I know I had felt I should never get used to the *Picannin Kaia* (little house) up the garden. When we had moved from the huts we filled in the first P.K. and planted on it a jacaranda tree which, by this time, was flourishing: Bryan called it the "Lavatree." Nkosi, in his anxiety to keep the new P.K. well away from the house, had built it at a distance of quite one hundred yards. Just before our guests had arrived, Peter had thrown a clutch of snake eggs down the hole — a nagging thought!

At one time I fixed up a system, whereby a flag went up when the place was occupied. This prevented many fruitless journeys, but one day someone forgot to put the flag down again, which caused much inconvenience to the whole family. It was not until 1948 that we had water-borne sanitation. It was a great joy and I christened it "Laughing Waters," and proposed breaking a bottle of lemonade on it, but Nkosi would not let me, as it might hurt the septic tank.

One afternoon, when we were about to take our guests to visit a neighbour, word came of trouble in the compound. It appeared that the very pretty wife of James, our driver, had snubbed the advances of a would-be lover, and the man had told her he was going to put magic *(mtagati)* on her and she would become ill and die. Unfortunately, she became sick soon afterwards and, believing in the Black Magic, she gradually lost strength. As usual, we were not called in until she was nearly dead. Nkosi sent for the police, but we were afraid she would die before they arrived with the Government doctor. I went to the hut where she was lying on her blankets. Round her head was a piece of string tied tightly.

When my eyes grew accustomed to the complete darkness and smoke, I saw that a horrible old crone was sitting in the dark corner behind the door. She had done her worst and was now glowering at me as a rival physician. I asked questions, but all the patient would say was, "Now I die."

"*Aikona,*" I said, cheerfully. "You will not die," but she repeated listlessly, "Now I die."

We were very relieved when the police arrived with the doctor. While the doctor examined the patient, the police dealt with the magician. He was later given a good hiding before the woman's eyes, which seemed to break the spell. She agreed to let me help her. The diagnosis was pneumonia, fever and an enlarged spleen. When the doctor had gone, I collected butter-muslin, rags, mealie meal and a kettle of boiling water, and set to work.

I had not the slightest idea where her spleen was, but when I examined her black body I found a place where cuts had been made recently to let the devils out, so I poulticed these. It was very difficult working in the hut, and when I had oiled her body I dropped the poultice face down on the floor, and it came up very gritty. I could not repeat the whole process, so the poultice had to go on as it was. She looked malevolently at me because I think it itched. Anyhow, whether on account of the magician's downfall, the doctor's medicine, or just the itchy poultice, she suddenly decided to live, and by the next day was quite well. I think it was the itchy poultice, because one may sink beneath a pain but never beneath an itch. I took my brother to town, where he soon found employment, and through hard work and his wife's clever fingers, they have made good in a marvellous way.

The legacy melted like snow, and what was left of the wood cheques also. We learned with great disappointment that the second cheque would not come until after Christmas.

A week before Christmas, Nkosi and I went to town to try to make a few shillings do the work of pounds. Very depressed, we called at the post-office for the mail. In it was a letter from an Uncle, enclosing a draft for £ 20. I think this was one of the most wonderful things that has ever happened to us.

With a jovial, Dickensian feeling we went round the shops. Peter had wanted a tricycle for years. Now we were able to take one home to him. I forget what Bryan and Nkosi had, but I bought a ready-made cotton frock for one pound. It was glorious to have something that no one else had worn: wearing other people's clothes makes one lose one's own personality. Kitty very kindly sent me her old tweeds, and I used to make skimpy shirt blouses of cheap Jap silk, buy outsize men's hats at sales, and outside women's stays, which I used to machine until they fitted me. I kept one pair of gloves and one pair of silk stockings, and wore this uniform for years.

We bought crackers and Christmas fare, and decided to

forget our troubles and anxieties and have a happy Christmas. We could not wait to give Peter his heart's desire. He was so delighted to be on wheels again that he rode from morning to night. On Christmas Eve he began limping and I found a swelling in his groin. He became very ill on Christmas Day and on Boxing Day we took him to hospital for an operation. We could not stay in, because we could not afford a hotel. Ronnie and Margaret, our most faithful and kindly friends, were away, so very unhappily, we had to leave him alone. We could have squeezed a cheque out of the bank from the Christmas present money, but the bank was shut. We waited until the operation was over and the doctor said Peter was quite all right, then we got in our car to go home, but it would not start. I remember the smiles of the other car owners as they saw us, one each side, pushing it along the hospital drive until it jerked to life, when we jumped inside.

A neighbour telephoned each day, and Margaret, when she returned, visited Peter. My brother and his wife also went to cheer him up. Before the end of the week we were told that we could fetch him on New Year's Eve. The car had now broken down completely, but Margaret arranged with our neighbour that she should bring Peter to her house and join in their tennis party, and in the afternoon, after he had rested, bring Peter back home. Nkosi, Bryan and I walked four miles, and found Peter in high spirits. We joined in the tennis, and when my neighbour suggested that we left Peter and Bryan with her for the night and went to a New Year's party given by our Scots neighbour, Meg, we allowed ourselves to be persuaded.

Feeling guilty but thrilled, we walked home across the veld trying to ignore the clouds that were looming. At home we bathed and changed into clean working clothes, then, packing our evening clothes into a suitcase, we started off in the opposite direction towards the hills, in spite of the heavy rain which was now falling. We took with us a boy who carried the suitcase wrapped in a sack on his head.

The first miles took us through the muddy farm tracks, then we went through tall, dripping grass which soaked us to the waist for another mile, and found ourselves on the banks of a river which was in spate and our usual fording place a wide stretch of muddy, tumbling water. Nkosi and the boy walked up and down looking for a place to cross, while I stayed with the suitcase in a frenzy of agitation. Finally Nkosi decided to try a spot where the river was very broad. In these cases one has either to jump over a deep ravine, or wade through a broader but shallower stretch. At this point a huge tree had been tossed down the river and had lodged against a tall upright rock, which divided the river into two streams. The native went first and then returned for the case, and we followed. Hand in hand we waded into the water. It was difficult to keep our balance and I had to fix my eyes ahead and upwards, for the sight of the water always mesmerises me, and makes me feel I must go along with it. One foot at a time we waded, and then Nkosi was on the tree trunk hauling me up. Along the slippery tree we advanced, and clambered up on to the rock. From here there was a wide leap on to a lower shelf of the high bank. As I was more frightened at the thought of going back, I had to follow Nkosi, who caught me and dragged me up the muddy bank. Then there was a long tramp through heavy red, ploughed soil with high wet maize, but now our bodies were tingling with health and effort. Finally, we came out on to the road track, walked another mile, waded through a small spruit, and saw the house standing high on its kopje. From the chimney thick grey smoke was curling, telling us of a good dinner waiting. The ascent was like walking up the side of a house, but at the door was Meg, with outstretched arms. "Come away in, hinney; I never thought you would be able to get here."

Inside we met the other guests, who had all more or less made difficult journeys. We were given hot water to wash in and changed into our evening clothes. What a happy party! All ages, all sorts, but all out for enjoyment, and though the rain continued to fall during the evening, it but added to the feeling of well-being.

I shall always remember the miner who insisted on reciting Shakespeare. He gave us the Mercy Speech several times, and as the night wore on and he consumed more drinks, he became more and more insistent. "The quality of mercy is NOT strained!" And he looked round angrily, as if to dare anyone to say it was.

When the party finally broke up about two o'clock, the guests emerged to find a clear, star-studded sky, only the roaring of the river in the distance and the drip, drip of the wet leaves told of the storm.

As we did not fancy wading through the river, we accepted the offer of a neighbour to spend the remainder of the night in his house.

It was a lovely sunny morning when we started to walk home along sandy roads washed as clean as the seashore. We found the oxen inspanned to the waggon, all ready to fetch Peter. We laid a mattress on the floor of the waggon along with pillows and blankets to make him comfortable.

We found Peter very excited. James was so glad to have him out of hospital.... natives insist on looking on hospitals as places from which there is no returning.... that he carried him to the waggon crooning over him, "Oh, Boss Peter! Oh, Boss Peter!"

Peter thoroughly enjoyed his importance and his drive in the waggon, while the rest of us either walked beside or sat on the tail. I loved it, for I realised how much we miss, travelling always by car. There is something so peaceful about a waggon. If you get off and walk, it does not leave you behind, and you have time to look at the country as you go by and enjoy hundreds of little things you have not time to notice when you are in a car.

So we began 1932 hopefully. The tobacco growing well, the maize not really bad, and the sunnhemp planted on the old maize lands. Things were going to be all right. I only meant holding on a little longer for Next Year, the wonderful mirage which kept us going.

Chapter 18 — Assorted Struggles.

The wood contract ended in February and cash was short, but the tobacco looked wonderful and our only anxiety was whether it would be saleable or not. To balance this little Hope, a small swarm of locusts settled on one end of the farm and ate several acres of maize, but, as it was very young some of it grew again.

The tobacco was reaped, carted to our partner's barns and cured. When it was sold, we had £300 for our share of the crop. Not only were we able to buy a few farm necessities and spread a little over the creditors, but we knew now that we had excellent tobacco soil, and that if tobacco had any sort of a future, we ought to be able to live. It would, of course, be many years before we climbed out of debt and replaced all our worn-out implements, but the business of sinking deeper and deeper into debt would eventually be stopped. So far, our payments to the fertilizer merchant only covered compound interest charged, but we knew that they and the other merchants now cared for our welfare, and would not like such a paying proposition to go bankrupt.

Bryan came back from school looking very ill. His last attack of asthma had been caused by the mistaken zeal of a new master, who had made all the boys run round the playground, a space of red dust. Bryan had asked to be excused because he was just out of hospital after bronchitis, but his request had been refused with scorn, and he was made to run until he collapsed with a terrible attack. I therefore decided that he should stay at home for the second term, and I would teach him by the Correspondence Classes.

If I had found it difficult to each Peter and the little girl, it was nothing to the job of teaching my own two delightful little sons. When I hear women say they cannot teach their own children I feel angry, because they can, guided by the Correspondence Teachers; but, of course, it is at a price. Teaching one's own children entails twice the time and patience needed to teach other children and three times the energy, physical, mental and nervous. Sons, one at a time, are possible, but two together are perfectly maddening. When, added to this, the mother has to cope with a thieving nitwit, for such was my temporary cook, then life is hideous indeed.

We "did lessents," as Peter called them, in the verandah, and the wind used to come along and snatch up the papers and chase them off into the veld. Only those mothers who have "done correspondence" know the vast amount of papers that are needed to teach one small child. As the children welcomed any diversion and loved dashing outside after them, I had to weight each pile down with a stone.

Earlier in the year, as my literary career seemed to be established, I invested in an old, rickety typewriter, which I bought for a pound. Evidently I lent it to Bryan during one of his many bouts of sickness, for I have among my papers a Birthday Card he typed for me:—

"Dear darling Mummy, I wish you many happy returns of your birthday from Bryan"
and then a huge "YOU" done in capital X's and underneath "darling, darling, darling."

Bryan never forgot my birthday, but at that time he was certainly not treating "darling, darling, darling," as he might have. He and Peter quarrelled incessantly, and I found teaching increasingly difficult. I suppose I should have found it easier if I could have been the jolly, laughing Mummie they loved, but I was worn out, cross and nervy.

At this time Peter kept rabbits. In our anxiety to earn quick money we had bought rabbits to rear for the Government Experimental Station, but when they were ready we could not bear to deliver them to the laboratories, so they became pets. Peter took them as his own. One morning he found a python, gorged with baby rabbits, lying bulging in the hutch. He called his father, who shot the snake through the head. It was only about five feet long, not fully grown.

Peter described the tragedy thus:—

> "A python swollod four rabbits of ours and we sor four lumps in his tummy. Daddy shot it with a shotgun, then he hanged it up. We cut it open and fond four rabbits and a rat. The fust one was Willy he was black and white, and the next two brown ones, they never had names. The next one was a black one, and his name was Billy. There was one more he kild but he lift it becos he was full."

I can remember the horrible look of the "swollod" rabbits. They were stretched out and slimed over and had bulging glassy eyes.

In those days Peter wrote vivid essays. One lurid one in which "me and the picannin kilt some rats" with reference to how they hit them and how they "bleeded" was kept by the School Inspector. At Christmas Peter wrote:

> "I want a big huge trumpit like the pleaseboys has and I will blow it and blow it as much as I can."

Life was very hard. The faint romance of battling against "fearful odds" had passed, and the shouts of battle had given place to the groans of the besieged waiting for deliverance.

Everything was so uncomfortable, especially in the cold weather, when we could not get out of the draughts and the fire still smoked badly.

We had only one reasonably comfortable chair, a Morris chair given us by the mother of the little girl I taught, and really only better than our two homemades in that the back did not fall out as often.

There was no ringworm this year, but both children had veld sores. In the cold weather Peter's legs became ingrained with dirt which no soap would remove. Every afternoon I put him on an old sheet and rubbed his legs with a mixture of melted candlegrease and paraffin. When he had rested I scrubbed this off with a brush and hot water.

Our tobacco partner had very kindly given us his old separator, and this was a great joy because it meant more cream and butter, but it was trickly to manage for it was badly worn.

One day, it was a Makaza, one of those mornings I have already described, when the sun comes up late and everything is in disorder and gloom. First of all, the tea was so late that we had to leave it and dash out and try to catch up with routine. Tom, my nasty cook, met me with the sad news that the cat had stolen the bacon. It appeared that "lo kits" had very cleverly opened the safe, which Tom, of course, had shut tightly and, unselfishly leaving half a cold dried fish, had unfastened the bacon, which, of course, Tom had wrapped up most carefully, and made off with it, leaving no trace. Before I could express my utter disbelief in this miracle, I was called off by a shriek from one of the children, who had cut himself. While I was fixing a bandage, the Chickinin (my omnibus name for the Chicken picannin) came up to say there was a snake in the fowlhouse. I took the gun and raced off, but, of course, there was no snake, but the hen it was presumed to have killed, a nice plump pullet, was lying stiff and stark.

When I returned, I found Nkosi demanding breakfast half-an-hour earlier than usual. There was a sick boy to be dosed, and Lupenga was held up for something or other which was locked up, and we could not find the keys. As I turned to the cook to give him his orders, I heard the separator being turned much too quickly. The milk boy, who was supposed to wait for me, had decided to get on with the job himself, and was simply racing the thing. I rushed to the hut and, above the noise of the rattling old machine, I shouted to him to go slower, but he mistook my meaning and, smiling good-humouredly, turned faster and faster. The children, who had followed me in, joined their shouts to mine, when, suddenly, the separator leapt into the air as a whole, and descended in many pieces. Just at that moment, as always, Nkosi put his head round the door, asking why the devil his breakfast was not ready? He saw his wife, his children and his servant staring at him in horor, the milk pouring down their frightened faces. He started to swear, "What the . . . . ?" Then something snapped, and he burst out laughing. We joined in, in joyous relief, and the spell of that bad day was broken. Then we brought in the dogs and cats to lick up the milk, picked up the bits of separator, and went in to breakfast.

One other unpleasant experience was when we were bringing my sister-in-law from town to stay. As usual, the car was bursting with purchases. We had a puncture and, as we had no spare wheel, Nkosi had to mend it. The tyre had some peculiar structural complication that Nkosi said was especially maddening. It meant that everything in the car had to be offloaded. Whilst he mended the puncture, the children and I tried to be helpful without being irritating, for Nkosi's nerves were a bit frayed.

The job finished, we re-loaded and went off. Three miles further on we had another puncture, a burst, and when he got out, Nkosi found that the pump had been left at the last stopping-place.

The sun was now beginning to sink, so plans had to be made. Even if Nkosi found the pump and could mend the tyre — which seemed doubtful — it would never stand the full load. My sister-in-law and I were jettisoned to walk home over the veld, while Bryan and Peter stayed to look after the car and Nkosi walked back to find the pump. As we left, Nkosi handed me twenty pounds in silver and notes, boys' wages, to take care of. We two women turned our faces to the twin Kopjes and walked as near in a straight line as possible. She, always wearing high heels, had wisely come into the country in flat ones, and I, always wearing flat heels, had gone to town in high. We suffered! Even though the sun was beginning to sink, it glared on our backs. When the car was lost in the distance and there was nothing round us but thick, whispering grass, we began to feel frightened. I remembered that on the Twin Kopjes lived some bad boys, a gang of villains operating in the district, with the kopjes as their headquarters. Once a policeman had come out to catch them, and had asked Nkosi to join him and bring some boys with him. The volunteers, all shapes and sizes, arrived, armed with heavy sticks. They put on a bold front but we knew at the first smell of danger they would be off. Nothing came of the raid, for from the kopje one can see for miles, and by the time the attacking party had panted noisily up, there was not a villain in sight. I told my shrinking companion this, and said I wished we had not brought the money. She said that what she was frightened of was that we might be raped, and she thought that if I carried the money openly, the villains might snatch it and run off. I agreed, and did as she said, but all the while I was trying to plan how I would convince Nkosi that the money had gone in a good cause.

No one attacked us, however, and we came out on to the road, not too far out in our reckoning. Then came the hard walk for two miles in the failing light. My heels were now blistened, so that I had to walk barefoot, quite painful, for except for a few sandy patches, the road was very gritty. On and on we plodded, and just reached the house before complete darkness. Here I handed my guest over to Lupenga for tea and a hot bath, and, putting on old shoes, I took water and food, mounted Bryan's bicycle, and started off to find my family.

The road was uphill and hardly distinguishable in the darkness. Reaching a long stretch of thick sand, the bicycle jibbed and flung me in the air. I landed heavily and lay moaning. Nkosi would come along and find me broken and bruised, with the food and water lying beside the bicycle. A Frances at last! I moaned a bit more and then tried my limbs, to see which were broken. None of them was, and I could not even feel a bruise. Every single part of me was in excellent condition; the sand had received me with utter kindness. This annoyed me intensely, and I cried awhile in sheer rage. Then I got up, picked up the bicycle, and found that the handlebars were twisted. Picking up the water-bottle and food, I started off again, but could see only the two white lines dimly before me and it was so difficult guiding the bent bicycle that every other minute I swerved off into the veld; but at length, by twisting my body into a strange position, I managed to make these excursions less frequent. When I had gone about three miles and was getting used to the pitch dark, I heard the car pounding along. I was delighted to see it, and was bursting to tell Nkosi of my terrible fall and bravery, but he got in first. He had found the pump and walked back. It had taken an hour, and when he returned the children ware beginning to feel a bit frightened. He could not mend the tyre, even if he could have seen. Finally, Bryan suggested that they stuff it with grass. This they had done, cutting the grass with a small penknife, and were now limping home. No one wanted the food, as the children had eaten a loaf of bread we had brought back for a native, and were not hungry. No one wanted a drink of healing water. So we crept home, with me hanging on to the back of the car and wobbling precariously,

"Oh, my brave little woman," cried Hugh, as he supported her exhausted form.

"There is no sacrifice I would not make for you and the children," said Frances, as she lost consciousness.

Chapter 19 — The Story of Marie.

Marie and Mealie, our pigs, had been a constant source of worry. In August of the previous year they had been due for the boar, but as we had not been able to buy or get the loan of one, they had escaped their duties. In November, when the butcher had loomed, a husband was offered. We accepted on the ladies' behalf with pleasure, and when the old gentleman had gone back in a Scotch cart, we watched them expectantly, the expectancy being entirely on our own part, as time proved. January had been too busy, February too wet, and so it was not until March that we could again fix things for these lazy creatures. To our delight it soon became apparent that Marie had done her duty, but as Mealie was as care-free as ever, Nkosi said we would wait for the cold weather, and then Mealie should provide us with bacon.

Left without her sister, Marie grew fat and sleek, but becoming bored alone, she would break out and eat the small bed of lettuces I was growing with the bath-water, trample my seedlings with her trotters, and even plucking my few flowers. Because she was "in an interesting condition," she got away with all this, and I remember seeing her roaming about with a red flower in her mouth, like an obese and obscene dancer. I did not make a fuss, for what were a few lettuces and a flower against a litter of pigs?

Nkosi, who knows all about animal obstetrics, had been too busy to study her case; all he did was to throw things at her when she got out, and call a boy. Then one day he looked at her with understanding eyes and did a few sums. The truth was that Marie had no intention of producing young; her fat was the fat of a luxurious life. She had outwitted us again, one whole year of wasted lives.

Soon after this she met the fate she so richly deserved.

"Murder! Murder!" shrieked the lady, as the boys caught her by various parts of her anatomy, and stood as firm as her flabby legs would allow her. At her ear-splitting shrieks, I let go of the bit I was holding.

"I can't bear it," I said. "I may not be fond of the animal, but I can't bear to upset her."

"Upset her?" growled Nkosi. "I wish I could upset her; haven't moved her an inch yet."

I stood aside while the boys renewed their efforts. Three leaned against her back, while the others tried to draw her forwards by her front feet. Oh, how she cried! The air was full of sound.

"Oh, poor Marie!" I cried, distractedly. "She is asking me to save her!"

"Don't be silly," replied Nkosi. "She's all right. You will credit animals with human feelings. She is only a dumb brute."

"Hardly dumb," I replied, for Marie, finding her balance gone, now gave the most piercing, long-drawn shrieks. "Now they are hurting her; Oh, Marie!"

"You'd better stay away, if it upsets you so much," said Nkosi, mustering his boys for another onslaught. I slipped away and brought the pig-pail.

"Let her go," I cried, "and watch."

Marie, finding herself suddenly released, lifted up her long snout and smiled Victory, and then started on a pumpkin.

Clink! Clink! What was that splendid sound? Missus with the pail! She looked up with her little black eyes under a thick ear. Yes, Missus with food! She trotted out of the pen with pleasurable anticipation, smelling the tea-leaves and potato rinds. Up to the waiting car, whose hood we had removed for the occasion. I led her and then all the boys jumped on her, and the next moment a sack with a hole in the top was popped over her head like a jumper, and another drawn up from her feet like a skirt, pinning down the jumper with her front legs inside it. A few heavy pushes and Marie was safe in the back of the car and we were off to town.

Marie grunted. She did not like the swift movement on rough roads and she missed her hands. Grunt! Grunt! she protested; this was no life for a self-indulgent pig.

"I do hope she doesn't make that noise in town," I said. "What will people think?"

"They will think that we are taking a pig to town," said Nkosi. "What else could they think?"

Grunt! Grunt! Grunt! I turned round. "Oh Marie dear, do be patient. It won't be long before all your troubles are over." Marie went on grunting, her head very near mine, so I leant back and scratched her scurfy neck with a match.

Once on the main road she ceased her struggles and dozed, so we were able to forget her existence. Suddenly a heavy weight fell on my shoulder and I screamed. There was Marie, released from her jumper, leaning between us in a most companionable way. I turned and tried to push the ugly head away, but could not move it, and she continued to breath down my neck.

"What is she doing?" asked Nkosi, feeling annoyed.

"She has one hoof out of the jumper, but seems quite happy," I replied.

"She can't stay there!" cried Nkosi, angrily.

"I can't move her," I said, pushing frantically at the immovable mass. "She is like a rock. Let her be. She isn't doing any harm."

"If you think I am going to drive to town with a pig's face next to mine, you are mistaken." He stopped the car, and greatly to her annoyance, Marie was fastened into her jumper with a safety-pin.

But she was not the sort of pig to suffer patiently. She made short work of the safety-pin, and soon not only a hoof but a heavy head was placed between us.

"Oh, hell!" cried Nkosi.

"It's no use," I said. "She likes to see the scenery. You'll just have to put up with it. At least she keeps still and stops that filthy grunting."

And so we went along, Marie's breath fanning our necks. Then another hoof joined the other on the back of our seat, and she pressed her heavy head so far forwards that it came between us. It was intolerable.

"I'll swerve and try to knock her off her feet," growled Nkosi, but Marie, like most fat people was an excellent dancer, and she swayed gracefully at every turn.

"You'll end by making her sick," I said, "and I can't think of anything that could be worse than that."

"Pigs can't be sick. If they are, they die."

"Well," I said, "don't risk it. To make her sick and then not be able to sell her would be too bad."

Wealthy neighbours, returning from a night in town in a beautiful car, passed us by and we could see their astonished faces.

"WHAT is it? A pig? Well! What next, I wonder!"

We were also wondering this. Marie seemed to know her time was near, and seemed to feel that she had never really appreciated us before. She leant further over, the sack slipping to her waist. Nkosi's voice came to me from somewhere beyond Marie's snout.

"We can't go on like this." At that moment there was a terrific bang. At first I thought that it was Marie, but one look at her smiling face beside me told me that all was well with her. The car swerved, slowed down, and bumped over the ground; the back tyre had burst.

"Now," said Nkosi, "we are for it! The spare isn't fit to carry the weight, and how the deuce am I to jack up the car with this sow in it?" He brought out his tools.

I will pass over the next hour: the struggle with the tyre: the hopelessness of fixing up the passenger in any other way. Nkosi suggested I should take a lift from a passing car, which I did. He told me afterwards what he suffered. How, when he was just in town, he had another puncture, and had to let the wheel bump along, and how people in the streets kept telling him he had a puncture, and how they laughed at Marie, who was breathing her sympathy in his face. He arrived at the butcher's shop at last. The butcher said airily, "Oh, take it round to the other premises." Then Nkosi broke out, and said he was damned if he would take the blasted pig another inch. The butcher realised that he must give in, and so Marie met her fate.

Chapter 20 — The Plagues of Egypt.

The maize was shelled and delivered to the siding with great joy, because we were depending on the first miserable pay-out to throw a few sops to creditors. To our utter surprise and disappointment, however, the maize inspector who came to the siding to take over the crop, said that the moisture content was too great, and he could not take them over for some weeks. We had to accept this, but we believed .... and still believe .... that the sudden enforcing of this rule was because the sheds in town were still full of last year's crop. It was a good move, because the maize lay in the sun week after week drying up, so that when at last it was taken over, most of the bags were underweight.

In September I crocked up. The continuous bilious attacks and continual anxiety, the strain of trying to run house, poultry and education all at once with what may be called broken tools, was too much. Bryan was little better for the term at home and Peter was quite out of hand. I realised, too, the truth that when everyting goes wrong, it is the fault of the mistress, because she is not supervising properly, not preventing as she should.

At last I became so nervy that I cried if anyone spoke to me, and dared not cross the road alone. Nkosi took me to a doctor, who said I was on the verge of a serious breakdown and was to go to hospital. We could not afford this, so it was arranged that I should stay in town for a week and be treated, and both boys were to go to school.

When my week was up, I went back to the farm and carried on, as other farmers' wives have done.

The children were rather ashamed of their part in my breakdown. I have Peter's first letter:

"Dear Mummie, I hope you are better. I doant like school."

The "doant" is crossed out, but not very firmly. Bryan wrote: "I hope you are better now. Peter was going to write, Dear Mom, but I stopped him. I didn't help Peter at all with his letter." But I imagined he had insisted that the "doant" should be crossed out.

This particular season, when it seemed we were, if not on the road to prosperity, at least standing in the right direction, the rains did not break, they cracked, and always it seemed on someone else's farm. In an early shower we had planted tobacco and this, having made a good start, stood quite still, wilting in the drought.

Early in December, when we went into town to fetch the children for the Christmas holidays, we got soaked through to the skin, but came home rejoicing at the thought of how our stricken crops would be greedily drinking in this glorious rain. Not a drop had fallen on our own farm.

The next week, in desperation, Nkosi ordered a hundred empty petrol tins to be railed to the siding; he was determined he would give each surviving tobacco plant a drop of water, carted from the spruit.

During the night a glorious storm broke and I remember wandering round the house, praising the Lord and catching drips. Until then I had always thought that David's psalms of praise were merely ingratiating, but now I could join with him and sing:

> Praise ye the Lord. Praise ye the Lord from the heavens. Praise him from the heights.
> Mountains and hills, fruitful trees and all cedars, beasts and all cattle, creeping things and flying fowl. Both young men and maidens, old men and children, let them praise the Lord. Praise ye the Lord.

In the morning, the hills, trees, tobacco, maize, cattle and chicken were all bursting with praise.

The tobacco was saved, quite fifty per cent. of it, and Nkosi was able to plant out the rest of the acreage in warm moist ground. The maize was replanted and it was heartening to see the farm become green and fertile.

The garden Nkosi had made for me by the river when I was ill, was, of course, swept away. Every raised bed was flattened and covered with a thick layer of sand. A huge tree trunk had been deposited in the middle of the garden and this had to be dragged off by a span of oxen. Brave little carrots, their bodies washed clean were still hanging on by their toes, very much, it seemed to me, as we settlers hung on during the slump.

When the new boy started on the new garden, he made a great effort to please. All the newly-sown seeds were labelled. There were: — "lettis," "tomatis," "hunyuns," "callots," "beatis," "peans." It is difficult to make a native distinguish between peas and beans, they are always "peans." There is wisdom behind this.

Shortly before Christmas I went into town to do the Christmas shopping and spent the night in a boarding-house.

The next morning I got up before dawn, because I had no watch, and tied my parcels together and started for the station. They were so heavy that I found I could only carry one block at a time and even then only for a few yards, which made the mile to the station three times as long.

It is an obsession with me that I shall miss any public conveyance I wish to catch. Though every clock I see tells me I have half-an-hour to spare, I am always sure the train will go without me.

When I arrived at the station, out of breath and very tired with that horrible neck pain that comes from carrying too heavy weights, I found I was forty minutes too early.

Nkosi met me at the siding, and as we bumped home we saw a thick brown cloud over the farm and wondered what it could be. It certainly was not rain.

As we drew nearer, a few locusts flew into the car, and on arrival we found the air was thick with them, like a heavy spotted veil through which the sun was unable to penetrate.

I changed my clothes and ran outside, a scarf round my throat to prevent locusts from going down my neck. Nkosi and the boys were already on the long stretch of land some distance from the front of the house, called by them "Nyasaland." Here was our best stand of maize, grown on the old tobacco ground. Usually, we could see a stretch of bright green; now all we could see was the brown of the locusts. In front of the house was the first planted tobacco, now growing well. The defence of this was allotted to me. The locusts would not eat the tobacco, but the weight of their heavy bodies, while they paused to see if this green were edible, would break the tender leaves.

I took my one black japanned tray and a stick; the children and natives had empty petrol tins and bits of iron.

Bang! Bang! Bang! Bang! Feeble little noises in wide open lands.

Shout! Shout, Shout! Shout! Feeble little voices lost among the whirl and whizz of the locusts.

They dashed in our faces, scratching us with their razor-like legs, and their excreta dropped on our hats, arms and any other unprotected part. Surely no insect has such a lightning digestive system as the locust

Up and down the lands we went, the locusts rising as we passed and returning directly. Beyond the tobacco was another small patch of maize and when I saw what the locusts were doing to it, I left the tobacco. Each evil-looking little creature was wrapping its hateful legs round a succulent mealie stalk and was ripping off huge mouthfuls with its great massive jaws.

Up and down. Bang! Shout! Bang! Shout! Up and down, up and down, while from Nyasaland came faint shouts now and then through the enveloping brown clouds.

At twelve o'clock I sent the children home for lunch and a rest and continued my activites. Bang! Bang! Shout! Shout! and louder and louder the sound of the hateful whizzing wings.

Then Nkosi came up, sweating, but clear-minded as usual. He may have groaned and fussed when trouble threatened, but when it came he was always cool, collected, alert and indefatigable. Only in his eyes was the hurt look that always makes my heart ache. He said:

"Nyasaland is finished. You go to the land behind the house. Do what you can alone, I have sent for the women to help you."

This land had been ploughed as a long strip, but as it was only fifteen acres, it was not so far to spread my aching body as the other one. The locusts, also, were not quite so thick. Up and down I went, beating my tray which now looked as if it had smallpox. I shouted and shouted, but when you shout alone, you become self-conscious, and do not know what word to shout. I cried "Hallo!" and "Hi!" and even "Yow!" Then I shouted invective, which was very tiring and not good noise. Then I resorted to song. I sang Effie's "Ah, Ah, my laughing Valley," and "Where the bee sucks." These two songs have lots of trills and high notes. I remember deliberately singing to an individual locust while it was busy feeding, and I saw it shudder. My strong raucous voice was never so useful as it was that day, but it was cracking up. I heard afterwards that Effie was singing "Elijah."

The women sauntered up chattering in their silly way. They were carrying sacks with which I thought they were going to thrash the locusts. I told them what I wanted them to do, but I soon found that their only intention was to catch as many locusts as they could to roast and eat. To do this they encouraged the locusts to settle. I should have been better off without them.

About two o'clock Nkosi came up and said I was to light smudge fires. He left me with instructions and some matches. It was difficult to find dried grass at that time of the year, but I managed with leaves and dry twigs. I made one, then two, then three little fires, at intervals down the side of the land. The idea is to wait until the fire is bright and clear and then to put on green branches. We had done this when smoking hams, so I knew what to do. With a maximum effort I managed to keep a minimum of smoke belching and then stood up to ease my back. I saw far away other smoke fires lit by poor Effie. She was trying to smoke the locusts our way, and I was trying to smoke them her way.

All this time, I had been praying between shouts and curses that the locusts might leave the farm. Now I realised that other prayers were going up as well as other smudge fires, and I wondered if it were fair to go on praying against Effie. However, just as my fires were going well, and I was about to continue the series, the wind changed and the fires blew their smoke steadily over the veld vegetation so that the locusts were free to concentrate on the maize.

For five hours now the locusts had been passing in a thick cloud. Every mealie was stripped and stood like a tiny broken mast. Shipwrecked hopes. I went on beating grimly, too tired now to shout.

It was four o'clock when Nkosi came up and said the main swarm was settling down for the night. He said they were all heavy with eggs and nothing would make them fly on. They would sleep in the lands and the veld, and there lay their eggs.

I crawled home with my battered tray and lay on my bed with a shattering sick headache, and the skin of my face and arms burned with the sun which somehow had managed to penetrate through the locust clouds.

By sundown all the locusts had found sleeping places in the veld. Only the tail end was on our lands. The trees round the house were laden with them, branches bowed to the ground. Looking towards "Nyasaland," we saw the brown earth — a hundred acres of young maize eaten to the ground. It could not possibly grow again. Nkosi said the piece in front of the house and the piece I had worked on might give half a crop if it rained soon, but we had suffered a severe loss.

It seemed to me as if we were to suffer the plagues of Egypt, caterpillars, locusts. I looked in my Bible to see what to expect next, but closed it with a sigh of relief, Locusts were the eighth plague; we need not expect the ninth and tenth.

It was not a very happy Christmas. One bright spot for me was the publication of my first book of poems which was selling well. It had a pale blue cover with the letter "T" on it. I experienced the deep private joy of all authors holding their first-born in their hands. I could hardly wait to hear my mother's appreciation: it was to be oil on troubled waters, champagne to troubled spirits.

We had been expecting the final pay-out on our previous year's maize crop, but nothing came until Christmas Eve, when we had a letter from the Farmers' Co-Op: saying there would be no further pay-outs and wishing us a Happy Christmas.

January was very wet that year, and in this bad spell Bryan, who had been ill on and off all the holidays, caught another cold and was put to bed. I treated him as I always did, but this time he did not respond. His temperature went up and he grew steadily worse. The cruel asthma gripped him and he fought for every breath. There was no hope of taking him to hospital because the rain fell incessantly, and even had the car been watertight, it would never have got through the water-logged roads with an invalid. It was too risky to try.

It was impossible to keep the house dry or warm. Heavy damp air rolled in through the front wire netting and over the walls from the open back of the house. Everything was damp to the touch. I shut the bedroom window tight, but there was no way in which I could keep the mist and wind from Bryan's bed. We made a charcoal bucket out of a petrol tin, but the fumes made the asthma worse. There was no fireplace and I could not move the child to the dining-room because the draughts were much greater, and sometimes the rain itself blew over the wall.

Night came, and another storm crashed over our iron roof and blew the candles out. I had to put a candle on the floor to keep it alight. I poulticed Bryan again and again, and blew the herb fumes into his face, but the bronchitis had turned to pneumonia. I was to ignorant to know this at the time, but I knew Bryan was seriously ill.

There was no telephone this side of the river. Nettie was always ready to help in time of trouble, but the river raged between us. No doctor could have crossed; no doctor would have attempted the journey from town, even if we could have afforded the twenty pounds he would have charged.

About ten o'clock I told Nkosi that I must have some help, advice and support. He said he would go over to an ex-nurse friend, Jeanetta, and ask her to come. Jeanetta was very fond of our boys; in fact, whenever we visited her Peter would secrete his pyjamas in the car, "In case she asks me to stay."

The farm was ten miles away over the most terrible roads, but fortunately our side of the flooded river. I could see little hope of Nkosi getting through but be would do his best.

On his way he called on Effie and asked her to come and sit with me. She came and it was nice having her, but there was nothing she could do but keep up the fire and heat water.

I knelt on the floor by Bryan's bed and held him in my arms. His face was nearly black and his breath came in harsh spasms. When he was conscious he would gasp:
"Do something.... Do something, Mummie."

I told him I was making him better and that if he would go on being brave, he would be well very soon. I knelt there and held him. I did not actually pray; but I felt that God and I and Bryan were all joined together by love, and if I kept the current going, Bryan would not die.

Nkosi came back about midnight. How he managed it I do not know, but when a thing must be done, he always does it. He told me he practically floated over the last spruit. When he arrived at the farm he found Jeanette up nursing her father, who was sick. Without hesitation she settled her father, left him with her mother, and came back with Nkosi.

I cannot describe the joy and relief she brought with her. She dosed and poulticed Bryan, and when he became easier said he must sleep. I was sent into the other room, but presently she came out and said that she could not get him off, and I had better see what I could do.

I went in and took him in my arms. He said "My Goatie!"

Then I began talking to him in a low, monotonous voice, telling him about the days when I was a little girl. I do not know how much he heard, but the knew that I was there and would not leave him. After some time he fell asleep, and I sat there holding him until I thought he was really off, and then very slowly I disengaged his arms and went into the dining-room.

The storm had passed and the sky was clear when Nkosi took Jeanetta home again and Effie went back. Bryan was still sleeping; I crept about the house, looking after the fire and airing warm clothes for the journey and trying to prevent any noise.

When Nkosi returned we took turns in having a little rest and as soon as it was light, we began to make preparations for the journey. Nkosi gave the car a thorough overhaul and patched up the spare wheel.

When Bryan woke he was a little better but his breathing was still very bad. I dressed him very gradually, so as not to tire him, in a rig-out that allowed no draughts to penetrate. Nkosi draped the car in mackintoshes and sacks, and made a nest for him with blankets.

The sun was shining, but we sent a native down to the river to report when it was fordable. When the time came — and with that particular river the flood goes down as quickly as it rises — Nkosi carried Bryan out to the car. Between gasps, he said, "Going *fagash?*" (spree).

We settled him in hospital, and Nkosi had to go back to the farm, but I stayed in. The nurse told me that he nearly died that night, but I knew he could be no nearer death than he was the night I held him in my arms.

Once out of danger, he recovered slowly. The Plague of the First-born had been averted.

When more than six weeks had passed since the locusts' invasion and no "hoppers" had appeared, we began to think that the heavy rains had washed the eggs out of the ground, and that all danger had passed.

Then, one morning, the young man who had taken the farm next door after my dear Afrikaans friend had died, came over, weak with fever, saying that the hoppers had hatched on the unoccupied land beyond his farm, and were advancing like a huge army.

Nkosi went over to see what had happened. Hoppers — tiny black things about a quarter of an inch long — were creeping along shoulder to shoulder over an area of three miles wide and ten miles in depth. The Police had sent a "Black Watch" (native policeman) to this unoccupied country to watch for the hatchings, when arsenical sprays would be sent out to destroy them before they began to move. Instead of doing this, the boy had fraternised with the squatters there and forgotten all about his responsibilities, and now the moment when they could have been disposed of had passed.

They had gone right through one of the young man's lands and were steadily advancing. Nkosi thought the best thing to do would be to try to trap them between two minor spruits which were fairly near each other. He sent natives for arsenic and sprays from the Police, and set to work. One neighbour sent a few boys and a pump to help, but the others would not realise that if we did not stop them, the hoppers would eventually come through their own farms. We used 300 lb. of pure arsenic. The natives carried the tins from the Police camp on their heads and I remember one boy arriving with a burnt ring on his wool. He was none the worse.

Although the hoppers were sprayed continuously, billions still advanced steadily. To his horror Nkosi found that they did not mind rivers. They found shallow places and crossed on their heaped-up dead. As the survivors landed they were attacked, and after ceaseless effort the main body was stopped.

Before we could congratulate ourselves on this, we found that a contingent had swerved to the right and was now advancing on our own lands. Nkosi returned to lunch that morning to get every boy he could raise, and I went back with him. During the time he had been away the hoppers had gone right through one of our lands of early maize which was cobbing, and had stripped each plant, cob and all.

The rapidity of their advance meant that our best red lands were in danger. We therefore left the stricken land and raced to this land, where we found the advance party had already arrived. The grass round the land was dense. We cut this grass and sprayed the arsenic thick on it, so that a wall of poison stood between the horde and our maize. All along the fringe of the lands we had boys on patrol with pumps. After a few anxious days it rained, and this seemed to settle the hoppers.

For a long time after this we had to keep the cattle from

wandering on the poisoned grass. All over the country we heard of farmers who had lost cattle, but it was surprising that with thousands of pounds of pure arsenic freely distributed over the country, more deaths did not occur.

In March, Margaret, her husband, Ronnie, and the two children went to America, via England. They left their dog, "Digger," with us. Digger was a white, shaggy dog of great personality, friendly and kindly, and one of those dogs who really smile and, who, if they do anything silly, give a self-conscious grin.

Before our friends left, they sold us their car, at a very low price and to be paid for when the tobacco was sold. It was a marvellous chance for us, for the "new car" was falling to bits, and for some time we had never been out in it without engine trouble as well as the usual punctures.

We soon found that "the Whippet" also needed money spent on it. The worn front tyres could not stand up to our country roads and were soon in ribbons, but we could not replace them, as we had no money at all and our credit was already strained.

Life was very drab at that time and I tried to rise above it by writing a diary, not of "daily happenings" but of "Thoughts." However, I found the thoughts very material and all leading up to the tobacco cheque.

"How I should love a new toothbrush! Every morning, when the soft bristles caress my gums, I realise our hateful poverty."

"Only evil thoughts this morning. Every day this week something has been killed. Yesterday it was a turkey. The day before a turkey, and to-day a hen killed by a snake. A hundred turkeys in January and now only seventy-six."

"When will Peter be ready to come home from school after measles? And how can I persuade the chemist to let me have codliver oil?"

"The postbag has come, solving one problem and, as usual, giving another one, so I shall not miss it. Peter must be taken home at once and Bryan is IN with measles."

We set off to collect Peter but had two punctures on the way. Nkosi had developed a grim patience over the old car, but when the new car began playing up, he was filled with rage. We did not arrive in town until the early afternoon, too late for lunch, so it was with rather an empty feeling that I approached the chemist for codliver oil.

The assistant told me he could not serve me, I must see the manager. Luckily, they made me stand in a hot, dusty passage for over half-an-hour, and by the time the manager came, I was feeling rather faint. I made no attempt to pull myself together and the manager was very sorry for me. He gave me codliver oil on credit and a free dose of sal volatile.

The great day of the tobacco selling dawned, and Nkosi left me with Nettie while he and his partner went to town.

During the afternoon we rested and discussed family matters, taking strict turns, as we always did. We discussed husbands and how they love to dash their wives' hopes; how they never give praise higher than "Not too bad," or "Might be worse," yet expect fulsome praise from us for any of their own undertakings. How they expected us to "Do Poultry" on nothing, and did not mind how much we tore our arms and spiked our heads on the rickety wire doors. How they grudged us crushed mealies and petrol tins and gave us for poultry-boy the biggest fool on the farm.

The airing of our grievances was pleasant, but while we were having tea, a large picture fell down suddenly, and we were very worried, wondering if our maligned menfolk had had an accident, which would serve us right for complaining of them.

When they returned, we learned that the tobacco had sold even better than they had expected, and there was much rejoicing. The only snag was that the crop was light.

The tobacco cheque stopped the Diary of Thoughts, and it ends: —

"We went to Nettie's party last night. I had an awful sick headache part of the time, but luckily it wore off. My blue silk dress split, because the person who had it first had got hot and made the material rot. It is a very bitter thought that I, who never perspire in any unpleasant way, should have to wear a dress which shows visible signs of perspiration. Still, it suited me very well and now it is split."

Bryan had had very little schooling that term. He had returned late and what with colds and finally measles, he came back before Easter looking very frail.

I wanted him to go to bed at once, but he refused, saying he was quite well, and I did not like to insist.

It made my heart ache to see him with his stick-like legs, trying to pretend that there was nothing in the least wrong with him.

He always had to give in in the end, and then he would

cry with rage and say he wished he could kill himself; but
the next day he was lying quietly in bed, docile and patient
as usual and full of hope.

When the attacks were very bad, he would say between
gasps, "Oh, Mummie, why DID you have me?" And I used to
sit and blow herbs until he got relief.

Peter was flourishing and, having no companion, he would
roam all over the farm alone without telling us, he nego-
tiated with the native squatters for the purchase of a donkey,
for which he paid with money he had saved from Christmas
and birthday presents. His method of riding was peculiar, for
he had neither saddle nor bridle. His legs and toes curved
inwards round the donkey's flanks, and to guide the animal
he merely pushed its head in the desired direction. When he
wanted to trot, he slipped back on the tail part, and when
he wanted to stop, he laid his head on the donkey's.

It was a great contrast to see the sturdy, healthy Peter
careering about the veld on his donkey and the thin, delicate-
looking Bryan creeping about in a thick coat, tending his
precious tins of plants. Though some inches taller than Peter,
Bryan was losing weight steadily, and was now the lighter
of the two.

It was very difficult to keep peace between the two boys.
I often wondered why Peter did not realise his superior
strength, but I think he knew that if they had a fight, Bryan
would never have given in. At school his nickname was
"Tough," because when stronger boys fought him, he would
fight on and on, however badly he was beaten. This made the
boys think twice before they started on a fight that would
last a long time. Peter was a little arrogant and selfish at that
time, as are all little boys of his age. Bryan, on the other hand,
took all the farm troubles to heart and was annoyed that
Peter took everything for granted.

As Bryan felt his inferiority very keenly, I bought him a
secondhand .22 rifle and taught him to shoot. Mothers talk of
the sacrifices they have made for their children: the only
sacrifice I made was running after them as they wobbled on
bicycles, and taking them out shooting in the veld after a
long day's work. I had to creep behind trees and bushes,
praying that a buck would have a moment's foolishness and
that the gun would not go off unexpectedly. I did this for
Bryan and later on for Peter, and how I loathed it. The
possession of a gun gave Bryan more confidence, and after
a few weeks I could trust him to go out alone.

One day when I had been to town I returned to find Bryan had shot himself through his foot. Luckily, Nkosi had heard him call and had found him with a bootful of blood. Used to gunshot wounds, he had bandaged the foot, so I was spared the shock. Luckily, the shot had only gone through the flesh between his toes. I made him sit with his foot in disinfectant and water for a whole day, which kept it clean.

When the new term began, Bryan was too weak to return to school. I realised that he must stay at home and I must concentrate on his health and teach him what I could. Peter had to go back alone, and a few days before he was due to leave, developed all sorts of strange aches and pains, even rashes. Once at school, he forgot all about these things and was perfectly happy. Harrowed by his apparent sufferings, I wrote the poem, "The Picannin Boss."

Bryan grew weaker and weaker. In June, I did not dare to let him up until the sun was strong, and I used to find him sunny spots to sit in. He would pretend to be well and very cheerful, but the next day he was in bed again.

I took him to the doctor, but all he could suggest was I should treat him like a consumptive and make him sleep outside. The result of this was that he caught a bad chill and, when I saw his temperature rising, we rushed him into hospital again. After he was out of danger, I visited the doctor, who said:

"I can do no more."

I stared at him. "Do you mean that Bryan will be an invalid all his life?" He nodded his head and my heart sank.

I went out and walked about the streets, longing for some place where I could cry in peace. A friend took me home with her and comforted me.

The next morning I awoke with my mind fully made up. I would take Bryan to England to see a specialist. I went to Thos. Cook's and booked two berths, tourist class, for May the following year. I chose the best cabin with two portholes, so there would be plenty of air. I did not tell Nkosi at first, but wrote to Kitty, Bryan's godmother, and asked if I might use the War Loan she had so generously given him, for his fare. She replied that I might. I then had to find my own fare and enough money to take us from relation to relation. When I broke the news to Nkosi, I warned him that this year every penny that he borrowed from my poem money must be paid back. He agreed. I should be paid out of the first tobacco cheque.

When the tobacco work was over, Nkosi agreed that the house must be closed in. We did not dare risk another case of pneumonia in an open house. He bought a window and closed in the back verandah, making a weather-tight bedroom for the children. As we could not do without this useful open room, we built another smaller one as a lean-to. This meant that now all the inner rooms were sealed from the elements. Winds, dust and insects could still make their way over the top of the walls and under the roof, but rats, bats and snakes could no longer enter at will. They had to await the opportunity of an open door. Ceilings did not come for many years afterwards.

Chapter 21 — High Hopes.

In the September of Hitler's first year of power the tobacco partners encouraged by their small success and by the faint whisper of hope for the future, which seemed to be reviving the country, decided to increase their activities. Frank, our partner's son, was to come and live with us, build our barns, and teach Nkosi how to cure in return for part of the crop. Every scrap of cash and credit had therefore to be used for building, and the effort for raising money for our trip home rested on me alone. I was determined that Bryan should have a chance of health.

Frank, who had constructed three sets of barns, was very clever at building, and while he was at work Nkosi did one of his lightning touches with the grading shed. The year before he had dashed up a shed of sorts, but as we could not afford glass or even imitation, the shed had to be lighted by holes in the roof and every time it rained natives had to climb on the roof and lay sheets of tin on the openings. We now needed something better.

Up sprang the walls; Nkosi could lay 2,000 bricks in a day, but of course they were not laid as well as those under Frank's careful eye. The walls up, Nkosi cut gum poles and fixed a roof. He put plenty of grass thatch so that it would be rain proof, and we were to have real imitation glass instead of holes. One afternoon during mid-term holiday — I know as both children were at home — I heard a loud rumble and terrific crash and ran outside. The grading shed had collapsed. The walls built without buttresses could not bear the weight of the roof and had caved in, or, I should say, caved out, and

Frank, perched on top of the barns, saw it go. Luckily no one was near enough to be killed, but Nkosi standing among the rubble was filled with shame and disgust. I went back to the house and routed out the children and any boy I could find, and we all set to there and then to pick up what bricks could be used again before any of the neighbours could see it and laugh. This was done in remarkably short time. The new walls were reinforced and the only thing to remind us of the tragedy is a limed brick here and there, which can be seen to this day.

At this time the Government granted us a moratorium on the farm. We no longer had to pay interest on the purchase price, but of course it still mounted up on the loans we had been granted. Also the first Air Mail to Britain started and that brought everything much nearer. I used to see it flying over the farm and away into the mountains and long to go with it.

> High in the air is an aeroplane sailing,
> White are her wings in the sun's golden light,
> Eyes that are anxious and eyes that are failing,
> Wistfully watching her sail out of sight.

As well as this the Government Roads Department was laying down the first tarred "strips" on the main roads. Things were certainly looking up.

This year the agonies of the planting season were even more acute because we all had so much more at stake. The rains came late, but when they broke they were good, and it almost looked as if we might perhaps, if nothing went wrong, grow a crop, which, if it had rain enough and not too much, might, if not eaten by army-worm or locusts or hoppers, bring in some money if prices did not drop to nothing. The spring of hopes was losing its elasticity. In the beginning I had hoped and feared with Nkosi, like a human barometer. Heights and depths I had touched in rapid succession, and I was now exhausted. I began to see through him now and all other farmer-husbands. If they do not get the weather they think they would like immediately they want it, they fall into a fit of gloom and predict Total Loss. The wives cheer them on with hopeful words, but these are greeted with a hollow laugh and all encouraging suggestions are disposed of summarily. Wives have to go on being hopeful, because it relieves the husbands to dash these hopes. If none were offered they would feel aggrieved. All farmers, I found, in the growing season love to come into the house and say,

"All is lost!"

It gives them a sadistic joy to see their wives' faces fall. If they do not fall far enough the husbands pile on the agony until the wife has reacted properly, then they will throw out of a few words of cheer, telling them they really must try to look on the bright side.

By this time, all had been lost so frequently that I sometimes felt I would welcome the promised bankruptcy. If it were our ultimate goal, it seemed to me that the sooner we reached it the better. In our position we had very little to lose. It would indeed be gain to say Goodbye to the Lands Department, hand over the farm to them, and let them whistle for the loan plus interest. To wave farewell to the grasping dealers; with their "End of Financial Years," their Raspberries and Compound Interest. They would regret our departure more than I should.

All I cared for now was to get Bryan home and no creditors would be allowed to take the money I was collecting towards my trip. Margaret, when she heard my plan, sent me a pound and said that she was sending me one every month until I left. This was a wonderful stimulant, for I could watch my savings grow. I hunted in all our boxes and sold everything I could lay my hands on. I stopped hair-cuts and an eleven o'clock cup of coffee in town which is a sure reviver to early travellers, and I put this money in my money box.

I did not have an allowance, neither for housekeeping money nor for pocket money, so the ways of saving open to most women were closed to me. The egg-money went to the grocers, and the cocks and old hens to the butcher. I had only my poem money and the odd ten shillings the Grannies sent me for birthday and Christmas, so something had to be done. I then wrote three short articles for the newspaper and the editors said I might continue. In this way, with the poems, I earned five pounds a month.

Rather heavy rainfall had prevented the tobacco from growing as it should have done. There is always a good selection of spots on tobacco, especially in wet weather, but one evening we found a new one. It had a halo round it and some of the leaves had rotted away. We looked it up in the book our partner had lent us. It was Wild Fire, the worst of all tobacco diseases. It spreads like its name. We pulled up all the diseased plants and hundreds of healthy ones around the infected area to prevent its spreading, but slowly and surely it made headway and half of the leaves were rotten before we would cure them.

Just when the leaves were beginning to colour and we were looking forward to the curing, another blow fell. Foot and Mouth disease broke out in the district and we were forbidden to send our oxen through the farm which separated us from our partner's barns. After a few sleepless nights our partner solved the problem by buying a tractor. In this way our oxen took the waggon to the boundary, where the tractor took it over the forbidden territory to our partner's farm. Once there his oxen were hitched to the waggon and took it to his barns.

The locusts abounded all that year and we had continuous fears and were in continual suspense. Once a swarm passed overhead for five days. We knew we were lucky that they should be in flight and that the millions we were beating out were just stragglers pausing for buffet snacks. The maize was eaten but not so badly that it would not partially recover. Nkosi evolved a system whereby natives carried the muslin used for shielding the tobacco seed beds cut into lengths of 20 yards up and down the lands. This did discourage the stragglers from alighting and was afterwards used to keep in check a small swarm, but, when a good sized swarm decides to alight on a certain farm there is nothing in the world the owner can do. I remember after one Locust Fight a cousin wrote from England, suggesting that Nkosi kept turkeys to eat the locusts! Towards the end of the growing season when a fair percentage of eaten maize had grown again and we had stopped worrying, a small but dense swarm descended on one outlying land and ate it completely, cobs and all.

Peter increased in size and weight, while Bryan seemed to shrink and the holidays were ruined by fierce quarrels. I felt that sooner or later there would be a deadly battle in which Bryan would be knocked out. It would only be what he deserved but at the same time a beating by a younger brother would finish off all the self-respect and self-confidence I was trying to build up in the boy. If only I could ward off the day of reckoning, when he returned from England strong and well I knew the quarrels would stop.

During the Easter weekend we were looking after a friend's dog while she was away. Jock, spoilt and vicious resented the worthy Digger so much that we had to try and keep them apart.

One evening Jock set on Digger and there was a terrible fight. Jock seized Digger by the back of his neck and slit it open. Digger showed remarkable courage and fastened on to an enemy leg. It was a most unequal fight for Digger had short bandy legs and a huge broad back while Jock was taller, stronger, smooth-skinned and more agile.

Charlie, the children and I and all the boys in the vicinity tried different methods of parting the combatants, but nothing was any use and pandemonium reigned.

I called for tins of water which the excited boys poured over anything but the dogs. I called for pepper and Charlie brought the tiny table-sprinkler which at no time functioned willingly. I called for the pepper-tin and again the dogs remained unscathed while the rest of us went into paroxysms of sneezing.

The dogs then got in a clinch from which no one seemed able to break them and the sand was covered with blood. The shouts and screams of the onlookers added to the commotion. I saw that unless I did something Digger would be killed. I swiftly swooped on Jock and caught him by the collar and the tail simultaneously. He was long and heavy and would not let go of poor Digger who was also fastened on to him by a leg. It was a heavy burden but I swung round and round hoping Digger would fall off; but no. The boys were quite useless and all they did was to make jabs at the dogs as they passed which only infuriated them the more. At last Charlie was able to get Digger and I was left with a length of snarling, snapping dog in my hands and dared not let go of either end. Luckily, Nkosi came up and released me.

By the time we had sorted out everything and Charlie had reclaimed the cruet, Digger had vanished. He could not be found and we were afraid the poor, game little chap had crept off to die. Charlie found him that night; he had crawled into an empty tobacco furnace and would not move. Charlie was wonderful. He made tempting dishes and crawled through to feed Digger, saying if we left him alone he would recover.

After the battle I went to change my frock, shoes and stockings, as I was wet to the skin and very exhausted. Bryan, who had been in a bad mood all day, had gone too far in his quarrelling with Peter and hearing renewed shouts I ran outside and found another bloody fight in progress.

Charlie who had just finished retrieving the weapons from the last fight came crying to me to stop the Bosses. He loved them both and could not bear to see them fighting. The ground was still covered with blood, so it looked all the more gruesome. There they were, the healthy young brother and the weak, thin elder, hard at it. I tried to stop them, but I soon realised that I must not. I hoped I was right because it was one of the most painful things I have experienced. Each blow on each fighter hurt me. To see lovely strong Peter not thinking quickly enough to escape a blow or take advantage of getting one in, and my delicate Bryan with his thin arms and legs and that fanatical look. Knowing I was watching, Peter tried to draw off. I think he felt I should say that he should not fight Bryan because he was sick, but I could not have that. I said,

"Go on, Peeps, use your head." I remember the hurt look Bryan gave me before he threw himself into the fray again. On they went, Charlie dancing round and almost weeping. Then suddenly, they both stopped and Bryan rushed away. Peter stood still, wondering if I should be angry. I told him that he had done right to hit Bryan if he had been annoying him. Peter was slightly relieved, but not very happy because he knew he was not blameless. I was not happy at all. I went to look for Bryan while Charlie was looking for Digger. I found him and he was crying bitterly. He said, "You TOLD Peter to hit me!"

I explained that I had to be fair. For his own sake I could not take his part just because he was not strong. He had been in a hateful mood all day. He would not see reason. I suppose I was the only thing he could rely on in those dark days of his, and he thought I had turned against him.

Later on I think he understood and since then they have never had a bad quarrel. It certainly nipped in the bud any tendency on Bryan's part to allow his weakness to mar his character.

The next day I wrote a poem, "The Dog Fight," which made us all laugh.

This fight made me realise more than ever that Bryan must really get strong. He must go to England whatever happened. I went on collecting and saving. I sold my machine and my bicycle. I made marzipan sweets and they were accepted by a new Home Made Sweet Shop in town, but when I went for my cheque I was told they had all gone maggoty and been thrown away.

Perhaps I should have made Nkosi put Bryan before the farm, and let the creditors wait a little longer; but in those days the farm was Nkosi's job and the children mine, and I had to take full responsibility for getting the child to England. It was a good thing really, that the responsibility was on my shoulders, because otherwise with the many set-backs we had with crops that year, I am sure the booking would have been cancelled.

Just before the first tobacco was sold, a fortnight before we were due to leave, we were told that no hessian was to be moved off farms in the infected area, as it might carry foot and mouth disease. This added to our difficulties because tobacco leaf is pressed down and sewn in hessian.

We heard this during the school holidays when Chris was staying with us. She tried to reason with me: the Government could NOT make us burn our tobacco; they must let us sell it. But I refused to be comforted, because I felt that there was nothing fate or the government could not do to push us back in the mud. If the tobacco was not sold then Nkosi could not repay me the money he had borrowed, and I could not take Bryan home, and he would be an invalid for life or die. I lashed myself into a frenzy, but I drew the money from the Post Office and paid the deposit on our berths.

Fortunately there was an uproar from the tobacco growers and the order was rescinded.

I had arranged the trip so that Peter would be at school most of the time I was away. He would have only the short August holiday without me, and Nettie and Effie had promised to look after him during that time.

Before I left, Lupenga who had been away, came back. That meant that I left Nkosi and Frank with two good boys, the first time I had had such a staff in my life.

Now all was settled and my ambition about to be realised, my heart began to ache for Peter. Before he went back to school he began singing to the tune of "My Bonnie,"

> My Mummie is under the ocean,
> My Mummie is under the sea.

This harrowed me, not so much for myself being under the sea but at the thought of poor little darling Peeps being sent back to boarding-school while his heartless mother and elder brother went for a glorious trip to England. I felt a complete brute. Instead of a fragile Bryan and a robust Peter, I saw a neglected little Peepy and a Spoilt Bryan. I felt almost angry with Bryan for being so heartlessly excited.

BETTER YEARS.

Chapter 22 — The trip Home.

A trip Home always seems a tremendous break, but when one returns, the two parts of life in Rhodesia close up until the time in England is like a dream, and looking back one cannot even be sure just when it was dreamt.

My kind friends, one and all, turned out their wardrobes and gave me a peculiar assortment of clothing, which, as I had nothing but my "uniform," I was glad to accept. Hardly one frock was my size, style or of a becoming colour, but I let out seams and took up hems so that they were all wearable. As I could not decide which made me look the least unattractive, I decided to take all twenty-four. There was plenty of room in my trunk and I could, when on board, decide whether I would look eldery and drab in a frock which was too old and big for me, or wear something that looked better but which entailed a ceaseless pushing and pulling into shape by the wearer. I told myself that it did not really matter how I looked; people would accept me as a plain woman in ill-chosen and ill-fitting clothes. They would not know that I could have looked better and would care less. This was galling but very sensible.

As we could only allot ten shillings for meals in the train, we took a basket of cooked food, among which was a cold boiled fowl. It is a great economy to take your food on a long train journey, because you do not eat anything. The cold boiled fowl haunted every meal. Roast chichen on the farm with accessories is very different from plain, cold, dried-up, sooty fowl on a tin plate. Any little appetite we had raised disappeared completely at the sight of the now hateful legs poking out of the paper. After a while, Bryan would bury his face in the upholstery and say he was not hungry. I tried to entice him with the more tasty bits, but he was not to be tempted, and he said he never wanted to eat a chicken in his life again. This depressed me considerably, as it had been bad enough to think of having to consume half of the wretched bird. The thought that I alone must finish it made me feel quite faint. Every meal, therefore, we looked at the hated carcass for as long as we could bear, and then ate some bread. I wished it would go bad, but no, it kept, marvellously. I suppose it was dehydrated.

The picannins at the sidings are always interesting and we remembered how, years before, we had pitied the poor, hungry little creatures and how callous we had thought some people, probably older settlers, who ignored the husky whispers and supplicating hands. The natives themselves must notice that the up-trains are more profitable than the down-trains. However, one picannin will, in future, always try to explode this theory, and maintain that there are rich pickings to be had on the down-trains. His look of delight was a joy to see. He immediately rushed off into the veld pursued by half-a-dozen little friends. The last I saw of him was a whirl of black legs and under his arm, the two familiar greasy, brown legs of the cold, boiled fowl.

Except for arriving on board without a proper ticket and the last-minute claiming of my trunk which, when the ship was about to start, was discovered lying alone on the quay, everything went well.

At St. Helena, all the able-bodied passengers went off to view the island. I, of course, could not afford to do this, and was delighted when some kind people insisted on taking Bryan. Watching the fresh-water lighter, I suddenly became aware of swarms of dark-skinned women surging round me with beautiful needlework for sale. I told them I had no money but they said they did not want it; all they wanted was old clothes. I went below and brought up an armful of the hated, secondhand garments, and was immediately the centre of a bunch of frantic women, snatching at the clothes and waving tablecloths in my face.

"Lady, don't listen to her! Lady, I asked you first!"

When I got rid of my armful, I took the cloths, beads and trinkets I had won down to my cabin, and brought up fresh supplies. At last, when everything I could possibly part with had gone, I had to retire to my cabin and lock the door, as I could not bear to see the reproachful faces of my would-be customers. It was lovely being rid of these many useless clothes, and now I had plenty of gifts for all my relations.

Towards the end of the voyage Bryan took a chill and became very ill. The ship's doctor gave him an injection and promised to return to give the second. I waited all day but he did not come back. He had spent the day in the bar, and when he arrived at six o'clock, he was quite drunk, and could not remember what he had given Bryan, who was now delirious. In rage, I told him to get out of the cabin. I then locked myself in with Bryan. I had kept him alive by love in the middle of the veld, and I would keep him alive by love in the middle of the sea. By the next morning, he was slightly better, and by the time we reached Southampton, he was well enough to walk off.

It was lovely being in England again, but I was disappointed to find that no one, except my mother, was the slightest bit interested in my life in Rhodesia, nor could they realise my impecuniosity. I had been able to afford the trip Home, so how could I be hard up? I therefore proceeded from relation to relation sharing their quiet lives, and it was only the week before we sailed that someone took me to the theatre. The main thing was, however, that Bryan went to a specialist, was given treatment, and his health improved wonderfully.

The day before we sailed I was down to my last halfcrown, but a generous uncle at the last moment, gave Bryan a tip for himself and Peter, and with this we limped home. Even then, we had only a few shillings left for food on the train, and should have had a very lean time, had not an elderly man taken a fancy to us, and insisted that we fed with him and his wife. He left us half-way, unfortunately, and we arrived in Salisbury without a penny and a bit flatulent with tea and bread-and-butter. It was good to be home!

It was well I came home free from debt, because when I arrived I found Nkosi in the depths of despair. The usual hope had not sprung, and fear for the future included locusts, tobacco disease and the uncertain market.

The truth was that he was thoroughly tired out and needed a holiday, but we knew that no holiday would do either of us any lasting good until we were free from the fear of failure.

Bryan was in excellent health, but when I found Nkosi unhappy and Peter looking run-down after whooping-cough, I felt that I had been thoroughly selfish in sacrificing these two to myself and Bryan. That Bryan would probably have died or been an invalid for life did not seem to count. I was worried because I could see that it was impossible for Nkosi and Peter to go to England next year, and as it would cost them a great deal more money to go than it had us, there seemed no hope for many years to come.

I found a surprise waiting for me. The tiny dining-room was now extended and in the new part was a handsome red-brick fireplace. I remember the old window was so eaten by ants it had had to be replaced by a new one, and the now inadequate curtains hung by Nkosi's inexpert hands, looked like a line of dingy washing. The bits of petrolbox furniture seemed lost in this large room, but Nkosi had spread them out, and when I produced some beautiful green Wedgewood plates my aunt had given me, he nailed up two rough shelves. Secretly, I made up my mind that I would somehow procure a couple of easy chairs.

The planting rains came very early, and the maize sprouted nicely and then died of drought. On one land we planted three times before there was a proper stand. Then it turned out to be a very wet season, and the week before Christmas was the wettest the country had ever known. The tobacco raged with spot. Nkosi put a pump on a handcart and sprayed the plants, but the rain washed the *muti* off after each application.

We expected and had a wet Christmas, but at New Year it cleared, and Nettie had one of her famous picnics down by the river.

These combined picnics are a very pleasant part of Rhodesian life. Three or four families join together, bringing with them all their guests and any friends who care to come out from town for the occasion. Husbands always set their faces against picnics and say they see no point in eating food uncomfortably when they can eat it in comfort at home, but for once the wishes of the women and children prevail, and picnics have always been one of Nettie's specialities.

Between green banks shaded by huge trees runs the Marodzi river, over grey rocks smoothed and curved by centuries of flowing water. Sometimes large slabs of granite set up a barrier, but the river only turns its course and finds an easier route. It does not mind how often it turns and twists, for it knows that in the end it will reach the great Zambesi. In the dry season, when the water is low, the trees and bushes, like daring children, venture further and further down into the riverbed and push their roots into the crevices of the rocks. When the rains come they are drowned, but manage to hold on tenaciously, and every year their chance of being

washed away lessens. Not only do they make this valiant
stand, but as the roots strengthen, they gradually split the
rock itself, such is the marvel of growing things. Then the day
comes when the large tree is struck by lightning and rots, and
soon afterwards the flood seizes it and carries it down the
stream.

This year the river was full. The floods had passed quite
recently, and high upon the bank we could still see the dried
grass and refuse which it had brought down.

Every living thing was now green and sappy, growing
luxuriantly in the bright sunshine. Here and there were shady
pools, fed by little waterfalls, where the children and young
people could bathe without fear, but the side pools, deep and
still, where the water-lilies spread in a thick carpet, must be
avoided, because under the lilies lurks the bilharzia snail.

Here we all were, then, about fifty of us, and after morning
tea the children bathed, whilst their mothers insisted that they
either put their heads in or their hats on. The water was so
tempting that even I bathed though my efforts at swimming
are like a tick in a tea-cup .... a round body with threshing
limbs that take it nowhere.

At one o'clock lunch was served under the thick, tall trees
and afterwards, while the young people and children formed
exploring parties, their elders lay on rugs and dozed. Back
came the children, demanding another bathe. Against my
better judgment I gave in to my own sons' entreaties, but a
little later, as the sun went in, I called to them to come out.
Unfortunately, I could only lay my hands on Peter, who was
very indignant and cross. Just as I had him dressed, the rain
dropped from the sky. No one had seen the dark thunder-
cloud approach. Immediately there was wild confusion. I
seized hold of Bryan and tried to make him dress quickly, but
his clothes were already wet and difficult to put on. Through
the thick veil of icy-cold rain, which poured down on the
party, I could see dim, wet, agitated figures packing baskets,
collecting children and rugs, and bundling them into cars,
which, with hastily erected side-curtains and slamming doors,
were bumping over the rough grass to the accompaniment of
lightning flashes and crashes of thunder.

By the time we had circled back to the fording-place, the
river was in spate, and little channels of water were racing
along the road with us, anxious to join the flood. When we
were in the middle of the river, the engine hiccoughed a few
times and stopped.

"Water in the damned plugs," said Nkosi, as he slipped calf-deep into the flood. He opened the bonnet, dried the plugs with his damp handkerchief and got back into the car, but after a few jerks it stopped again, and Bryan sneezed.

Nkosi helped the children out of the car and waded with them to the bank. He said:

"Run towards home as fast as you can, and we will pick you up on the way." Then, to me, standing knee-deep in water, the rain pouring off my hat, he said, "Give me something dry!"

There was nothing dry on me, except that part of my vest which was held tightly by the new stays I had been given in England, but feeling that a heroine should stick at nothing, I broke my shoulder-straps and pulled it over my head. It felt warm and cosy as it passed over my wet face. I then struggled back into my sodden frock and saw that the dye had come off on the precious stays.

When the plugs were dry, Nkosi threw me back my vest and said:

"Go behind the car and push, and go on pushing." The river was filling rapidly, and I could hardly keep my balance, but in a series of jerks we managed to get the car shorewards and, finally, off the stones of the crossing. Now, however, we had the steep, muddy slope, submerged in a foot of water, up which the car could not mount with the few plugs in action.

Nkosi handed me a large rock. "Push this under the back wheels every time I stop." I did so, and as I stooped, the water ran over my neck; and I realised that even had I not sacrificed my vest, it would by now be very wet. Gradually, we crept out of the water, but we still had Effie's hill, a thick morass of mud, to climb, and my orders were:

"Follow with the stone, and every time you see me stop, push it in place." This was more strenuous, because sometimes the car leapt forward a couple of yards and I had to leap after it. As the car made better headway I had to run faster, and often I slipped and fell full length in the red mud, but by this time it did not matter. It is only when you are clean that you mind mud. After strenuous pushing and panting, it is quite pleasant to lie in its soft embrace and rest.

We picked up the children and arrived home to find the native in charge had gone off, leaving no fire and no hot water.

That night Bryan was very ill again, and as I dosed and poulticed him, I felt very bitter. All my trouble had been in

vain. Once again the river was flooded; there was no doctor,
no help, and it was all my own fault for foolishly giving in to
him, and letting him bathe a second time. I could not expect
yet another miracle. I watched him all night.

The next morning he was no worse, and to my great joy
he recovered far more quickly than he had ever done before.
When it was suggested that all users of the ford over the
river should club together and, with Government aid, build
a low-level bridge, we joined in gladly. Apart from its drowning
capacities and the fiendish way it seemed to rise whenever
there was a sick child the wrong side of it, this river was a
great trial. It flooded without warning and each year it caught
me with short supplies. At Christmas time it had caught Nkosi
without meal for the natives, and in desperation he and
Frank had gone to the river and attacked a huge tree with
the idea of felling it right across the chasm, making a sort of
bridge over which an agile native could climb with part of
a sack of meal. To their surprise, as the tree fell, the flood
picked it up and in a moment had dashed it downstream out
of sight, as if it had been a matchstick. Then they went higher
up, where the river was narrower and the banks steeper, and
managed to throw a tall tree to the other side, where it lodged
in the branches of another tree. Both ends of this tree were
then secured, and the bridge was usable. Coming back from
town once by train, I had had to use it. First I was pushed
up a tree and then told to climb over the trunk high up in
the air, with the rushing, tumbling water far below. Nkosi
led the way on all-fours, but I insisted on sitting astride the
log and propelling myself by hands and seat, my handbag
hanging from my mouth.

The bridge then, was the first real comfort in our rather
difficult lives. After this, when the children were ill I knew
that I could get them to hospital, or, if we could afford the
fee, we could even have the doctor out on the farm.

Bryan grew stronger and my mind was at rest. Immediately
it seemed to me that Peter was not looking very well. He
had never picked up after whooping-cough. When I had
taught him I had found him bright but fidgetty, but once
at school he had made no effort to become educated. He
enjoyed his companions and the sports, but in class he was
always near the bottom. His report ran:

"Peter's position is by no means satisfactory. He takes things
in far too casual a manner."

When asked what position he held in class, Peter would

count from the bottom and say:

"I beat three boys this term." This sounded better than saying he was beaten by twenty-nine. In one of the letters he wrote at this time he said: "I am as happy as ever I could be, as I have nothing to worry about."

When he came back for half-term he told me that he was always getting bad headaches. I had had him tested for bilharzia several times, but the report had been negative. My doctor gave him a blood test, and the dreaded bilharzia was found and treated.

This made me determined that Peter should have a holiday, and the only way I could possibly do this was to take advantage of the Children's Welfare Holiday Scheme, by which Rhodesian children were sent to a holiday camp at Beira for a month. Other children than those selected were allowed to accompany the party on payment of £10. I made arrangements that Peter should go in the August holidays.

When the children were home at Easter Nkosi attended a sale and took them with him. When they returned, they rushed to me:

"Mummie, the most wonderful thing has happened!"

"Daddy has bought a horse!"

"A white horse!"

"A tall horse!"

"An old strong horse!"

"And it only cost five pounds with the saddle!"

"And it's coming to-morrow!"

Jimmie arrived the next day. He was over sixteen hands, and looked like a carthorse. Nkosi rode him, and made him trot and canter, but it took persuasion, for he was a hardy old gentleman, and had decided to take the remainder of his life easily.

When it came to actual riding there was a slump in the wild excitement. Jimmie was so tall that it was impossible for anyone under six feet to mount without a step-ladder. Even Peter could not bounce into the saddle. They were undeterred by this, and I never knew a quiet moment while they were on Jimmie.

I decided that I, too, would learn to ride. Jimmie had to be halted by a certain rock before I could be pushed up on to his back, and then I felt as if I were sitting on a steeple in a high wind. The only comfort was Jimmie's giraffe-like neck, on to which I could cling. I had always thought of horses as noble beasts like "Black Beauty" or Dick Turpin's "Bess."

I never guessed there were horses like Jimmie. He had been ridden by hundreds of settlers and knew all the ropes. When Nkosi rode him he galloped like a warhorse at Creçy, but when the children or I mounted (a good word!), he did as he liked. He also had the habit of brushing his riders against wire fences and under low trees. Nkosi said:

"You should try to guide him by pressure of the knee."

Jimmie had a mouth like a Wellington-boot, and what was the use of pressing the knees when our impotent heels bounced off his hippo-like sides unnoticed?

Nkosi's official reason for buying Jimmie was that he would save petrol. Jimmie saved nothing. When he was wanted he would be at the furthermost end of the paddock, and nothing would induce him to be caught. Nkosi soon realised that a stable of sorts must be provided, so my turkey-house was taken and made over. After this the old horse was of some use, for he had been trained to step daintily between the rows of maize — his sole accomplishment!

By the end of the holidays Peter was riding fairly well but Bryan, as usual, was in constant danger of being thrown. I, therefore arranged that he should have a few lessons while at school at my own expense. My regular earnings of about ten shillings a week was wealth.

Chapter 23 — Progress.

When the tobacco cheques began to hold their own against "Accounts Rendered," I went into Salisbury and bought for £5 a huge settee made out of an old car seat, and two enormous chairs made out of something unwieldy and wounding. These were railed out and filled my beautiful new room, and when I had covered them with some cheap cretonne, they looked quite comfortable, if bulky. The springs played tunes when we sat down, but it was something to have a spring to sit on. We luxuriated in these — at least Nkosi did, because he has very long legs, but I had to choose whether I would lean back and have my legs shooting out straight, or my legs resting easily on the floor and a wearing gap between my back and the back of the chair.

By this time both children had bicycles; both had the use of the gun; both had the horse to ride; and the thing I now needed for their development was a tennis court. From the first we had decided on a level space which would one day be made into a court, but there was never any time, money, or labour to do it. One of my ways of getting Nkosi to do what I want is to attempt it myself inexpertly, and then wait for him to come, see, disapprove, snatch it out of my hands, and do it himself. This was my plan when I started to level the tennis court, but it was many weeks before my groans were obvious enough for Nkosi to come to the rescue. He finished it with a full complement of boys in two days. When it was finished, we rolled the court with a cement roller Frank had made out of a dip drum. It was a fine heavy roller, the only fault was that it dragged one's inside out to push it, and once on the roll, being solid, there was no guiding it; it went its own sweet way.

For wire netting I robbed the chickens, for I felt a shortage of wire, entailing hens all over the place would receive attention sooner than a tennis-court. The net was a problem; three guineas cash and four pounds entered. One day Nkosi gave me three guineas to pay a firm which, unlike others, set its face against discount for cash. Without hesitating, I bought the net and let the merchant wait.

Peter played well naturally, but Bryan, as usual, was unhandy. Nkosi undertook to teach him to serve properly, so that though he might not hit a ball, he would miss it in style.

Peter, with some of his schoolfellows, went off to Beira in July, some time before the end of term. I found out later that on the morning of their departure, he awoke with a rash all over his chest. He tried to hide it from the matron who was supervising his bath, and luck was with him, as she was called away, and by the time she returned Peter was dressed. Off he went with fifty other children, and German measles full out on his body. It was a very mild type and so he was not isolated for long. He wrote:

"I am as happy as a bobby-john (babbijaan .. baboon). I have collected some shells. Yesterday we went in a big steamer and saw the engines, it was very, very big. After that we had such a big tea. We had coloured ice cream. I had three cakes, samiges, jelly, lemonade, orange drink and tea."

This invitation was from the B.I.S.N. Company.

He had been at Beira for nearly three weeks when we received a letter saying it was regretted that our son Peter had developed scarlet-fever and had been sent to the Fever Hospital, Beira. We dashed into town to try to get news but were told that nothing could be done, and that even if we went to Beira, we should not be allowed to see the child. As we could not afford the expense, unless urgent, we had to be content with this. I lashed myself into a frenzy, picturing Peter dying in a foreign country. Bryan had gone to England, but poor little Peter had been sent away with a lot of rough children who had given him an infectious disease. I might have paused to remember the measles, and what the other parents thought about it, but I was too upset. We managed to get a Beira resident to send him fruit, and I wrote every mail in a fury of love. He replied:

"Do not think I am as wonderful as all that, darling. How can I be your baby when I am 40? I will be much too old."

He told us afterwards that the Portuguese nurses were very nice but there was no night nurse. A native slept on the floor by his bed and if he wanted anything during the night he just poked the boy.

It was a very mild attack; scarlet-fever in Rhodesia is always slight; and he was back in the camp long before the holiday ended. All the children who had had the infection stayed on another fortnight, so my Peter lost nothing. He wrote:

"We have a pet monkey here; it belongs to a little girl who is sick in the opesit dormetry to me. I do not mind getting ill as long as I get better again. I was not bad at all. All the boys and girls were pleased to see me when I came back. I am having a good time with the little girls."

In spite of measles and scarlet fever, Peter arrived home looking a picture of health, and I felt that he would survive now until I could send him to England.

Though the 1935 tobacco crop had been disappointing, the maize was marvellous. Frank, who had bought a virgin farm near by, left us, and we missed him very much. The partnership thus ended, unique in its way, for between the three men there had never been anything but goodwill and co-operation. Ruth, Frank's bride, came as a cheery welcome addition to the district.

We were now slowly catching up on our debts. It would have been a relief to wipe some of them out altogether, but to earn a better income we needed to replace our worn-out tools and to put up more buildings. The joyful day when we could pay cash with order and so achieve the Heaven of receiving discount was still far away.

October came along and with it the new season, and Nkosi, now on his own, sowed his tobacco seed and tended his plants so carefully that they grew big and beautiful with an almost unearthly delicacy. The beds were always placed near the spruit for handy watering, but the rest of the farm, including the house, was a desert, quite waterless.

A water supply was one of the vital things we had to do without. We had built our house on a rock, and it soon appeared that this was the top of a range of underground mountains, for wherever we dug we came upon granite. Our original well supplied our simple needs in the wet weather but every year, one blistering October day the boys would say that the water was finished and after that every drop had to be carried from the shrinking spruit.

Finally, Peter, who often stayed with Jeanetta, our ex-nurse neighbour, told me that she had water carted up from the spruit by donkeys, four tins on each donkey, say, fifteen gallons per journey, allowing for spilling.

Peter's donkey had now a grown daughter and a baby son, so when we had purchased another adult, I had four wooden saddles made at the blacksmiths and prepared twelve new shining petrol-tins. Thus equipped I sent the animals down to the spruit with three boys and, feeling the water problem was now solved, I sank on my bed for a siesta.

I awoke with a start; there was a terrific din. Bangs, clatterings, hoarse shouts, and screams like a brass band gone crazy! What could it be? Too sudden and violent to be anti-locust measures, and anyhow locusts did not come when everything was dried up. Dried up! Water! I ran out and saw boys running from all directions and then I saw the donkeys. They were rushing towards me, full pelt, their tins flapping at their sides, pursued by shouting, screaming natives. The more noise, the more frightened were the donkeys, and every beat of a tin was a spur to them to go faster.

Finally they were caught and willing hands held the wretched animals until I came up. I found my beautiful tins battered out of shape and, of course, not one drop of water remained. I tried again with two natives per donkey. The donkeys, surly brutes, had to be dragged to the water, but when it came to the return journey they sped home. After several attempts, during which sometimes they brought a pint of water to the house but generally nothing at all, I gave up the whole idea. Water was not for us.

In February 1936, Nkosi picked and cured his first barn of tobacco. The second morning he came to me and said, "I've spoilt it! It's all turned black!" This was a tragedy, and the next day the second barn also turned black, and Nkosi was terribly upset. We had several days of misery and anxiety, and the blackened tobacco was destroyed; then he found out his mistake, and went from strength to strength.

At Easter, it was Bryan who came back thin and ill and when it was discovered that he had bilharzia I was quite glad, for I had dreaded a return of the asthma condition. I arranged that he should have injections at school, and as there was no other way of getting him to the coast, I decided to send him to the Holiday Camp in the next August. This made him one up on Peter, but he was still far from strong, and Peter was going to England whenever it became possible.

As the season advanced the Whippet began do deteriorate and Nkosi, after he had sold the first tobacco, boldly bought a new Ford lorry. Our joy at this possession was intense. We were like four children and had to force the smirks off our faces when driving in town. Now we had a real car, an accelerator that leapt to the command and brakes that answered to the call. Whereas we had formerly rebelliously dragged stones to fill up the holes before our chariot's wheels, now they were so many flowers strewn before the pathway of our king.

As Bryan was nearly fourteen I did not expect him to be as thrilled with his trip to Beira as young Peter had been at ten, and unfortunately, instead of the nice children Peter had had as companions, this time there was a large crowd of very rough children from a mining camp. Bryan wrote:

"This is the most pugnacious crowd I ever saw. They flare up on the slightest provocation. I have had several offers to fight but have only accepted two. There is on an average a disagreement every five minutes. It is rather funny hearing arguments in Dutch and English with epithets in Kaffir."

Bryan looked so well when he returned that I felt Peter should have something to make up. He was very musical and had often asked if he could learn to play the piano, so now I arranged for him to have lessons when he went back to school.

As things were certainly looking better and Nkosi was feeling tired, he suggested that we two should go to Beira also for a week, for a breath of sea air.

In packing, for some reason or other, I had to reopen a suitcase and was immediately stung on the thumb by a scorpion that had decided to accompany us. It was my second sting, but nothing happened. The first one, some time before, had been on my thigh. Nkosi had been very frightened and during the morning he kept coming in to see if I was swollen up or dead. After several abortive visits, he said:

"I think it must be the same as when a snake bites a very fat pig, the sting does not penetrate."

Beira was the first holiday we had ever had together. My memories of it are sand and heavy, rich meals at the hotel. I put on seven pounds in seven days.

We had intended to relax but found we had forgotten how to do so. After a few days Nkosi became restless and his only real pleasure was to go to the docks and watch the ships loading and unloading. The high light was when he saw his own sacks of maize being handled. As the loaders ripped up the beautiful new sacks painted with our number, Nkosi wished he could take them back to the farm. We were forced to use brand new sacks which were a great expense.

Soon after our return we had the news that Nkosi had inherited a substantial legacy from an uncle which we could hope to receive early in 1937. This made the opening of another season less of an anxiety.

We were able to pay back the money borrowed from Nkosi's mother and help to provide for an old servant who had been overlooked in the will. Having bought a new plough and other things urgently needed for the farm, Nkosi put a few hundreds away for a Rainy Day. The farm and the loan could be paid off gradually out of income. He also booked passages for himself and for Peter to go to England Next Year.

It was a season of great content. Both boys were looking healthy and well. The scales would soon balance.

Bryan did very well at school and won several prizes. His Latin, however, was a disgrace. In Rhodesia, Latin, which should be started young, was at that time not taught until children reached the senior school, and if a child was ill or absent and missed a few lessons, he became muddled from the start and seldom or never caught up. It was so with Bryan. He did not understand it, and no one had time to explain. This particular examination is written on one sheet of paper, without a margin and his pen had wandered over the sheet like an inky-legged fly.

There are blots and words crossed out, black-eyed "E's" and words popped in. The Latin-into-English is bad, but the English-into-Latin is hardly attempted.

But at the bottom of the sheet is the school motto printed very perfectly.

TANTUM FACIENDUM PARUM FACTUM. And written underneath in red ink by the master is, "Very true!"

Chapter 24 — Nkosi goes Home.

The legacy was no Aladdin's lamp turning a homemade house into a mansion, but it was like an oil-can; a drop here and a drop there, and life became a little smoother. On the farm Nkosi had now been able to buy some of the implements he needed, and no longer had to see a job done badly through lack of the right tool.

All these years we had had no privacy. Going to bed, we could join in the conversation of our guests without raising our voices. I often thought it hard on the visitors not being able to exchange nightly criticisms of their hosts. Nkosi now put up ceilings in the original four rooms and these were a great improvement. It was delightful to lie and look at a ceiling instead of the inside of a corrugated iron roof with Nkosi's name painted on it in black ink, and the name of the siding to which it had been railed years ago.

In most Rhodesian farms you could always find out who built the original house by looking inside the iron roof; the name is always there.

People who begin married life with a well-equipped house do not taste half the joys we tasted. From the day that I bought a real enamel slop-pail with a lid .... a luxury, because a petrol tin did just as well .... I savoured pure joy in every new acquisition. We all did. In an age when the word "necessity" covers such things as electricity, water-sanitation, refrigerators and radios, people have lost the joy of acquiring inanimate things gradually, and they pity those who have to do without for many years. They are like dogs who swallow luscious lumps of meat at a gulp and, unsatisfied, look for more. We, on the other hand, were like cats, who eat slowly and deliberately, savouring to the full each morsel and, having finished, lick their lips and polish up before, fully satisfied with good food, they curl up and sleep, dreaming of delicacies to come.

As Peter said, he could not be expected to play the piano properly when he could not practise at home, I bought a piano for £17. When it arrived in the waggon it seemed a little bronchial, but we put it down to the extremely wet weather and hoped it would improve.

The thrill of that piano! I unearthed yellowed sheets of music and Nkosi and I took turns in playing our "pieces," telling each other, as our stiffened fingers fumbled over the notes,

"I used to play that perfectly."

The next complete joy was when I bought the horse "Gracie." She was six years old and Nkosi said a bargain. To me, Gracie was a fat, wide, grey horse, with no nice neck to which I could cling. After Jimmie, it was rather frightening to have a horse which, when eating, shelved away from me and had a habit of jerking her head down when she coughed. It seemed as if she tried to put her hoof in front of her mouth. An account of my early riding activities runs:

"Nkosi always rides in front of me and never hears anything I say. He suddenly begins to trot and I race after him, taking the bumps on my suspender. I groan, and he says I should not wear them for riding.

"We go follow-my-leader all over the veld, stooping under the branches of the trees. I look fearfully at the stony bits, hoping that Gracie will not choose that sort of spot when she decides to get rid of me. We reach a waggon-track and break into a canter. I am secretly terrified because of Gracie's lowered head, and I put one finger in a little ring in the front of the saddle and remove it when Nkosi looks round.

"We trot again, and Nkosi says something about day-light between me and the saddle. Under his critical eye I force elbows down, hands down, back straight, feet well in the stirrups. I wish my mother could see me, but when Gracie puts her foot in a hole, I am glad she cannot. Nkosi turns round and asks what I am doing, hanging round Gracie's neck. I say, 'Brushing off the blind-flies that are biting her!' "

There is nothing more lovely than to ride off over the veld in the freshness of the early morning. On horseback in Rhodesia, we go right back to the day when the first daring young man threw himself on to some wild horse and enjoyed a few thrilling moments before he was tossed off into a thorn bush. The same untouched, primitive land survives to-day in the veld; the graceful clumps of trees, the patches of brilliant wild flowers, the coloured lichens on the rocks, the perfect, natural rock-gardens. All these are trimmed with birds, butterflies and insects, forming some glorious design, utterly independent of Man, which his hand can only spoil.

In the cool of the early morning, we mount our eager horses and plunge into the dewy grass which is sparkling in the sushine. Over the clean, fresh veld we trot and then pass into the shade of the trees, winding our way in single file the sun glinting on us through the leaves. Then out again into the sunshine, we ride carefully through a damp vlei, daintily over a running spruit, we jump over a water hole, scramble up a bank, and rounding a kopje, we plunge into the long grass again, till suddenly we come on a cleared land where natives are working. A rest, during which the horses nibble the green grass, then up and away, and reaching a chosen, clear stretch, we canter for home. With wind-swept cheeks we race along, aglow with the glorious feeling of a healthy body, riding a willing horse, controlling, encouraging, joining it in the joy of speed, a glory which the rich man pressing his accelerator, can never know.

You can fly over Rhodesia, motor through Rhodesia, take long, tiring walks; but you will only find Rhodesia's heart when you set off on horseback in the early morning into the veld.

The best thing of all was that Nkosi was now able to make his plans to go Home. He did not intend to stay long in England and was hiring a car, so he could move about as he liked.

He engaged a young man to look after the farm. The only important work was the reaping and shelling of the maize and nothing should really go wrong with that.

Shortly before he left, I found my friend, Edna Boddington, who ran a little weekly paper called "The Weekly Advertiser," was in very bad health. She could not leave the paper to go for a holiday, so I offered to run it for a few weeks while Nkosi was away. It was arranged that I should stay with Margaret during the week and, on Friday afternoons, I should collect Bryan from school and return to the farm to see that everything was all right.

Thus I found myself in the editorial chair without the slightest idea of how to "put a paper to bed." I discovered that you take last week's copy, cross out all the items you do not want and substitute those you do. How a first edition is started I cannot guess. There is also an agonising time when the printer sends round for six inches in five minutes. The experienced editor has odd paragraphs ready for this emergency, but I had nothing and had to sit down and compose with the messenger standing by.

There was a clerk who was very kind and helpful. She did the typing, but of course the procuring of advertisements and writing of articles was my job. I had the use of Mrs. Boddington's rickshaw and the mournful boy who pulled it. He really had a very easy life but he liked people to feel sorry for him. He never ran with the rickshaw, but walked slowly and on principle never made way for any traffic, so that his passenger often stood up ready to jump to safety. He also liked tipping the rickshaw so far backwards that all the passenger could see was the sky and had great trouble about her skirts. Mrs. Boddington was far too kind to him; I could see that. She was far too kind to everyone. Half the people who came to her office came for help, and however busy or sick she was, she always listened, cheered them up, and gave what help she could.

I started off in fine style. The first issue was put to bed, taken out, and distributed on Friday morning, as per schedule. With great satisfaction I called for Bryan and we drove home. Here I looked into the farming department, the housekeeping department, the poultry department and felt very capable. During the week-end a boy whom Nkosi had set prospecting for gold came up with a promising piece of rock. We panned it and, sure enough, there was a nice long tail. This was thrilling. I already ran a weekly paper, a farm, a house and poultry; I could also run a gold claim; I would take it all in my stride.

We went out to see where the gold had been found, but did not take any more samples, as nothing could be done until I had obtained a prospecting licence from town.

Full of bounce, I started my second number, but the office was at the end of a passage down which a cruel south wind rushed wildly, and I caught cold. By the end of the week the paper was put to bed, but I was feverish and my throat full of ulcers. I knew that the third issue of the paper must be started at the latest on the following Tuesday and as I could not see how I could recover in time I worked myself into a panic until I could get no breath through my rapidly closing throat. It was only tonsillitis made worse by panic. In self-defence I must say that the fear was not of the sickness but the thought of breaking my promise to Mrs. Boddington and defaulting with the weekly issues. I went to hospital and became a model patient, doing everything I was told. But it was not until Wednesday that the doctor allowed me to leave hospital. Feeling like death, I mounted my rickshaw and went on my rounds. It has always been hateful to me to ask favours, and though advertisements are not actually favours they were so to me because I had to have them. This week the agony of asking was more intense because it was crowded into one short morning, but luckily my deathlike appearance inspired pity.

One could not refuse a dying woman's last request for two-and-a-half inches, and I did quite well.

When the paper was out I went to the Mines Office, bought a licence, collected Bryan and went back to the farm.

At home things did not seem quite up to the mark, but I could not put my finger on what was wrong. Even in the slack season, Nkosi was always busy, but Fred, the young man in charge, seemed to do nothing and stayed round the house with Bryan and me all day.

Directly we had finished tea that evening, we went out to peg our claim. The spot where the piece of quartz had been found was in some thick bush, and we had to decide where the pegs should be placed to advantage. We pondered and argued a bit because we knew Nkosi would say, "You should have included the whole reef!" When we had decided where we would begin, we marked a tree and Fred with his long legs went ahead counting the yards. Bryan and I followed, heads bent.

"Here!" cried Fred, triumphantly, and raised his head, then gasped.

Bryan and I raised our heads and gasped.

In front of us was a stake holding a Discovery Notice!

Someone had jumped our claim!

There were no miners in the district and we had had no notice that a prospector wished to look for gold on our farm. How on earth could our secret have been discovered?

I found out later that the man who had pegged a claim employed a special native to prospect the district. He may not have known that the boy's way of prospecting was to visit farm compounds and listen to the boys chattering about their master's business. We found that this boy had come to our compound while I was in hospital.

To finish this particular incident, the owner of the claim sent nine boys. They cut down trees and built huts, and when this was done, they dug trenches. Later on we received a letter offering us a share in this mine. Our part was to put up the money and supervise the boys' work. We refused. In justice I must say that the miner was within his rights. The law allows prospectors to stake a claim on any farm they please, provided it is not within a certain distance of a permanent building or on ploughed land. He may also help himself to wood and water, and demand grazing for his cattle. When the mine is established, the farmer may claim certain small payments, but it seldom pays, and if it does, then the whole of the farm is quickly pegged by other miners, and, as well as his land, the farmer loses his crops by the natives employed. Farmers and miners do not see eye to eye.

Much later the claim was abandoned, for no further trace of gold had been discovered. We think now that the large piece of gold-bearing quartz had been carted from somewhere else, for no one has ever found any more gold. The miner, as is the way of miners, left us to fill in the holes.

During my five weeks in Salisbury, I had in the course of business found a secondhand chesterfield suite which was going at a very reasonable price. It was not too modern and in good preservation. The old car-case-couch was a Blot and a Menace. A "Blot," because a tomcat had made it so, and a "Menace," because we had tracked down an elusive rat into its interior, where we had discovered a flourishing colony.

I had Nkosi's Power of Attorney and I allowed Bryan to persuade me to buy the suite. Nkosi had made the lounge extension as a surprise for me while I was in England; I would furnish it as a surprise for him.

Except for being a pack of nerves and tired to death, I enjoyed those weeks in town and used to take various friends home with me for the week-end. One Friday, I took back a complete stranger. I had met her somehow and found that she was very poor and sick, and lived in one room. She was a shrivelled, shrunken old lady, but her mind was active. She told me how much she longed to go out into the country, and I could not refuse.

When we called for her and lifted her into the front of the lorry, she said:

"You know my doctor would not agree to let me come, but I persuaded him at last, and he said I could, as long as I brought my tablets in case I get a Bad Turn."

When we heard this we wished we could leave her behind, but felt committed. We drove home with the utmost care at a funereal pace, and every time she shut her eyes we slowed down to get the tablets. On arrival I put her straight to bed and wondered if she would last the night. I lay awake listening for the death rattle. In the morning I crept into her room and thought she had died in her sleep, so corpselike did she look without her teeth. I kept her in for breakfast and told her to stay there until lunch. Then I attacked my many duties.

About eleven o'clock, when Bryan, Fred and I were making

cakes in the kitchen, we heard music. Who had put the gramophone on? Bryan went to see, and came running back: "Mummie, the old lady is simply doing it on the piano!"

We all rushed into the lounge and looked in. There was the old lady sitting bolt upright at the piano, her shrivelled hands plucking at the keys. DUM-di-diddle-dum! TUM-ti-tiddle-tum! We were amazed, but she called us in and played us several sprightly polkas, and then sang "Annie Laurie" in a cracked and quavering voice. We were very appreciative, but feared any moment the "turn" might happen, and as soon as she had had lunch we hurried her back to bed.

When on Monday we delivered her alive to her room, we sighed with relief. We found out afterwards she was only fifty-five.

In the window of an auctioneer's shop I had seen for many weeks a refectory table with six heavy handmade chairs. The price was £20. I looked and longed, and Bryan looked and tempted. He gave some very convincing arguments: one was, I remember, that the table we had bought the year before could still be sold for the money we gave for it, as I had bettered its condition, and the remaining bentwood chairs were literally on their last legs. I fell! I have nursed this table for many years, and now it is a thing of beauty.

Then Bryan and Fred planned the refurnishing and redecoration of the lounge. The walls were to be of light fawn, and the cement floor painted green and polished: this would go with the chesterfield suite. As the piano was black, Bryan said touches of black must be introduced elsewhere. This was done by enamelling the shelf holding the Wedge-wood plates, and by painting a black wainscot round the floor.

It was then that my son decided that the piano must be ironed. The veneer was peeling off and he had been told that the only thing to do was to take it all off with a hot iron, sandpaper it, and begin again with three coats of paint, the last a lacquer.

One unhappy Saturday morning we started ironing the piano. At first we brought the irons to the piano, but Bryan, racing round our many corners holding a hot iron was extremely dangerous, and the mess he made carrying the burnt paint about the house on his shoes was not to be endured. We therefore took off the flap and finished it on the ironing table in the kitchen, while Lupenga looked on gloomily.

The coats of paint carried the job on to the next two week-ends, but before that Bryan had become interested in the inside of the piano and one day I came in from the kitchen to find all the notes lying scattered on the floor. He explained he was trying to find out why the piano was bronchial. He mended some of the notes with seccotine, and then we had the unpleasant job of putting them back in the right order. We then sprinkled every part with moth-powder, and the tone was certainly improved. Since then Bryan and I have often on a dull evening taken the piano to pieces.

To continue with our redecoration schemes: every picture, piece of china or brass we possessed, was first considered, to see if it were worthy and then put in the one position which showed it to advantage. Bryan then declared that the petrol-box sideboard must go; it spoilt everything: but here I put my foot down. I loved my sideboard, and would not part with it. If he liked he could give it its long-wanted back, but get rid of it? No! He gave in, but insisted that the room must have a ceiling. The old part had been sealed, but Nkosi had left the new because the wall above the archway was built up to the roof so the new ceiling would have to be put up from below, and it was a hopeless job. Bryan, however, was determined and ordered planks and sawed them. It was a formidable task, but he stuck to it though the air was thick with curses and hammers. I begged him to leave it for his father, but he said he was doing it himself. I left him to it, because it is distressing for a mother to realise her adolescent son knows more bad words, has a prettier blending of adjectives, verbs and nouns than she has. The ceiling was put up: I was shamed into buying new fawn rugs: and the room was finished.

Chapter 25 — Camping Out.

The "Weekly Advertiser" efforts had left me tired out and the responsibility of the farm and house pressed heavily. I knew that Fred was not looking after things properly but could not put my finger on what was wrong. The knowledge that Nkosi would so immediately he returned did not make it any better. When Gracie spurned my advances and gave me a violent kick — luckily where the bone was well protected — I might have realised that the fault lay in the fact Fred was leaving everything to the boys.

After years of only doing as I was told, each decision I had to make was a great effort, and having had each shining idea

put through the furnace of common sense and economy, the
freedom to plan, do, and take the consequences was unnerving.
Jeanetta told me the other day she will never forget how, when
she met me in town one day about this time and asked me
when Nkosi was coming home, I burst into tears.

I missed Nkosi terribly and was frightened by the amount
of money I had spent on farm needs, wages, not to mention
furniture and paint. The lorry was still our most prized
possession and again I suffered greatly, for I had not realised
that cars need a continuous supply of petrol and water and
had thought that oil was only used for putting in holes, as with
a sewing machine. Now I had to continue to teach Bryan to
drive and was, unfortunately for both of us, in a perpetual
hysterical dither. The lessons ran like this:— "Not that, you
fool! You Idiot! Oh, darling! I didn't mean that, but don't....
Change gears! Oh God! Change Gears! Change Gears! Not
that way, you blithering ass.... do as I say! Darling, I am a
brute and a beast but.... Fool! Fool! Now you've done it!
Heavens! Oh darling!"

Bryan was very patient. He was determined to learn to drive
the car while Nkosi was away. He had always wanted to go
camping but Nkosi, having slept on the ground for the war
years, said he could see no point in doing so when he had a
bed. I wanted Bryan to have a nice holiday, so, although I
knew nothing about camping, we started off directly he came
back from school. We decided to go up to the Zambesi, and
as this meant passing through wild country, I prepared for
every emergency, and the lorry was laden to capacity. There
were tinned foods and bread and butter, teapots, kettles,
bacon, frying-pans, eggs, snakebite outfits, water bags, all
homely remedies, knitting and First Aid. There were guns,
spirit stoves, methylated spirits in a bottle, matches, lamps,
candles, warm clothes, mackintoshes, blankets and pillows.

Among my budding fanmail I had received a letter from a
woman in California, who had, years before, lived in Rhodesia.
Her husband had been mining in a Native Reserve and had
died during the 1918 'flu epidemic. He had been buried on
the mine, which was now abandoned. She had left the country
and re-married. A Rhodesian friend had sent her a copy of my
poems. She had written to tell me the poem "A Tribute" (to
miners' wives) was exactly what she had experienced, even to
the sewing machine which had been dropped in the spruit.
We corresponded for a while, and she told me that she was
worried about her late husband's grave. She had left money

in Rhodesia for its upkeep, but had heard nothing of it for years. I had promised, if I ever found myself in that district, I would visit and report on it. Now the opportunity had arrived. Bryan and I would go there on our way to the Zambesi.

We set off, had lunch at a friend's house, and were directed to the Reserve. After miles of vain wanderings, we found a deserted-looking mine and from an old shanty emerged a miner in his best clothes. He was about to climb into his old wreck of a car to spend a few days in town. He told us the grave was quite near. Hearing that we were camping, he suggested we chose a spot by the river just outside the Reserve.

"But," he warned us, "if you are sleeping in your lorry, be careful not to let your toes hang out, for there's a hyaena in the district that bites people's toes off. Quite a lot have been lost in the Reserve."

We thanked him for the directions and advice, and went off to find the grave. Growing beside it was the most wonderful msasa tree we had ever seen. It was enormous and its leaves were showing the shining red of spring. I took several snapshots including it and then a close-up of the grave behind its iron rail so that the lettering could be seen clearly and my correspondent would be able to see that it was well kept.

It was getting dark when we found the river outside the Reserve, and we decided that we must make camp without delay. The approach to the site was very bad. We had to go dead slow, while each wheel in turn bumped down a step. At the bottom we turned sharp round an anthill on to a flat green verge which was slightly boggy. While Bryan hunted about for sticks to light the fire, I tried to find our immediate necessities, which had disappeared in a remarkable way. When I had food ready to cook I found the kettle was sitting on the sticks, sulkily not attempting to get warm. As it was getting dark and we were being bitten by swarms of mosquitoes I decided to go without tea and just cook eggs and bacon.

Leaving Bryan to do the washing up in the river, I attacked the bedding and, after an exhausting time, had it laid out on the floor of the lorry. I had not realised that when all the space of the lorry is needed for sleeping, somewhere else must be found for the luggage. I got Bryan to pack what he could in the front cabin, and what was left under the car itself. His complaint that he was very cold and bitten to death hastened my preparations. I took the mosquito net which I had provided with a piece of string, and tried to fasten it to the top of the roof, but the canvas was attached to the beam and there was no way of tying it. I then laboured with a nail, a safety-pin and my shoe as a hammer, and secured it. At last we undressed and gingerly crept into our lair and lay down. We soon found that we had stopped the lorry on a slant and however much we doubled our pillows, the blood raced to our heads in the most painful manner. At last Bryan said he could bear it no longer and was going to move the lorry. We got out, moved all the things underneath in case they got run over, unpacked the cabin, and drove the lorry further along the grassy bank. Cold, itching and miserable, we climbed in again, but an unwise movement brought the net down on top of us and suddenly we were both enveloped in its voluminous folds, fighting for existence like two caterpillars in the same cocoon. By the time we had fought our way to fresh air and freedom, the bed was like a bundle of dirty washing. We were lucky to find the torch and the swarms of mosquitoes and hosts of moths were also glad. They forced us to put the torch out and work in the dark.

When we were once more trying to sleep, the cold air on my extended feet reminded me of the special hyena. I said nothing and we lay there, each hoping the other was asleep.

Then I heard the cry of a hyaena.

Even when you are safe in a brick house with a husband near, this cry is frightening, but now alone in the open it was terrifying.

"Bryan, did you hear that hyaena?"

"The miner said it would bite our toes."

"He was only pulling our legs."

"No, he wasn't. Hyaenas do eat bits of people. I have read of them eating people's ears, and if an ear, why not a foot? And ours are hanging out, simply inviting a hungry hyaena to set to. You must do something."

"Very well, then; we must lift up the back flap." He crawled out of the lorry and fastened the flap and as I pressed my shortened legs against it I was comforted, and lay there looking at the beautiful black sky.

After some time when Bryan seemed to have fallen asleep, I heard a rustle: the hyaena had arrived, but our feet were safe. Surely it would realise that it had drawn a blank and go away, but the rustling continued. A leopard! That's what it was! A leopard could easily leap over the end of the lorry and Bryan would be torn to bits before my eyes, and I had not the slightest idea where I had put the gun.

I shook my sleeping son. "Bryan, do you hear that rustle, I think it is a leopard. At any moment it may spring upon us. What shall we do?"

"Nothing," he replied, sleepily.

"But you don't want to be torn in pieces, do you?"

"I don't mind. I'm sleepy."

"Well," I replied, crossly, "I suppose you mind if I am torn to pieces before your eyes?"

"What do you want me to do?"

"Close and fasten the back curtains."

This took some time to do, and when it was done and we settled down again, we grew hotter and hotter. I said,

"Bryan, are you awake?"

"Yes. What's the matter?"

"Did you see any veld fires about?"

"Only one in the distance over the Reserve."

"Then," I said, "it will come and we shall be burned to death."

"Oh, Mummie, don't be silly!" He turned over to try and sleep. I lay there and worried. What would Nkosi say if we were both burned to death? But, of course, we should most likely have time to plunge into the water: but the lorry? We could not possibly move it in time. I tried to plan how I would break the news to him that his beautiful new lorry was burned right out. I suppose I groaned a bit, for Bryan turned and kissed me and said:

"What is it now, my Goat?"

"I am terrified of veld fires."

"Darling, the veld fire is miles away, and it could not get us here because of the water and the green grass, Besides, it is so hot I think it is going to rain, and that will put all the veld fires out."

Rain! That would be good and I lay awake for what seemed like an hour. Then I thought I heard a distant roll of thunder, for though it was the dry season, sometimes an isolated thunderstorm comes along, as it did in the first year in the huts. Anyway, it was hot enough for rain, I thought, quite forgetting that the inside temperature was caused by lack of air.

Bryan was now sleeping peacefully, but I lay worrying. We were disobeying Nkosi's orders and disaster would fall upon us. The thunder rolled unmistakably now, and there was no sign of rain. Then I remembered that, although the sky was clear, if it rained at the source of the river, the flood would rush down in a wall and overflow the river banks. We were hardly two inches above the water. Even a couple of feet of water, and then what would happen? The first thing we should know would be a roar and before we could fight our way out of the lorry we should be swirling down the river, probably upside down, with the blankets and mosquito net paralysing our every effort to get out. I could bear it no longer. I woke Bryan. He knew by this time I was beyond reasoning with.

He said, "What do you want me to do?"

"Get out of this death-trap," I cried, "and go somewhere, anywhere!"

We got out and set to work while the storm increased in violence far away. We cleared the cabin, and then the torch flickered out and died. We could not find the refills I had brought. We hunted on the ground by candle light for things we had put under the car. This done, I tried to back the lorry, but after I had gone a couple of yards, Bryan shouted that I was nearly over the bank. I went forwards and tried again with worse results. Backwards and forwards I went until I had only three inches either way, and the battery was getting weak.

Then Bryan took charge. I started to give him frantic directions and warnings, hopping about on the boggy grass in my pyjamas. Suddenly, snap went the elastic and, being of the cheap, slippery, satin kind, they fell to my feet. Luckily, the darkness covered me, but I told Bryan to stop operations while I looked for my clothes. I climbed into the lorry but they were nowhere to be found. I found the kettle and the tinned food, but no clothes. I had to give up the search and hold my trousers on while I gave Bryan the directions he asked for. I had left the lorry on a slant between the thick trees and the river, and he had to straighten it before he could begin to get out. When he was back in the old position he was faced with the problem of backing the lorry round the sharp turn up the steep incline into the road. One wheel would have to mount the anthill if the other were not to go into the mud, where it would probably stick, for everything was getting pretty well churned up by now.

It was the day before Bryan's fifteenth birthday and he had barely learned to drive on the straight. Suddenly, with a great lurch, he turned the lorry round going over the anthill and my bare foot at the same time. I gave a loud cry. My foot was not hurt much for it had sunk into the mud, but I nearly lost my trousers!

He said, "It's all right now, Goatie," and stopped the car. He then walked back with the candle to see what we had left behind and I waited for him in the pitch dark. Suddenly I felt I was being watched and turning, saw two eyes looking at me from the rushes. I screamed loudly and Bryan, thinking I had really met my hyaena, ran to my side. A native was standing motionless in the rushes, a chopper in his hand. For a moment we all stood staring at each other, and then Bryan said in his gruffest voice, "*Ini funa?*" and the wild, murderous savage turned into a humble, travelling native come to see what all the noise was about.... He directed us to the nearest village.

It was so pitch dark that we could hardly see the faint tracks and soon found that we were lost. We stopped a band of natives. Unfortunately, they were returning from a beer drink and, thinking that the two treble voices belonged only to women, some of them jumped on to the running-board, shouting at us. Bryan accelerated and I hit the clinging fingers until they were pulled away. By luck we arrived in the village, which was completely deserted. This was not the end of our adventures. We found another car and, as we drew up to ask for help, a man dashed out.

"We are in great trouble. Can you help us?" he cried. "I'm just bringing my wife and new baby from the nursing home and we have run out of petrol. We've sent a boy for the store owner, but the children have had nothing to eat for hours and are crying with hunger. It will be hours before we get home."

Bryan got out and, rummaging in the chaos at the back, produced part of a loaf and a bottle of milk, which were accepted gladly. We said we must get on and I told Bryan to go to the only farmer we knew of in the district. We were surprised to find lights in the house. The inmates had measles and were feeling rather depressed, but when they saw us muddy and draggled and me still clinging to my trousers, they burst out laughing and I thought they would never stop. They took us in, fed us, provided us with baths and beds: as I snuggled down in peace and safety, I vowed I would never go camping again; and I never have!

Chapter 26 — Further Fields.

In novels the heroic couple, having weathered the storm, shooed the wolf away from the door, and caught Love flying out of the window by its shirt tails, should live in peace and

plenty, in fact, "happily ever after." Frances, whose story
ended in 1933, would by now have become plump and homely.
Her house would be an example to all and her children, step
and own, would be all beautiful, good and clever. The
passionate love affair I had allowed her to have, in order to
show the nobility of her character when the renunciation came,
would have been completely forgotten, and the little wistful
look she sometimes had when sitting alone would have given
way to fat complacency. Frances would have been living
"happily ever after."

In real life we do not know we are living happily ever after.
The "happily" we do not realise and the "ever after" we do
not trust. So we remain busy, full of ideas for the future and
regrets for the present, and we go on and on until suddenly,
the bell rings for the curtain to go down. Our living happily
ever after has finished before we knew it had begun.

Nkosi had returned looking wonderfully well and longing
to start work. Although he was quite pleased with the new
furnishings, he was very angry to find the farm had been
neglected. The best cow had died of starvation and the maize
crop was greatly below his expectations. Drastic economy
must be practised, for the money we had put away for a rainy
day must not be touched.

To our surprise we found we had been granted a telephone.
It was, of course, a party-line connected to a small country
exchange which was shut at half-past four on weekdays and
all the week-end. It therefore behoved us not to get ill during
those periods; a disadvantage, but it was nice to have five-
and-a-half days on which to be ill.

Party-lines can cause unpleasantness because sometimes
you answer the wrong ring and people are rude. At other
times, when you are in the middle of an interesting conversation, you hear heavy breathing and know someone is
listening-in. Women with babies are easily detected and
mining people have no chance because directly they take off
their receivers you hear the stamp, stamp, stamp of their mill,
and if you know how many stamps you know who it is.

Meg and I used to have nightly free conversations. We sat
on chairs and when cold we wrapped ourselves in rugs.

During the Christmas term, 1937, Bryan walked into town
from school and bought himself a car for £12, and parked it
outside the boarding-house. As no one had done such a thing
before there was no rule against it.

The following Sunday a party of schoolboys set off in the car for a day in the country. Each contributed something. One a driver's licence, others cash towards petrol, and another the hospitality of his parents, if they drove to their farm some fifteen miles out. Directly they were out of sight of the school, Bryan took over the driving, but when they arrived at the farm the family was out. They raided the larder and spent quite a happy day, but on their way back to school the car stopped and nothing would make it go. Finally they had to push it to another farm, leave it there and ask for a lift to town.

Bryan then had to confess to us what he had done. Nkosi was very angry and, as it was half-term the next week-end, we called for the car on the way and towed it home. Bryan was very sorry for the trouble he had given us but nothing could dim his pride of ownership. I suppose he got some enjoyment out of it, but it gave him constant and gruelling work. Every day he was to be found under it, and would emerge black with grease and red with exertion and fury.

As Nkosi had said in anger that he would never have an old wreck of a car on the farm again, it was not possible to ask for help. Peter, who had no knowledge or interest in things mechanical, handed the tools. Sometimes I would see them flying past in perfect happiness and at others I would see Bryan kick the car and throw spanners at it. At the end of the holidays he sold it with great relief.

During the Hard Years we had had to let our insurance policies lapse and now things were a little easier we renewed these and in January, 1938, we sent the lads to another school, Plumtree, a school in the desert.

It was from Plumtree that Bryan brought Pukuyoni in his shirt. Night-apes abound in that district and the natives catch them when young and sell them to the schoolboys.

A *puka,* as we call them, is so tiny that you can hold it inside your hand with only its little triangular head and long tail showing. Its body is most decently covered with thick, soft fur like chinchilla, and it has the most delightful little hands. This is the only simian thing about these little lemurs, for their faces are more like those of a squirrel. They have tiny mouths filled with very sharp teeth, and their enormous brown eyes have such a soulful expression that it is hard to believe how full of mischief the little animals can be.

My Puka would be sitting on top of a picture about eight feet away, when suddenly, with a thud, she would alight on my shoulder. If I jumped at the impact, she would steady herself by clutching at my hair. Puka seldom touched the floor. She lived on pictures, chairbacks, and the mantelshelf.

She loved my hair. She liked to grasp a strand and then swing on it. She sometimes tangled it and got it wound her interfering little fingers, and nothing would make her let go until she wanted to do so.

If she saw anyone reading with glasses on nose, she would make a sudden spring and the next second the reader would find the glasses over one eye and Puka hanging on with both hands. I really felt angry with her when she meddled with my sewing. She got the cotton wound round her body, and then bit it to free herself, and I was always finding short threads, or my knitting wool would suddenly come to an end, severed by her sharp teeth.

In their natural state night-apes sleep all day and hunt all night. Our little darling used to sleep all day in my hat. She insisted on this, so I had to remove and lock up my best one and leave her an old one which she did not like so well. I used to leave it turned up for her, and she would line it with pieces of paper, no letter was safe. Sometimes Puka would be seen racing through the air carrying an envelope like a sail. Once, when I lost five postal orders, I found them crumpled up in her nest. One evening, jumping about on the mantelshelf, she dropped a letter on the hearth and immediately jumped down and picked it up again. This seems impossible, but when you remember letters were leaves to her, naturally when she dropped a promising-looking one, she picked it up.

When Nkosi came in and the lamps were lighted, I used to release Puka from her day quarters in my bedroom, and she would come jumping in from picture to table. She always made a bee-line for the shining silver sugar-bowl first, and grabbed two handfuls of sugar and licked them before she was shooed off. She loved sundowner-time, and would climb up the bottles and lick all the drips. If we were not watchful, we would find an inverted Puka on our glass-rim helping herself. When chased away from her prized sugar-bowl she would cling to the door-post, and chatter her rage. She very seldom knocked anything down, but after she had broken one valuable vase, I wired the rest to the shelf.

She knew the preparations for bed, and when we turned out the lamp, instead of sitting happily in the dark, she leapt from picture to picture into the bedroom, or just rode on my shoulder. As soon as we were ready to get into bed she would follow her tin of grasshoppers and saucer of milk into the next room, where Bryan and Peter slept when at home. Here she would spend the night as she pleased. Often she would get close to the wire gauze and chatter insults at any cat, dog or nocturnal visitor. When Bryan and Peter were home for the holidays she tormented them. Sometimes she would creep down into bed with them so that they were afraid to go to sleep lest they squash her, or if she felt particularly lively, she would suddenly jump on their stomachs and wake them up. Early in the morning she would sit on their faces and lick their closed eyelids. If that did not awaken them, she would try to force them open with her little cold hands. Directly she heard the first rattle of the morning tea-tray, she would spring on to the door handle and rattle it with her feet. From our side we would see the handle being turned and we would let her in when, of course, in two springs she was on the sugar basin.

Periodically, Bryan would insist that she was bathed. Puka hated this and chattered and bit. Wet, she looked like a miserable little mouse; but dried and dabbed with my face-powder, she was beautiful.

Sometimes in the evening I would take her for a walk perched on my shoulder and clinging to my ear lobe. From this position she would chatter rude remarks to our very large and dignified Great Dane, Faro. At other times she would creep down the front of my frock. With her little triangular furry head she looked like a brooch.

We grew to love Puka too much. Although he could not afford it Nkosi had to finish putting up ceilings because otherwise he had to climb on to the existing ceilings calling "Puka, Puka!" while I stood in anguish below. I do not think I have ever loved an animal as I did Puka. She loved me, too, and whenever I lost her I only had to stand in a room and call her and then, suddenly, with a bump, she would arrive from some unexpected place. She loved me to stroke under her chin and would turn her tiny head nearly completely round so that no spot should be missed. This done, she would lift up first one arm so that I could scratch under it, and then the other.

In spite of our precautions, naughty little Puka would sometimes escape and then we left whatever we were doing until we had caught her. One night, however, the boys left a door open and she was gone. I rushed outside calling, but no Puka. Nkosi, just as worried as I was, joined me and round the garden we went calling. Then suddenly, there was a scream like a baby, and we realised that a cat had caught our Puka. Nkosi and I charged about in the darkness, calling "Pst! Kat!" which generally puts cats to flight. After some time our torch light fell on Puka. She was lying on her side on a granite stone. Gently I picked up the precious little body, and put it against my cheek. I could hear her little heart thumping. We took her in and examined her. One little arm was stiff. We gave her drops of brandy and stroked her. She lifted up her chin, but for once the arm was not raised. We gave her her favourite grasshoppers, but she would not touch them. We brought the shining silver sugar-bowl, and put sugar on her lips. She sucked it off, but did not grab or gobble as usual. I then got out my best hat and lined it with tissue paper and put it near my bed. I lay awake until midnight stroking her and talking, so that she would know I was there. This is the most pathetic part of taking little wild creatures and taming them. They forget their own kind, and are so dependent on us and we, of course, fail them.

In the morning, I woke with a start and put my hand out to find the soft, warm body, but no Puka. Then I found her on the floor, quite dead. She had tried to jump into my bed, but the wonderful little body had not obeyed for once, and she had fallen on the cement floor.

II.

Since his return from England, Nkosi had not felt as happy with the lorry as he had before. I believe he thought I had spoilt it. This was unfair and unkind, as I had treated the lorry far better than it had treated me. We also found on long trips Peter used to feel very sick when at the back. Anyway, as the crop was quite good, Nkosi bought a coupé. This new car was not satisfactory, as only three of us could sit in front and Peter had to lie on the tray behind our heads. Lying in a peculiar position was no hardship to Peter, and I remember when we took him back to catch the school train, how he lay there playing his mouth organ to cheer us up.

Soon after this we were ambling along a country road when the tie-rod broke. We were glad of this excuse to get rid of the coupé, and we bought a V8 five-seater.

If the lorry had been a thrill, then this beautiful shining car was a cause for ecstasy. I used to make Nkosi drive slowly through town so I could see our reflection in the shop windows. We now lay back in complete comfort and proudly hooted older cars off the tarred strips. For Nkosi, driving was no longer an ordeal, it was a pleasure, and he suggested we drove to the Victoria Falls for a few days' holiday.

We started off in high spirits. Not only the comfort of the car but we were going to stop at hotels on the way, a wonderful prospect for a weary housewife.

The only snag was the seating. If Bryan and Peter sat together at the back they argued, quarrelled and fought to such an extent that there was no peace. If Peter sat in the front his fidgetting irritated his father, so most of the time I had to relinquish my rightful seat by Nkosi and sit at the back with Peter bouncing like a ball.

The face of her child is always indelibly printed on a mother's mind. The innocent eyes, the soft little mouth and rounded cheeks, combine to form a loved picture.

As Peter spent most of his waking hours upside down, the picture printed on my memory is of brawny arms with jabbing elbows, sinewy legs with heavy boots and a hard, round, butting seat.

By the time we reached the Falls I had had enough of Peter and was glad to stay in the hotel with Bryan, who went down with fever on arrival, while Nkosi showed the Falls to Peter and was responsible for his safety.

When finally the four of us did explore the Falls together, there was so much precautionary pushing-back of one by the other, that it was a wonder we did not all fall to destruction. However, it was our first holiday together and for that reason will remain unforgettable.

With the first tobacco cheque of 1938, I brought out my plans. The bedrooms were enlarged and a handsome stone veranda was built in front of the house. A Rhodesian farm is a builder's paradise. As well as billions of tons of granite and soil suitable for brickmaking, we had unlimited supplies of washed sand for plaster, unwashed sand for cement work and small quartz for concrete. For lesser buildings we could always use gumpoles and thatch.

We now had a resident builder-boy living on the farm. Gaston had a collection of huts and as much land as he wanted for a garden, and when we had no work for him he went to the neighbours.

When he had made the house alterations, he asked if he might build a Church and School for our natives. Nkosi and I had thought that, as we had come to the Good Years, we might build this as a thank-offering.

When Gaston had finished the brick walls, Nkosi nailed on the gumpoles for thatching. I remember his sitting on the roof swearing, as he tried to make the long nails pierce the tough gumpoles, and refusing to stop when I told him that it was hardly the spirit in which a church should be built. To make up for this, he put on a tiny steeple. This was for ornament only, and I still feel that he put it on the wrong end.

The East End of the building was curved like a bow window, and this was the Church part. We put in a tiny window, which I covered with coloured paper to give it the subdued light needed. Nkosi made a Communion Table and a Cross and Peter carved two wooden candlesticks. I bought two brass vases for flowers — we only used wild flowers. Then I took some tobacco hessian and cut large curtains, to keep this part away from the school room. I tried to make the mfazis help me stitch them with wool, but they were too silly, and in the end I finished them myself. Nkosi made some long forms, and the next thing was a blackboard. We made this by smearing the wall with a mixture of antheap and lampblack.

The Church provided a native teacher, and we paid and housed him. Our boys paid one shilling a month for night school and a morning school was held for mfazis and picannins.

We called it St. Mary's but it was not consecrated. One day the clergyman on one of his visits gave me and the school teacher Holy Communion. Although it was conducted in the native language, I could follow it. It was strangely impressive.

The school flourished. I remember going down one morning to see how the pupils were getting on. There they were sitting in rows with slates. On the blackboard was a sum:

$$5 - 3 = \ ?$$

The juniors, that is the picannins and females, were puzzling over the problem with knitted brows, scratching their woolly heads. This manner of thought seems universal. After a while I looked at the pupil next to me. He had put down, "Ans. 5." The boy next had copied him and on all down the row. I had not realised how naturally the natives would cheat. I said to the first boy,

"If you had five bob on your ticket and I *pusa'd* (ate) three, how much would you have left?"

He answered promptly, "Two," and wetting his finger, made

the correction, whereupon the line of cheats followed suit without a pang of conscience.

At the end of the term we were invited to a Drill Display and, sitting on forms, we felt like Royalty watching them.

From that day the school went down with a bang. The next term the teacher, unknown to us, opened another school at the siding, the fees of which he kept for himself. He cut down the morning classes to one hour and was too tired in the evening to give our boys their money's worth, so that the number of pupils dwindled to nothing. It all ended in a great row, Nkosi sacked the teacher.

As this is a family record, I have not mentioned World Affairs. Now, however, our little lives were to be affected by world happenings. Churchill was hammering away trying to make Britain and the Empire see what was going to happen.

"If war breaks out in Europe, no one can say how far it will spread, or who will have it in their power to stay out of it."

Every evening we used to listen to the news and I would sit there feeling we were drifting into something hideous. There seemed no help for it. It was just as if I had been waiting all my life for the horror to come, and now it was coming nearer. I used to seize on any tiny bit of hopeful news, but in my heart I could see no hope. September was an uneasy month and in October Mr. Chamberlain told us we should have "peace in our time." We listened-in when he arrived back at Downing Street after his visit to Hitler. Meg was anxious to hear but she had no wireless, so I put ours on full and held the receiver of the telephone so that she could hear. We were told he had brought "Peace with Honour," and we could hear the wild cheering of the crowd. It seemed too good to be true. Meg said:

"God bless him," and she hoped Mrs. Chamberlain would put him straight to bed, and how she wished that she, Meg, could give him a plateful of her most nourishing broth.

I felt sad, for, strangely enough, "Give us peace in our time, O Lord," has always seemed to me the wrong type of prayer. Perhaps because our vicar at Home in intoning it used to stress the "our." It seems so selfish and I cannot pass a prayer that has a flavour of selfishness in it. I felt as I did years before when I was beating trays and dear Effie was also beating trays, that I could not pray that the locusts should go her way.

Churchill said, "I will begin, therefore, by saying the most unpopular, unwelcome thing. I will begin by saying what everybody would like to forget or ignore, but which must, nevertheless, be stated, namely, that we have sustained a total and unmitigated defeat."

Through the next month we began to realise that Churchill was right. Hitler was having his own way, and we all knew that nothing would stop him now. Again came the voice of Churchill:

"Are we going to make a supreme additional effort to remain a great power, or are we going to slide away into what seems to be easier, softer, less strenuous, less harassing courses, with all the tremendous renunciation which that decision implies?"

And yet I must continue with the story of the petty doings of unimportant people. "Peace in our time." Yes, but not in everybody's time. Someone's husband would have to fight, somebody's sons have to die.

Peter was thirteen and a half. Bryan was sixteen.

PART VII

THE WAR YEARS.

Chapter 27 — The Rainy Day.

THE season 1938-9 started with a good shower early in October, which brought up the weeds upon which we pounced delighted to be one jump ahead of them. Early in November we had another shower on which we planted a little tobacco and maize. We then waited with increasing anxiety for the rains to come but nothing happened.

In other districts good rains were falling and we had to listen to other farmers talking of the acreage they had planted while our own planters lay idle. When the farm was a desert and the surviving plants had all been eaten by starving insects, suddenly the rain fell, and the rain fell, and went on falling. Twenty inches, a year's rainfall, fell on our luckless farm and the ground became sodden and cold.

The tobacco looked like small starved cabbages and the maize turned blue, and every acre was crowded with sturdy luxuriant weeds. I have never understood why the adjective "weedy" is taken to mean pale and sickly. A weedy man should be one who is gross and fat and strong with an enormous appetite, a roaring, pushing egotist. Our crops were so bad that year that Nkosi said it would have grown no crops at all. Very reluctantly we had to draw on the money we had put away for a Rainy Day. It is strange how annoying we humans find it, to use the Rainy Day hoard for the purpose for which it is saved.

In sight of his examination, the then goal of Rhodesian education, Bryan wrote to say he was always tired and his brain perpetually in a muddle. I had not striven with him for all these years, to allow him to give up on the last lap so I had him tested for bilhazia and when this was once again found and treated I took him away for a few weeks to the coast. On his return he set to work and in spite of the gloomy forebodings of his headmaster, passed well.

But before the year was over, war was declared and our personal troubles and anxieties were overshadowed.

In Rhodesia, everyone leapt to the call and was told not to be a nuisance. Every able-bodied man wanted to join up and later, conscription had to be introduced to keep them at their jobs.

Women who had taken part in the last war, expected to be able to take up war work at once and were disappointed when they found there was nothing to do. Bottles were collected in such numbers that one firm had to employ a special native to break them and many miles of bandages were rolled. First Aid classes were started and after a few batches had been turned out, the streets became unsafe. One slight stumble or a wan look, and members of the public were pounced upon by eager first-aiders.

It was a strange war, some people called it "phoney" yet the Poles were being shot to pieces. Churchill said,

"I cannot forecast to you the action of Russia. The key is Russian national interest."

We did not realise then that we were one of a line of schoolboys waiting for punishment, whose master will deal with each in turn.

Bryan was blissfully happy on the farm. As he had missed the curing season, he was able to devote himself to forge work and used to come in black with soot and grease. I felt sorry for myself, because Bryan had the brains of the family and I had hoped he would follow my father's family and become a docter; but no, he preferred farming and of all farming jobs, blacksmith's work was his choice. My only comfort was that he read widely and intelligently.

When he first came home we had battles about vests and cold mixtures, but I had to give in. Immediately, his health became established and he started on a course of Health Exercises. The latter entailed dieting and Fast Days. He tried to make me fast, but Nkosi found me so disagreeable when I had to watch him eating bacon that he forbade my fasting further.

Bryan was very good to me, he earned only five pounds a month but he was always buying me presents. He bought me a music stool at a sale, and when it arrived tried to destroy it because it was not good enough. He made me a screen of such solid proportions that it took two natives to move it, and was warranted to kill anybody it fell on.

He drew up a plan of how he hoped the farm would be developed one day with trees, dams, and fences. He rode Gracie my horse violently, and was often thrown off. I tried to make him take interest in girls, but he would not. All he wanted to do was to work on the farm or in the workshop.

His ideas were generally far above his possible achievement, and often things went wrong and then the tools used to fly. A heavy hammer went through the workshop window and to this day the pane is missing.

Although we enjoyed having the sedan car we missed the lorry and finally had to buy a second-hand half-ton for farm work.

James, now the boss-boy was very put out when he heard that Bryan would only have a year on the farm before he would be of joining-up age. He said that Nkosi, who was now in the forties, was getting very old and that Boss "Brown's" (Bryan) place was on the farm helping him. Why should OUR Picannin Boss go and fight? I explained that it was the duty of Boss Bryan, just as much as it was the duty of other Picannin Bosses to "*enza fight.*" James turned away muttering;

"*Ini indaba lo English zonkeskat enza fight?*"

What is the reason the English always make fight?

I called him back; I had to justify England in his sight. Telling him to wait, I went into the house and fetched an atlas and opening it I pointed to the sea.

"*Lo manzi makulu.*" (The big water.)

He nodded, he had heard that there was a great stretch of water bigger than Lake Nyassa and salt. Then I pointed to the land.

"*Lo veld.*" He was not impressed. When you are trying to instruct a native about things he has never seen or heard of you can feel behind the polite silence a barrier of disbelief.

"*Manje,*" (now) I said, "*lo* Germany tells *lo* Austria, '*Mina bamba wena!*' (I catch you) and *lo* Austria say, '*Aikona!*' and *lo* English tells *lo* Germany '*Aikona enza so!*' I paused. "*Manje, lo* Germany *bambele lo* Austria."

A flicker of interest spread over James' face.

"*Manje,*" I went on, slightly heartened, "*lo* Germany tells *lo* Czechoslovakia, '*Mina bamba wena!*' and *lo* Czechoslovakia says '*Aikona!*' *Manje lo* English tells *lo* Germany, "*Aikona enza so!*" Pause. "*Man je lo* Germany *bambele lo* Czecho-slovakia!"

"*Uh, uh!*" said James, "*lo* Germany *meninge* cheeky!"

Then I continued with the sad tale and could see that James was enjoying repetition for, like children, the Native appreciates most the stories told on these lines. When we came to the fatal part when Poland was *"bambele,"* James agreed that *lo* English could do no less than fight, but he was sad.

"Muhle lo Boss hamba fight," he said, relinquishing his dearest dream that a young and vigorous Boss should help a decrepit Nkosi on the farm. Then with pride, *"Manje lo* Boss "Brown" *yen'azi lungissa lo* Germany!" (knows how to fix.)

On March the 30th Churchill said,

"All's quiet on the Western Front; and to-day this Saturday nothing has happened on the sea or in the air. But more than a million German soldiers, including all their active divisions, are drawn up ready to attack at a few hours' notice all along the frontier of Luxembourg, of Belgium, and of Holland. At any moment these neutral countries may be subject to an avalanche of steel and fire."

In spite of this warning we were all thoroughly surprised and shocked when on April 9th Germany invaded Norway.

To Churchill we listened. On Churchill we relied. We lived on the sound of his voice coming to us across the world.

"Come, let us go forward together with our united strength."

Nkosi, with other ex-soldiers, spent every minute he could listening to the wireless. We heard the same news over and over again, in case there might be one new item.

When war had been declared our local Broadcasting Station, inspired with patriotism, filled in the time before the news by playing stirring marches. It seemed at the time quite suitable, but now with terrible things happening and a great threatening cloud hiding the future from us, these little tin-soldier marches became infuriating. We knew each one by heart, from the first Tiddly-Tum to the final blare and flourish.

Then came the British Expeditionary Force to Norway and the heart-break of the withdrawal. Hot on this we heard of the invasion of Holland and Belgium.

Oh, God! those days! And nothing we could do! Subscribe to the Red Cross, to the Navy League, to the National War Fund. Collect salvage, knit socks. Food and Luxuries were still plentiful, but necessities for farming hard to get. There were marvellous clothes in the shops for rich women, but a scarcity of children's clothes.

Nkosi could not leave the wireless. He would sit there and groan, "If only I could be there!" He had fought all over France and Belgium and every name brought back memories. It was his place to go. Bryan could manage the farm; would have to manage the farm. Poor Nkosi. Then Dunkirk.

I used to sit on the stool by his side and listen as the scanty news came through. How many more had got away? How were they getting away? The little boats? Oh, if only he could have been in one of them.

The five dread days dragged past, and Nkosi was with the troops all the time. Then the dawn of hope. The wonderful unbelievable news of the successful evacuation. Oh, dear England. Oh, dear English people. Our own people and we not there to help.

Later came the business of the French Fleet. The news was like a thrilling instalment of a book. I often said to Nkosi it seemed so terrible that with all the suffering, destruction and slaughter, it could be so interesting, arresting and absorbing. It seemed wicked that we should find it so.

Finally came the Battle of Britain. London was bombed. Again Churchill spoke to us.

"This wicked man ... has now resolved to try to break our famous island race by a process of indiscriminate destruction."

One morning my sister-in-law phoned me up to tell me that a cable had come from London saying that my younger brother's house had received a direct hit and that he and this wife were both killed.

This was a terrible shock. I had worried over my mother living at the mouth of the Thames, but I had not thought of my brother living in the heart of London. The news had been delayed because all communications were disorganised.

My mother had been evacuated to a stranger in Somerset, and the cable warned me not to mention my brother's death to her. She wrote to me as she always did, but now her letters were pathetic. Bunny never wrote to her; she did not know what she had done to offend. She had heard that they had left their house and given no address. If only they would let her go and live with them she would be no trouble at all. She was so lonely by herself.

How cruel we are to old people in the mistaken desire to spare them. I wonder what makes us think that those who have braved the troubles of life so long should be incapable of taking another blow. When at last they broke the news she was not in the least upset. She wrote and told me how sorry she was that she would not see me again, but she was longing to be with my father and brother.

"Perhaps," she wrote, "I shall be able to help you from that side. If I can, I will."

On June 5th the Germans attacked the Somme and the
Aisne, Nkosi's own particular fields of activity, and he was
frantic. Swift on this came the declaration of War by Italy,
and once again Churchill gave us the words we wanted....
"Jackal."

Then the fall of France and his speech.

"We have become the sole champions now in arms to
defend the world cause. We shall do our best to be worthy
of this high honour. We shall defend our island home and
with the British Empire we shall fight on, unconquerable."

When he had finished Nkosi said,

"I feel better now we are on our own. At least we know
where we are."

Chapter 28 — Anxious Days.

With the farm ready for planting and the intention of
growing bumper corps, Nkosi and Bryan were anxious to start
the new season, but this year no rain fell until Boxing Day,
and thus six weeks of the precious growing season were
wasted.

For Christmas we gave Bryan a dog. Becky Sharpe was
bought as a pure-bred, short-haired fox-terrier, and by the
time she had grown a long shaggy coat it was too late to
complain for she was his constant companion. Becky adored
Bryan, loved Peter and quite liked Nkosi, but towards me
or any other female she was completely indifferent.

Frank had given Bryan a semi-wild kitten. He called it
Phyllis as it was his "only joy," and "Spitzes" because she
did nothing but growl and spit. Phyllis had kittens regularly
and secretly. The first we would know of it was on finding
little, dead, striped bodies on the tennis-court. This was
Becky's doing for she disliked sharing her master with Spitzes.

Rhodesia was now filling up very rapidly with R.A.F.
training camps, with German and Italian internees and with
Polish refugees. Food was therefore badly needed. There was
no longer a surplus of maize and the farmers were asked
to grow as much food as possible. We therefore pulled down
our school, which was slowly rotting away, and with the
bricks built another block of pigsties, which we called St.
Mary's Piggeries. Strangely enough, soon afterwards these sties
were struck by lightning, and three pedigree sows were
eltctrocuted.

We country women welcomed the arrival of the R.A.F. boys, as here was a chance of doing something beside the inevitable knitting and helping with fêtes.

The first contingent of ground staff had been a mistake. The type sent were unable to grasp the position and the obligations of the white man in a black country. They cat-called after our Rhodesian girls, and when repulsed fraternised with the Coloureds and natives.

We old settlers had brought up our children to believe that England was a wonderful country, and the English a wonderful race. So anxious had we been to instil in them the best of the English traditions, that we had lead them to believe that the English type was the ideal and should be their example.

When our sons saw these under-privileged, under-nourished, under-educated lads with their bad teeth and bad manners, they were aghast and when they saw them with the Coloureds and natives they were horrified. These English lads who, most of them, had never left their home city were prompt to notice the disapproval, and so, instead of settling down and gradually suiting themselves to their new surroundings, they were on the defence, and showed their shortcomings and none of the sterling virtues we English-born knew they possessed. Later on, a different type was sent out, and these boys coped with conditions and learned from our boys the correct and fair treatment of natives. The ignorant newcomer so often begins by treating the native as an equal, which the latter does not expect or want, and then suddenly switches over and treats him like dirt. The Rhodesian born boy accepts, with the servant's work, the responsibility of caring for him and protecting him.

Peter and Bryan were very good with the many R.A.F. guests we entertained. They showed them round and in-structed them in the rules of the house. Bath and change into longs for dinner, and not to take Father's chair.

During the war we had many of these R.A.F. boys to stay and grew very fond of some of them, but though a few seemed to belong to the family for a time, I am leaving them out of this story. We never experienced anything but good behaviour, gratitude and affection from our boys. My ten-dency to spoil them was balanced by Nkosi's apparent, but really non-existent, sterness.

In April the telephone rang one morning. It was the aide-de-camp's Secretary asking Nkosi and me to tea at Govern-

ment House next Sunday. I was very surprised as we had not
met Sir Herbert and Lady Stanley, and I could not see why
we should be asked.

Arriving at the gates, we waited to let other cars go first
but when it was a minute to the time and no other cars had
arrived, we went on, Nkosi putting me in a panic by saying
that I must have made a mistake as to the date or time. As
we came up to the long, low, white building, we saw no trace
of another car and felt like going home. Our relief was great
when Colonel Holbech stepped off the veranda to welcome us.

We were introduced to the English actress, Ivy Tresmand,
and after tea I found out the reason for our visit. Ivy was
getting up an entertainment for War Funds in Rhodesia later
on, and I was to give her what help I could. I thoroughly
enjoyed myself and Nkosi said later I ate more than I should
have done, but when I meet real actors and actresses or
stage-lovers something goes singing inside me and I forget
myself. I did mean to nibble my food, but they were talking
to me and I kept finding that in my anxiety to answer I swallowed things whole.

Ivy Tresmand, whom I was to meet again and love, introduced in a light-hearted manner a form of raising money
for War Funds called a Pyramid Tea. She invited eight
women to tea at Government House. Each paid a shilling and
had to go home and invite seven guests to tea, and collect
a shilling per head. These seven had to go forth and invite
six to do same with five, and so down to one who having
eaten her tea and paid her shilling was a free woman and
£ 5,000 would be raised.

By the census of that year the population of Salisbury
district was 11,000 and with the proportion of 19 men to 14
women this leaves about 5,000 females. From this number
must be subtracted all female children. Then again the country
women would not be able to attend, and many of the women
living in the suburbs would not be able to spare the petrol to
accept an invitation to tea.

From this one can estimate how many women were left
to eat the 109,000 teas.

Off went Ivy back to the Union never guessing what she
had left behind. The teas went happily along for the first
week. The women who would anyway be having many
delicious morning teas, felt very content that by paying one
shilling they could clear themselves of all guilty feelings. The
next week, with three hundred and thirty-six teas, was not

quite so easy, but being war work it was accomplished with a smile. It was the following week when 1,680 tea drinkers had to be found that things began to get difficult. Telephones were constanly ringing, "Will you come to tea on Friday?"

"I'll be delighted," then, "It isn't a Pyramid Tea, is it? Yes? Well, my dear, I am sorry but I must flatly refuse. I've already had one dose and had the greatest difficulty in getting my number. I'm not going to be caught again. So sorry!"

The next week the number of guests to be invited reached, 6,720, and Salisbury was in a dilemma.

Patriotism was still strong, but life-long friendships broke up when one friend refused to accept an invitation of another. "I helped you with yours and now you won't help me!" When the 20,000 mark was reached a gloom began to descend on the City. The tea givers were all behind and no one would visit anyone else, in case they were caught.

The Lady Mayoress wrote a letter to the paper encouraging Pyramid tea givers and telling them not to give up hope. What happened when the desired guests numbered 40,000 and when each of these had to find *one* other I do not know. I believe there was collusion, blackmail and black marketing, for women were gladly paying for the privilege of not going out to tea.

I wrote a poem about it which appeared in one of the weekly papers and I sent Ivy a copy. She wrote: —

"The Pyramid Tea Poem makes me smile. In sheer defence I must tell you the number I suggested for the first was seven not eight. I would not have been so unpopular if it had been carried out, but perhaps the results would have been the same in such a small town. Should I come to Salisbury again I promise not to bring any new ideas."

I think 13,000 would have been just as bad, for the conscientious women of Salisbury, bent on doing their duty might have struggled longer thinking that determination and bicarbonate of soda might have brought victory.

As the war news became more serious, Rhodesians grew more and more anxious to help, but the only thing that could be done on a large scale was to raise money. Of the many war funds, the Navy League was first favourite, as we knew that most of our necessities and all of our luxuries were brought to us through the might of the Royal Navy.

In this effort to raise money Rhodesia was plunged into one long spate of amusement. Enjoy yourself and help the "Air Raid Distress!" Give yourself a rattling good meal and incidentally provide meals for homeless children! Buy a paper favour and provide medical aid for some poor wretch who has been dug out of a wrecked building! Take tickets for a dance, a concert, a ball, a raffle for a pearl ring! On and on it went until every night in Salisbury was a Gala night. True, some people bought tickets and did not attend, or gave them to young people, but the whole spirit was one of unwanted enjoyment.

Ivy Tresmand's show was one of the high lights of the war entertainments and I was amazed at the enormous amount of hard work professionals put into their shows. We women may think we have an exhausting day spring-cleaning or working for a Charity Fête but it is nothing to what Ivy and her troupe did as usual routine. All the time they are on top of their job, slick and smart. I was struggling all the while to keep up and though Ivy would keep the others on their feet for hours, she was always saying "Sit down 'T'". I shall never forget her, for it was one of the most marvellous things that ever happened to me.

Bryan went to his annual camp in August, and a wave of militarism swept over the farm. A native regiment had been formed and there were many letters in the paper asking to what use these boys would be put. One of the Mashona Chiefs was asked why few of his men volunteered for service. He replied that the reason was because they did not want to be killed.

On the farm, a very old native, Shumba, who years before had been Askari, collected a dozen farm-boys and drilled them with sticks. So began the craze for "soja-ing."

Shumba brought his troop one Sunday evening to the back door, and asked for "The Captain" (Nkosi.) We appeared and watched the drilling. It was an odd assortment of boys, and each had a round cardboard hat, like the English Boys' Brigade hat, which he had made from the long rolls in which the tobacco paper is bought. With them was Chunga. Chunga was the post-cum-milk-cum-flower-garden boy. He had a wandering eye and the mentality of a child of four. When he was watering the garden, he would play like a child. Sometimes he was a motorcar and with heavy tins of water he had to change gear. Other times he was a train, and very slow, never having seen a train go more than a few miles an hour. Sometimes he would be an aeroplane, which was quicker, but spilt more water. When he was not a vehicle he would sing and dance. I have seen him stretched out in a real ballet movement, while the last drops from the can dripped on a flower.

Now he was crazy about "soja-ing," whether watering, milking, or going to the siding he was always on duty. When spoken to he would stand to attention and salute, then sharp left turn, and forget everything he had been told. On his hat he had written "No. 1. Soja."

After his camp training Bryan took his lorry and set off on a tour of the Eastern Districts. When I was beginning to get anxious at not hearing from him, I found he was staying with my brother in Salisbury. When climbing one of the steep mountain roads, he had been run into by a drunk miner. All his holiday money was spent in repairing the lorry and he returned to Salisbury.

In November my mother died. Snap! the last real tie with Home was broken. I could only be glad for her sake, for she was very sick and lonely and longing to go, in fact she was like a child waiting for a party.

So went my Audience, my Partisan, for no one ever loves you as much as your mother does. I know my limitations and faults well, but it was so comforting to have someone who refused to recognise them. Children love you when they are young. Husbands love you at first because you are their choice and property, and later because they are used to you, but mothers love you for yourself, the real self you were meant to be and would be if the everyday did not make it all so difficult.

Bryan's time went quickly. In September on his nineteenth birthday he went in to Salisbury to enlist, but the Government would not release him until the new year.

At Christmas Dinner it is the custom in my father's family as far back as they know that when the dessert is brought in the lights are turned out, and the Father lights a little coloured candle and puts it on his plate. The eldest son at his right takes his own candle and lights it from his father's flame, and so on round the table. No other match may be used. The father then stands and drinks the King's health, and after that a health to Absent Friends. This year all the R.A.F. guests had warned their parents in England to pause at 7.30 and think of them. Nkosi timed it to a second, and we stood and thought of those we loved.

Chapter 29 — Then there were three.

In January 1942 Bryan joined up. He bought a second-hand baby-Morris car so that he might use it while in camp.

He spent the day in Salisbury and at five o'clock he telephoned to tell me that everything was all right, but that he would have to drive to Bulawayo that night if he wanted his car, because he had to report at the camp at half-past six the next morning. The other lads were going down by train.

I said that it was late; that it would be dark; that it would be stormy; that he could not drive alone, that he could not carry enough petrol. He said all that had been arranged: he did not mind driving in storms, and another chap had promised to go with him.

I was very worried all night, especially when a heavy storm broke and raged. I could imagine him speeding on the tarmac strips which his little car could hardly span, and skidding on to the muddy sides and so into the waiting dongas. I could see the rain streaming through the leaky hood and the swollen rivers overflowing the narrow bridges and the little car being swept away and dashed on to the rocks.

When the first letter arrived I felt better.

"Just to tell you that all is well and that I reached Bulawayo safely and spent the rest of the night here (hotel). I was very touched that you did not go all sentimental when I left, and I mean it." This letter had the desired effect of calming me down, and preparing the way for the truth which was disclosed later.

It appeared that as the "chap's" people had refused to allow him to accompany Bryan in his hazardous journey Bryan had therefore decided to go alone. The petrol difficulty had been solved by going from pump to pump, filling up and then syphoning the petrol into bottles given him by our grocer. He was probably the first Rhodesian to buy rubber tubing for this purpose. He started off just before dark in a heavy storm. It was sometime before I pieced together the details of the story, but when I did I found that he had travelled through sheets of water and over flooded bridges, and had only paused to fill up the petrol tank from his store of bottles. He did the three hundred miles in under nine hours. Arriving at the hotel about three in the morning, he had slept for a short time, bathed, breakfasted, written my letter and arrived at the station in time to meet the train. Lounging in his little

car he sat watching his friends being loaded on lorries and
followed them to the camp, in grand style.

Peter delighted to have left school, threw himself into the
work of the farm. Instead of buying the bulldog he had always
wanted, he took Becky, who already loved him dearly. This
was as well for Becky would never have countenanced another
dog in her life. She tolerated Judy the spaniel but when Judy's
soft silky ways irritated her, she would suddenly round on
her and send her yelping into the veld.

The natives whose craze for "soja-ing" had worn itself out,
now asked for a football, and when this was provided they
rigged up two rickety goal posts, and on the first Sunday
play began at dawn. After breakfast we went and found the
game in full swing. Fifty natives of all sizes from picannins
to fully grown boys were racing about the "field" kicking
the ball in any direction. There was no indication of sides,
each boy's main idea was to kick the ball whenever he could.
Although natives' feet are hard as leather it is a horrid sight
to see them kicking the ball or stubbing the ground with bare
toes. On and on they went, and as the exhausted retired behind
the goal posts to recover, others joined the fray, friends and
brothers from other farms. One boy who had played football
on a mine arrived in shorts, muffler, football boots and red
stockings. When he wanted the ball he would call out "Boss
UP!" and the amateurs would fall away from the ball while
he kicked it high in the air. At sundown the game ended
and the next morning many of the boys had to be treated for
bruises and cuts. After work the next evening they were at
it again, and Peter tried to show them the rudiments of the
game. They stood and watched with Uh Uh's of admiration
when he shot a goal but they preferred to play the game
their own way. In a week the ball was kicked to death and
football passed out of fashion.

The temporary relief we had felt when America came into
the war was short-lived when we heard of the fall of Singapore
and the Malay Peninsula. Hitler was boasting that he had
the strongest Army and Air Force in the world and was
congratulating himself on the grandeur of the times and how
the world was being forged anew.

Churchill said, "We have at present a very long road to
tread. The arrival of a new enemy, very fresh and powerful
has prolonged the journey which Europe must travel."

The strenuous effort to grow food meant that more fowls,

sheep and pigs were raised and the surplus maize was soon used up. This year there was a large deficit and extra supplies had to be imported from the Argentine at great cost. A committee was formed to encourage farmers to grow more maize and more food for the thousands of newcomers now in the country. The future of farming was bright and Nkosi gladly took over the voluntary work of the committee in his area.

In June Bryan wrote that he could not fly solo. His tutor had no patience with him and shouted at him which only made him worse. I know how he felt, for I am always helpless before a critical audience ready to pounce. I wrote and told him not to give up, because I knew he learned very slowly but surely. In spite of this I was worried because I knew that if he failed he would never get over it, and the self-confidence I had tried all his life to build up would receive a serious set-back. I hated his flying, but as he had set out to fly, I wanted him to succeed.

Later he wrote:—

"Dear Mummie, I wrote yesterday despairing of being able to fly. To-day I had a test to see if I was fit to go on with it, and all is well." He was given another instructor, and after this he learned quickly.

The fall of Tobruk brought the war very near to us for the casualty list of Rhodesians and South Africans was very heavy. Through the dark cloud of depression which followed, we could not see the first streaks of hope in the stormy sky.

My continued ill-health now began to intrude on our lives. The doctors said there was nothing the matter with me, yet I could not do what I considered a day's work. When I forced myself to do more, back came the migraine, but to take things quietly and carefully when Bryan was flying, Peter nearing the age of joining-up, which had been reduced to eighteen, and the whole world suffering and struggling, was quite impossible. If the doctor said there was nothing wrong, then it could only be laziness and incompetence, and I must force myself on.

In November Churchill said,

"General Alexander with his brilliant comrade, General Montgomery. has gained a glorious, exciting, victory in what I think should be called the Battle of Egypt."

Hitler for the first time had stopped boasting.

"It is understandable that in this world-wide struggle one cannot expect to gain a new success week by week."

Then in December Churchill told us:—

"The years of defence, of stubborn, outnumbered ill-equipped almost miraculous survival are behind us. Everywhere the United Nations turn to the attack."

Chapter 30 — Then there were Two.

Early in 1943 Nkosi sent me down to the coast. I felt guilty at leaving Peter during what would be his last year on the farm and I hated the thought of going out of the country while Bryan was still in it, but he told me that he had no hope of having any leave while I was away. and if I went we could see each other on my way down and back.

Instead of staying at an hotel, I spent my holiday at a cottage at one of the Bays. It was not a great success from the point of view of comfort but one interesting incident arose out of it.

The old lady who owned the cottage told me that she had had a brother who had died in Rhodesia and asked if I would like to see a picture of his grave. Of course I said that nothing would give me greater pleasure and I stood in the dark, narrow hall while she delved in a great wooden chest. At last she brought out three huge enlargements. Directly I saw them I recognised them as the snaps I had taken of the grave in the Reserve!

On the way home Bryan and I spent a happy afternoon in an hotel making plans for altering the house. After great argument we decided that the ex-bathroom, now office and lumber room, should be thrown into the Living room and form a sort of dining alcove, with subdued lighting. I remember Bryan rolling on the floor of my hotel bedroom holding his stomach and saying, "No one makes me laugh like you do!"

When I got home I found that Peter, having turned eighteen, had reported for enlistment but had been told that he must not leave the farm until all the crops were reaped. I was rather worried about Peter. Just as he had longed to leave school and begin farming, so now he was longing to leave the farm and join up. He was already regretting the loss of the last year at school and I was so afraid that once he was in the army he would regret losing his time on the farm.

But there was nothing to be done, he was anxious to be off.

Bryan got his wings and the doctor said his health was now perfect and that the asthma would never return. I knew this meant a great deal to Bryan and would wipe out the years of frustration.

The need for pilots was so great that even his last leave
was curtailed. He came home and changed into mufti and
we all tried to pretend he was living at home again, but the
inevitable parting darkened the days. He spent some time in
his hut putting his possessions away, for he knew that once
Peter had left we should probably have an assistant in the
hut. He gave his old toys away to the people who had been
kind to him at Gwelo while he was training and had children
who could enjoy them.

I planned each meal so that he had every single dish he
liked and he made me promise I would do exactly the same
for his friend Dick, who would be spending his last leave
with us, the following week. He said that when we saw him
off by train we were to think of it just as if he were going
back to school.

The R.T. Officer had booked him on a train leaving Salisbury at 7.30 p.m., so we started for the station in plenty of
time. As we drove off, I saw Bryan look round at his beloved
home as if he wished to take the picture of it with him. We were
using the lorry and I kept looking back through the window
at Bryan and every time I did so he smiled at me. I felt that
if I could keep smiling until we got to the station, then in
the bustle and confusion of the hundreds of other people I
might be able to get through without disgracing myself.

We found the station strangely deserted and when we made
enquires were told that there was no train that night. The
R.T. Officer had made a mistake and the office was shut. This
was bad news, for Bryan had to report at daybreak the next
morning. In ordinary times we could have set out in the lorry,
but with petrol rationed and all the offices and petrol pumps
closed it was impossible.

I do not remember much of what happened, for all my
attention was needed to keep the smile fixed on my face and
my throat ready to give a laugh every time somebody tried
to be funny.

After a long wait it was suggested that Bryan went down
of the night goods train, if the guard would let him sit in
his cabin.

We had to find the guard and find the train, and this
necessitated our walking over many lines. It is all very con-
fused and I know everyone was very cheerful, and made jokes
at which we all laughed heartily.

It was found that a youngish woman was also stranded,
and she, too, was to spend the night in the guard's cabin. This

was a great help in the joke-making. The goods train was very restless and kept leaving us and coming back on another line. This meant more scrambling over the rails in the pitch dark, and great activity in preventing each other from being run down. The hands of the station clock were very slow, but we did not dare to leave the station for refreshment.

Finally, the train decided to stay where it was, and we kissed Bryan goodbye. We saw the young woman sitting in the dim light of the cabin, and made more jokes. Margaret and my sister-in-law were most valiant. Bryan climbed into the cabin and we handed up his belongings, but the train did not start and he got down again: these ten minutes were the worst.

Then the guard called him and everyone kissed Bryan goodbye again, but the ends of my mouth were stiff and I could not release them. I dared not. I knew if I did and felt his soft cheek on mine I should scream, so I just stood there grinning, and said when he came towards me,

"Goodbye, darling," and could not kiss him. He hesitated a moment, and then climbed up. The engine hooted, and drew slowly out of the station, and he stood there in the lighted cabin and I kept my mouth fixed hoping he would see the white of my teeth and think it was a smile. At last the train turned and all we could see was the red sparks flying up into the black sky.

They hoisted me on to the platform and I was allowed to cry. Ronnie and my brother were holding on to me. Then my poor sister-in-law crashed her head on to something very hard and my brother rushed to her. Poor girl, she was in great pain, but it helped me for it took my mind off my own troubles.

Nkosi and Peter and I sat in the front of the lorry and drove back to the farm. Peter was very good to me and for the first time I realised that he was a man.

The next morning I wrote to Bryan asking him to forgive me for not kissing him goodbye. He wrote on arrival at Cape Town,

"Have arrived safely. Co-passenger quite harmless and the guard played duenna." Then scrawled on the back "parting at Salisbury O.K."

I told myself there would be weeks and weeks of training, before Bryan went on Ops. and the war might be over before then.

I then prepared for Dick's final leave, and when he had gone I asked the W.N.S. League to send me pilots on last leave, and I treated each one as I treated Bryan and Dick.

Nkosi was feeling things badly. The hope of Better Times which had kept us going for so many years no longer functioned, for what did better times matter when the Picannin Bosses were not there to share them? Like many other parents we turned to our work and worked even harder than before, but instead of the shining goal of prosperity we worked to help end the war, to save for the future of the Picannin Bosses, if they returned.

Prosperity came. It always does to farmers in war time. That year we began paying for the farm. We were a little afraid of this prosperity, because we wondered whether we could expect prosperity *and* our sons when millions of other people had lost everything. Nkosi decided he would not have an assistant, but do all the work himself, besides the voluntary work of the Food Production Committee. I helped him by taking pigs to town, by raising more poultry; and to help the war funds, I made it a rule never to refuse any demand for help in entertaining or writing or concert work. It was a miserable enough war effort.

As soon as we heard Bryan had arrived in England I bought a duplicate book and began to write what he called "The Book of the Goat." This book contained all the daily events and details which could not be written in an airgraph letter. They were very badly written but he enjoyed them. I used to write in bed, but not every night, because "I deliberately did not write yesterday because I don't want to get into the habit of writing every day, because if I do and then don't, I'll worry because I haven't."

In re-reading our letters I find that we were always telling each other not to worry. I wrote,

"Re worrying. The truth of the matter is that I don't want you to suffer anything, not even inconvenience. I don't want you to worry or feel homesick or have a pain or be bothered . . . in fact what I really want to do is to put you to bed and wait on you. That is the real ridiculous physical Mother-love, and most destroying to an adult male. But the spiritual love wants you to succeed and feel pleased with yourself by going through things. Luckily this love is the stronger, because honestly, if in return for signing a paper never to see you again, I'd know you were perfectly happy and married, I would do so very readily, though you know how much I enjoy being with you. I am trying to stifle the love that wants to blow your nose for you, and practise the other."

Praying was very difficult then, because the physical mother only longs for her son's return .... anyhow. But Bryan had had too much sickness, and Peter so gloried in his health, that I could only pray that neither of them would return, unless fit enough to enjoy life. It hurt very much.

Bryan wrote regularly, though most of his small spare time was taken up with writing to relations. They were all very kind to him, especially Kitty his godmother.

"Kitty," wrote Bryan, "has huge jambouts in the village. She browbeats women and wasps alike."

Every evening we used to listen to the radio from London. Sometimes it was clear and at other times it was muffled and we used to wonder under what difficulties and hardships this programme was being sent to us.

It was sad to listen to the music halls and hear the sentimental songs. Sitting in my high-backed chair I used to listen. The black sky showed where the curtains had been drawn back, bright stars, peaceful night. Not a sound but the music coming over the air. I was one of a great host of sad, anxious, ordinary people all over the world, listening to the same music.

How critical are the cultured public of these sentimental songs in peace-time! Emotions and feelings are private and should not be broadcast to the world. Perhaps not, yet to me, sitting listening, there was dignity and beauty in those sentimental songs. Poets capture words to express their feelings and the cultured can read these poems and share in them without troubling themselves to find suitable words but the ordinary people, mass educated, can find no words and "the burden of them is intolerable." A song written with a tune which is easily remembered and words that fit. Behind the words "I'll see *you* again." I could hear the cry of the ordinary people, and the ache of the world's heart.

Then silence, the flicker of the dim lamp, the falling of a log, the ringing of the bell for dinner. Good food in plenty, a safe, soft bed, and on the morrow the little vexations of lack of petrol, lack of ploughparts, difficulties of every petty necessity among unwanted luxuries. A fine war effort indeed! What could I do but seize every miserable job and do it hard? "Since all that I can do is nothing worth."

Becky, by some freak of nature was unable to have puppies and when kaffir suitors came visiting Judy, she used to fly at them in rage. We called her The Virgin Queen. Bryan used to like hearing about the animals. I wrote:

"Judy is very expectant. She makes excuses to come into the house and lie on the carpet, and when told to go out, lies on her back, lifts helpless paws and refuses to move."

One evening, when the house was in a state of siege by swarms of bees (a thing that happens regularly every year) Judy gave a sudden yelp. We thought it was a bee, but is was a pup and Nkosi only just managed to get her outside before the others were born. I sent Bryan the notice.

"To Judy, wife of A Kaffir Dog Esq., of six puppies at the back door. Thanks to Father, not in the dining-room."

"We made Judy comfortable in her basket," I continued in my letter, "and Becky went up to her."

"Hallo! What you got there? Rats?"

"Hands off my children!" shrieked Judy, snapping at Becky viciously, I clapped my hands at them and got them apart, Judy all outraged motherhood, and Becky giving half-hearted snarls and looking up at me sheepishly.

"It wasn't my fault. I never knew she would cut up rough. She surely can't think I want them!"

True but no doubt Judy remembered the Spitzes Kits on the tennis-court.

In September we were listening to the wireless when the news came that Italy had surrendered. When we heard the headlines we stopped and looked at one another. I thought afterwards that the world in its course must have given a sudden hitch as everyone gasped with surprise. After it was over I knew that millions of parents were feeling as we were, excited, relieved, with a wild hope that their sons might return safely. This good news took off any unhappiness we felt in parting with Peter. It was evident he was disappointed and hoped the war would not be over before he was trained.

He went off to Umtali very cheerfully, and wrote saying that he had never been so happy in his life. It was like school, but a hundred per cent better. He came up with two friends one week-end, and we invited them out to dinner. When we met them outside the hotel we found them all polished up to perfection, and as we came up they stood to attention and saluted, eighteen foot of the best Rhodesia can do. I felt so glad to think the war would be over before they lost the joy they felt in the army.

That October was very hot, and we were still besieged by bees. Smoked out of one room, they came into another. I wrote to Bryan,

"Foully hot, boys foul, fowls foul. Foul 'phone out of order.

Ef wanted me to get an urgent call through, and Ruth arrived with cattle inspector who had to get through on foul 'phone. Whole morning foul."

And, "House besieged by bees again. Have drawn curtains, shut doors and windows, but it makes no difference. Have sprayed and sprayed and swotted and swotted all day. The times your father comes in they are quiet, so he won't do anything.

P.S. Your father met the bees on Sunday and got stung. He is having them destroyed immediately.

P.P.S. I have been stung every day for a week!"

One day we received a cable saying Bryan would broadcast on the following Tuesday, and luckily Peter was home on leave.

Well before the time of the broadcast we were all assembled in the lounge. James and Lupenga as old retainers, in attendance.

There was the usual agony of tuning in, because since Bryan and I had mended a sort of string fanbelt which had been bitten by a cockroach, we had to guess where the stations were. As Radios always go wrong on important occasions Nkosi had put on a newly-charged battery. He tuned in quite ten minutes before "Songtime in the Laager" was due to begin. I said, was he sure he was on the right station? and he said he was sure as he could be: and I said that it wasn't sure enough, and he said surely he knew when he was sure, and we felt quite angry with one another. But sure enough the clock struck when a song was just starting: no sign of the "Laager." We were on the wrong station! There was an agonised minute while Nkosi found the right place, and when we found the "Laager" going strong I was quite sure we had missed Bryan's message. It was a great strain listening. Nkosi stood with his back to the fire and there were tears in his eyes. Peeps, as usual, was lying on the floor. I huddled in my tall chair and the two natives stood in respectful and unbelieving silence. They frankly did not believe that Boss Brown's voice would come out of the box. Then suddenly,

"Hallo, Mum and Dad! I have been drinking all day long . . . ." a dead silence — ". . . . your health. Cherrio, Bryan."

There was a deep silence, we just could not understand. It was some time before we realised that what to us was a dramatic moment, was to Bryan a bit of fun shared with dozens of his pals and fellow-Rhodesians, before whom we could not be sentimental or even serious. Peter, remembering my antipathy against the word "Mum," for he had been threatened with an egg whisk in his face if he repeated it — which he did and I did — could not understand why Bryan had deliberately used the fatal word. Long afterwards we received his letter.

"Got there at 3 o'clock and they gave us tea and let us write out our message. They asked us to be amusing as the audience got so bored with the same messages. I am sorry I said 'Mum and Dad' but all the others did."

In our worry and anxiety we had turned the gay, fun-loving, ridiculous Bryan into a tragic, brave airman on active service.

Peter went back to camp, and just before Christmas sprang upon us the news that he was boxing in the Championship: Army v. R.A.F. He had never been keen on boxing, because he was so large for his age that the boys he met were all much older and wilier. Now it appeared his unit had no one of his weight to put in and he had agreed to slim and take on the fight.

Nkosi was delighted, because he himself had been a boxer, his highlight being when he acted as "feed" to the school's prize boxer at a demonstration before the parents. The star, knowing that Nkosi was only acting as a punch ball, began some fancy tricks and Nkosi promptly put him over the grand piano. He was, however, afraid Peter would have no chance, for he had had no experience at all.

Nkosi and Frank went to the fight, while I stayed with Ruth waiting for the news that Peter had been sent to hospital.

He had been put against an ex-instructor of thirty. He was not knocked out. He had been on the defensive all the time, and won a medal as runner up. Nkosi was very proud of him and said that if only he had had more experience, he would have seen that the older man was getting tired, and, had he known it, there was an opportunity when he could have knocked him out. Peter was quite happy: he said he knew he had no chance of knocking his opponent out, and was resolved that he himself would not be knocked out, hence the caution. All his pals had been knocked out.

Chapter 31 — Dark Days.

We were entirely dependent on lamps. Older settlers had, years ago, bought good, solid lamps, but we had never been able to afford even one. When things became a little easier we had bought a pressure lamp, which gave a better light and was cheaper. Now of course this was wearing out and we were unable to buy spare parts, with the result that in the evenings we sat in gloom.

When Bryan's airgraphs came we put on spectacles, took a magnifying glass and stood under the lamp but had to wait for the bright sunshine before we could read them properly. I therefore asked him to write by airmail instead, so he changed over. Unfortunately, just at that time the airmail service was suspended and all such letters were sent by surface mail which took up to two months. We did not know this so suffered many weeks of acute anxiety waiting for letters.

During the hard years, the only garment for which I had not been able to find a use was a pair of long thick woollen underpants sent to me by Nkosi's mother. My sons had viewed them with horror hardly able to believe men in England could wear such things. They had haunted me until the appeal for clothes for Air Raid Victims was made and then I sent them to the depôt with joy. Bryan, suffering a Scottish winter wrote;

"I now wear under-pants down to my ankles and like them." He also wrote of the "beautiful moonlight nights with the snow lying glistening" and "lovely frosty mornings with rime and ice all over the place" and how he amused himself riding his bicycle over the frozen puddles and hearing them crack.

He spent what leave he had in London, because he loved it and felt at home there.

"I went to a Mosley Protest Meeting in Trafalgar Square and contributed a few irrelevant remarks about shooting him. However it started to rain, so I spent an hour in a penny arcade. I DO enjoy myself."

He went to the theatre whenever he could and on one of his leaves he was joined by a girl he had met.

"Jo and I wander about like a pair of sheep, and don't get much done. She is extremely nice and we get on well. She is twenty-five so things will remain as they are. We argue for hours without agreeing on much." They wandered round the London antique shops and bought six tiny wedgewood plates, "Like ours, only five inches across. I am having them sent to you."

He said the beer was so short that he and his friends had to go "from pub to pub sipping every flower as it were." He was delighted to find and recognise snowdrops and said he did not think he would be on Ops. until March.

As the letters telling this comforting news did not arrive for two months, Nkosi and I worried solidly and unnecessarily. Meanwhile I wrote:

"I know I am not a brave woman, the sort of woman in books who bears her troubles without showing them and looks interesting and anxious-eyed." (Still a lingering hankering after Frances.) "When I have a letter from you I feel full of beans and happiness, but when letters don't come, like now, I feel like throwing things about and screaming. I shall be relieved when I have you home safe and sound, I hope with a wife. It will be lovely when we are six, you and Peter married. That's something to look forward to."

We needed something to look forward to, as Nkosi was struggling on with bad crops and I with bad health. I had to spend a great many days in bed, at least bed was my base. I sometimes thought it would be less tiring to be up. I learned to make cakes and puddings in bed, even to roll pastry, but the climax was when Nkosi, for reasons now forgotten, one day killed a three-quarter-sized pig which was brought to my bed for partition.

It was decided that my health might improve if I had my tonsils out. Ruth, most courageously, had had hers removed with a local anaesthetic and encouraged me to do the same. I allowed her to persuade me and since then have tried to persuade Effie, but she has too much common sense. I wrote to Bryan.

"Well darling, the blood a hero's sire has shed, still nerves a hero's son. Luckily it does not mean a hero's dam or you would not be much of a pilot. What an ugly expression "dam." POEM, a dam fine poem.

> Who pushed me in my little pram?
> My Mother dear my darling dam.
> Who gave me lamb and ham and jam?
> My Mother dear my darling dam.
> With lessons who my head did cram?
> My Mother dear my darling dam.
> Who, *muti* down my throat did ram?
> My Mother dear my darling dam.
> Oh what a lucky man I am
> To have Mamma, my darling dam.

Then followed a description of the process ending; "When the surgeon begins it seems as if you are listening to some sort of clanging smith work. There is also a horrid moment when they put scissors into your mouth and you hear the sound as of linoleum being cut."

Soon after this we received a letter referring to the reactions of the relations to his engagement. As we had not received the letters about his leave and Jo, we were astonished, but we sent off a cable of congratulations to them both.

Later on we heard all about it. That they now agreed on all points more or less.

"Jo knows all the songs we used to sing on the veranda in the evenings and she speaks of "the little man who" like you do, which makes me laugh."

Jo, he said was well-built with auburn hair, freckles and a sense of humour. She was just perfectly right and would fit in well with the family. They would probably be married this year and he would not be on Ops. until May. He criticised me strongly for imagining him on Ops. before.

"What a fool I would feel if you told everyone I was and then I never went." He said he had been changed over to heavier and heavier aircraft so often that it looked as if I were "prayin' agin" him.

A minor criticism, "I may not be able to spell "beautiful" but surely I can do better than "antitthiumins." And then, "Well me dear, unlike the war, I have no difficulty in ending." And "I heard 'In a Monastery Garden' the other night. It's funny what memories it brings back."

In April we received a cable to say Bryan had been given a commission, and later on a letter telling us he was now "the lowest thing in officer life, a P/O." Following this, that he looked beautiful in his uniform and that the first day he wore it, he was saluted by an American and was so astonished that he had not time to return it.

In May everyone was strung up, waiting for the Second Front. We knew Bryan would be in the Invasion and longed for it to be over and the war won. Peter was studying hard for a commission and this was cheering because if he got through the examination he would stay longer in this country.

Nkosi was so run down with overwork and anxiety that he decided to take a holiday. I should have gone with him but I wanted to stay with Peter whom we had been allowed to borrow for one month. Peter told me that even if he did get his commission he would be leaving Rhodesia in July and so

I felt that if anything happened to him later on, I should never forgive myself for not spending this last month with him. We had not been taking his soldiering seriously, so sure were we that he would never see active service. Now it was quite likely that Bryan, over whom I had been worrying incessantly would come safely through and Peter would go to Japan and be killed or worse. I therefore sacrificed Nkosi to Peter. It seemed I was selfish whatever decision I made.

Peter, along with sixty per cent of his friends, did not pass the examination and he was quite pleased to have a month on the farm.

Nkosi went off mournfully and he had no sooner gone when a cable arrived saying that Bryan and Jo were being married on May 18th our own wedding day. After this came Bryan's letter:

"Darling, you have been so very kind in writing about Jo and she is pathetically longing for a mother, and she seems to love you already. I have told her all I can, mostly anecdotes, and all the things, you do, silly and otherwise.

I begin to realise more and more all the things you have done for me all my life, and this commission is only through the confidence you have managed to instil in me. I do love you both very much. I think it is marvellous the number of parcels you have sent me, my Goat, and I am very grateful. It is difficult to write to both of you separately because I love you both the same, and you love each other so that you are like one. I know you are pretty worried, with both Peter and me away, and seeming to be able to do without you, and all that, but there is nothing like having you always as a source of inspiration and comfort, to draw upon when one's own self is exhausted temporarily in some way or other. You may think I do not know what an effort it is for you to keep cheerful and appear normal, but I do, and I wish you didn't have to."

Then came the long expected Second Front. It was a great comfort having Peter with me, and I knew that though Bryan was on Ops. at last, he had a wife to love and comfort him. I blessed Jo and her wonderful love for him.

Nkosi came back looking much better but he had not enjoyed his holiday alone. He had booked for me later on at another hotel. Bored to death one afternoon, he had accepted the invitation of a fellow guest to visit an hotel nearby little dreaming that this act would lead to a change in our lives years afterwards.

Peter went back and after bouts of illness it was decided I should have all my double teeth out.

I went into hospital, and unfortunately Peter's embarkation leave came unexpectedly at the same time. However, it had to be done. That night I had a temperature and could not sleep for the pain in my wretched septic gums. I remember lying awake and watching the beautiful black starry sky, and praying that if Bryan was somewhere up there he would be kept safe. Worries are always intensified when one is in pain, and in spite of a sleeping draught I could not feel drowsy. About three o'clock I fell into a beautiful, deep sleep.

The next morning I was still in pain, but I felt I must go home. The doctor said no, I must stay: but I refused. Peter was home, and though I was of no use to him I could watch him, and store up memories of him for when he was away. I went home by train, a long, slow journey.

The next day my face was swollen up both sides, and kind Ruth came and poulticed me for my mouth was white with sepsis. I looked a fright, but was determined that Peter should have a farewell sundowner party. The Invasion was not going very well, and Japan was still to be feared. I was worried about Peter, and then he broke the news to me that he had joined the paratroops. I thought of my bouncing little Peeps learning his letters; progressing along the road head over heels; the older Peter lying on a tray of the Ford Sedan playing his mouth organ; the grown up Peter always lying on the floor upside down, and smiled at the choice he had made, while I hated it.

The day of the sundower party was dull and cold, and I was in too great pain to do anything more than sit by the fire with hot poultices on each cheek. Occasionally I would get up, go to the kitchen, prepare some savoury, and then return to the fire.

About the middle of the morning I heard the police motor bicycle. It stopped at the back of the house, and went on again.

Nkosi came in and said in a strange, set voice.

"It's happened!"

I said "Killed?"

He said, "Missing." It took ages to say this, and the words came out slowly, like wading through water. After a few minutes I went to the telephone and rang Jeanetta; and asked her to 'phone everyone that there would be no sundowner party. She asked me for the numbers and addresses, and rang off. She, bless her, did not ask any questions though she loved our boys.

In this way the news reached Peter as he was having lunch at a friend's, and we did not have the pain of breaking it to him. When he came home I opened the door. His face was white and strained and I could see that half his horror was how it would affect us, so I said, "He is only missing. Perhaps we shall hear tomorrow that he is safe."

The neighbours came along, each one trying to persuade us that there was every hope of Bryan's safe return. Jo cabled, "Dearests I feel sure he is safe the waiting is so awful but we must hope, love."

We cheered each other up, and even laughed, but when I worked out the time that he was missing I found that it was that night when I lay awake in pain and fell asleep at three o'clock.

Peter went off the next day. He wrote: "I know when I am leaving, but I am not going to tell you, as I don't want to have to say goodbye all over again. It is not that I don't want to see you, I want to very much, but I think it is best that we leave things as they are." He did not 'phone up at all, so we thought he had gone, but some days later we ran into him in town. I wished I had had him those last few days, but it would have been selfish. He had a lot to bear, and if not seeing us helped him, then we had to do as he wished.

I bought a duplicate book to write a daily screed to Peter. In Bryan's book I burned the last pages I had written to him, and continued writing to Jo.

"It hurts taking up this book again, but it is such a comfort to have you to write to. I shall not write as much, because all the little details that interest him would not interest you: but I must tell you all I can, so that you will feel that this is your home and I your Mother."

My brother and his wife took some leave and came out to the farm. With our mining friend they fixed up our electric light, which was a great comfort and joy.

Everyone was most kind and abnormally cheerful, so cheerful and cheering that they left me with the feeling that they thought I was a sentimental fool to think for a moment Bryan was anything but safe and well. I knew how Cheerers-up hated to see us look stricken, how they wanted us to smile and show a bold front, but they did not understand. If I mourned over him and he returned, they would say I had been a pessimistic fool, but I preferred that to the thought of letting him go

without a tear. Of course, there was the agonising thought
that he might be in a prison camp, be wounded, unattended,
ill-treated. I thought of all the times that I had nursed him.
I knew what his face looked like when he suffered, the slanting
black lashes; I could imagine him very clearly. I thought of
the prayers I had managed to put up that neither of my sons
would return unless they would be able to lead a normal,
happy life. Perhaps God had taken me at my word. That night
I lay awake he had been shot down, and somehow I believed
my prayer had been answered.

Jo's letters were a great joy and comfort. She was so like
Bryan that it seemed his letters were still coming. She was
also full of hope. She asked me not to stop writing my journal
letters and that she wished I was with her as it would help to
have someone who loved him as much as she did. She said she
had received four parcels for Bryan, one the wedding cake
which she would keep unopened, in case he came back for
their birthdays, which were in September.

In July, just before my birthday, a parcel came, a small
sweet tin, and packed in cotton wool were the six little green
wedgewood plates. Inside was a card. "To Mummie darling,
wishing her very many happy returns of the day, Bryan."

I did not want to go to the sea, but Nkosi insisted,
thinking it was for my good, but I do not think I should have
gone alone. As Peter had flown north he had sent cables, and
while in Egypt and later in Italy he wrote regularly.

But I was very lonely and unhappy. Strangely enough while
there, Ivy Tresmand wrote to me asking if I would join her
on an eight weeks' tour all over the Union and Rhodesia. Of
course I could not accept, though it was the most wonderful
chance I had ever had. I could not even be very disappointed,
for it was one of those dreams that could never come true.

I was very much better in health when I arrived home.

The Invasion was at last progressing favourably, and Nkosi
used to listen in, and I knew he was hoping that as the
countries were freed, he might hear that Bryan was safe. Jo
also wrote cheerfully. "The news is so wonderful, I am always
expecting Bryan to walk in. I imagine myself looking my
best in a pretty dress, but most likely I shall have my face
covered with cold cream, and my hair in a net. I feel we shall
hear soon."

Whenever we were in town we called for the mail, and one
day I collected a cable: from Jo.

"Cousin in Belgium writes good grounds for stating Bryan is certain to return but can say no more have written fully."

That evening we went over to Frank's. Ruth had her parents with her. They all greeted us with congratulations. They said the news must be true because no one would say as much without being sure of even more. I could not let myself hope, though I had to pretend I did. I felt that if he were alive then there was plenty of time for rejoicing, and if he were dead he would not like my hopes to be raised, then dashed. But Nkosi and I went to bed a little happier that night.

We waited anxiously for Jo's letter, and then received a strange communication from the Red Cross. It told us that six of the crew were killed that night, two of whom were identified, four unidentified. It continued, "As there were eight members of the crew it will be appreciated that it is impossible to state precisely who were the four unidentified members, but it is considered that you would wish to be informed of this report." We puzzled over this. Taking note of Jo's cable it seemed that Bryan and another must have escaped, and sent some messages through her cousin. Such extra-ordinary things were happening that it seemed a sensible solution to the mystery. There was no confirming cable from Jo, so we waited, and when her letter came tore it open frantically.

It appeared that the cousin had written to his wife saying that she was to tell Jo that he was certain Bryan would turn up and not to worry. She ended, "Oh, darlings, now perhaps it will be all right again, and I shall come to you and see his joy at being back with you and have the farm shown to me by him."

Soon after this we had a letter saying she too, had had the Red Cross Letter and she hardly dared hope that one of the missing two was Bryan. To Nkosi and me, who knew Bryan, it seemed very strange that he should be safe and his crew killed.

Then at last came definite news. The cousin had sent the message without any shred of evidence. In Belgium, he met a woman who was an active member of the Underground, and had sheltered and helped our airmen to escape. She had procured food for them by selling whisky to the Germans in her estaminet; and when the liberation army arrived the towns people were all for arresting her, as a collaborator, but she produced letters and photographs proving she had helped 476 boys to escape. When the cousin had shown her a very small snap of Bryan she had said, "Tell his wife that there is every chance he may get back."

Jo felt this far more keenly than I did, and after this she wrote beseeching us to try and get her out to Rhodesia. Nkosi and I went to town and chased after people, but no one would or could help us get a permit and passage for her. Jo herself did everything she could think of. At Rhodesia House a "Colonel Blimp" told her there was nothing to be done, and he realised it must be worrying. She wrote, "Just as if it were my dog I had lost."

In November a letter came from England enclosing one left by Bryan to be forwarded in the event of death or missing from Ops.

"My Darling Mummie and Daddy and Peter, If you should receive this I should be presumed lost, stolen or strayed. I am sure you don't care for anything weepy. I should like to express my gratitude for your many kindnesses and your unremitting care of me. I always think of you and have never done anything worse than be extremely drunk. I have loved you always and will always do so.... I have loved the farm and everything on it. I need hardly say the R.A.F. has been a great experience, though a great disillusionment. Well, dears, I should have loved to have seen you again, but it can't be helped, I suppose. That's about all there is, so all my love, Bryan.

P.S. I would not die for my country, I'd just do it by mistake. No heroics."

Peter took his jumps safely and went to Italy. I sent him as many parcels as I could.

Margaret invited us to spend Christmas with them in Salisbury. In the morning Nkosi let me take the car and visit the hospital and talk to some of the sick R.A.F. boys. I arranged for one to come and convalesce later on the farm.

Before dinner in our bedroom Nkosi and I lighted the candles for the four of us.

Chapter 32 — Next Year.

In January 1945, Jo wrote that she had been to Rhodesia House again, signed all necessary papers and that she should be leaving England in April. This gave us something to look forward to, and I renewed my preparations.

Peter wrote regularly. He enjoyed the many parcels I sent him. He used to say that he was sure that Bryan would just walk in one day. In his heart Nkosi still hoped this might be so, The war clouds were lifting, and it was only a matter of waiting and hoping that Peter might return.

Meanwhile, the sound of the policeman's motor-bike used to send me into a frenzy.

Some months previously we had been surprised to receive a letter from an ex-farm boy who had joined the R.A.R.

"dear Sir the Captaine. I am very glad I have been the good opportunity to write this letter sir. I staid with you a long time sir. Here (Burma) is very good country. Better than our country but what very very wet. Give my best lick to Missis and Boss Peter and Sir Bramin." (Bryan). "My captanin Please sir answord me as soon as your possible. We still going forwards with our jobs. We shall be Victory. Remaining your cincierry Peter Muza."

Nkosi refused to answer as he had no recollection of Peter Muza, but although I knew the boy had no real affection for us I felt that as he had joined up and had taken the trouble to write, his letter must be answered. I also sent him some cigarettes.

He was delighted to have my letter and answered at once.

"Dear Sir, But I was very glad to have your letter and I was very glad the day I reseaved your letter. I still looking about my cigarettes I hope you will send me somethink on your Christmas.

"I shall see you if Gold (God) saived me to be life. I shall see you my Lord. I wish you sen me a letter sir remaining your senceriry fathfurry Love. Your servantry man. Peter Muza."

Then Nkosi said if I wrote again it must be under my own name. The reply came.

"Dear Nkosikasi. With much thanks to have your letter I was very happy about that letter I thing and know you still remember me. I stil going my best power for the job in Army. The japanese is ver bad indid.

"But I was very sad about Sir Bramin that to say he was shout down over germani. (Bryan.)

"We do not know when we come to Rhodesia. We shall come if God knows as he saves us in action. Oh but it was very dangerous in action but we still Twinkle twinkle like stares in the sky."

In March Jo wrote that she had had a letter from the Chief Passport Officer, saying that the Ministry of Labour were unable to grant her a visa. She said she could hardly believe it. She had given them a letter from the C.O. of her Unit saying that she was being released when her passage came through.

Then a letter came from Peter saying that he was volunteering for Japan. He said that if he was really needed on the farm he would come back. But "I don't think you can see me staying behind for no particular reason and seeing the boys going off." We told him he must do just as he wished.

In May, Jo wrote more cheerfully. She had obtained permission to leave her Unit and could get her visa. She went up to Rhodesia House to see the man who was dealing with the shipping.

"He rang lots of bells and summoned all his minions and told one of them to bring my file. A large folder appeared inside which was a piece of paper with my name and nothing else. That rather shook him and he said that Records must have slipped up somehow. He was horribly vague and knows absolutely nothing, but will let me know as soon as he finds out. However I don't think it will be long now, dearests, before I am with you."

Peace came in May, and Salisbury decorated itself with the flags it had been hoarding. Those who know our city will remember that the heart or centre is generally taken as the intersection of First Street and Stanley Avenue. To my great astonishment I found that the Salisbury Municipality, not wishing to go to the great trouble of erecting an island, had utilised the Public Conveniences which are as near the centre as possible. I suppose the sight of those firm iron railings on which heavy poles might be lashed was too tempting to resist. This edifice was, therefore, decorated with flags and pennants, and round the iron fence were ferns and flowers in tubs. On closer inspection I found that most of the tubs were the old-time sanitary buckets which used to be collected nightly in the city. Through the green paint I could see "S.M." clearly. I thought this was a pretty touch, the old and new sanitation grouped together, to show how much our country had progressed. The interesting thing was to see self-conscious Salisbury business men diving through the flags. On the top of all was the Royal Standard, and I was told that in the evening the band was massed round the flags and played to the assembled citizens.

In June, Jo wrote to say that when her visa had been refused all her papers, even her passport, had been destroyed by Rhodesia House, and now she would have to start all over again. However, nothing mattered because we should be together.

Later she said that she would be sailing at the end of July.

I turned to and finished her room and decorated it with the presents sent by neighbours with words of welcome attached. Every day we expected the cable but we quite realised there might be more delays.

Early in August I called in at the G.P.O. to see if the cable had come. There was none but there was a letter.

Jo was remarrying and going to America.

It was a great blow but we understood. Nobody could have tried harder than she did to come out, but she had either to accept or refuse the offer immediately and she had chosen wisely. Young people cannot live in the past.

A week later we received a communication from the War Office, saying that Bryan was to be presumed as having died the night of June 21-22, 1944.

Peter wrote rather bitterly,

"Now we know that Bryan has gone for certain, we shall have to carry on as best we can without him."

That was true, the whole hurting truth. We are no longer a family of four, but three.

Before she left England, Jo sent me a copy of a little paper she had found hidden away in Bryan's writing case.

"My six ambitions.
1. To be fit enought to join the R.A.F.
2. To be able to fly solo.
3. To get my wings.
4. To get a commission on merit.
5. To go on Ops.
6. To live to tell the tale."

Against all except the last one was the date on which the ambition had been realised... Underneath he had written, "If I can do these then I shall have justified my parents' faith in me."

That October I was standing by the window looking at the storm, when I was struck by lightning. Nkosi carried me to the couch. When I came round I said,

"Where have I been?"

He said, "Nowhere."

Then I asked if my mother were dead? He said, "Yes."

After a pause I asked if Bryan were dead; and again Nkosi said "Yes."

I was only out a few moments, and yet I had been with the two I loved, and since then death has never meant much to me, for I know that they are both waiting near.

Peter arrived home looking so big, brown and handsome. Nkosi seemed to shed years, for after all there was a Picannin Boss to carry on.

After Bryan had left the country, every time Becky saw a uniform stepping out of the car, she rushed up barking with delight but was of course always disappointed. Later on when Peter left she would greet every car expectantly. She was pleased to see some of our R.A.F. guests when she got to know them, but they were always second best.

She was beginning to lose hope when Peter came home. When he stepped out of the car and said "Hallo Becky!" she was puzzled for a moment and then after smothering him with love and licks she ran madly round and round in a circle.

He had his twenty-first birthday, and we had our silver wedding, and then Nkosi and I decided to have our first real holiday together while Peter ran the farm.

We had hoped the Government would let Peter have a farm under the scheme for returned ex-servicemen, but they refused. Their reason was that under the scheme no father must train his son. Nkosi had trained Peter, and all he now needed was one more season to pick up what he had forgotten.

Nkosi said he must finish training him himself, and on these grounds his application for a farm was refused.

In 1947 I decided Peter must have a really good holiday, and as he kept putting off the finding of a suitable place and hotel, in desperation I managed to get him a room in the hotel Nkosi had booked for me three years previously.

Here he met Elaine, and they became engaged at once.

In January 1948, we found a large virgin farm for Peter, and he and Elaine were married that April.

After the honeymoon the children came back to us and lived in the hut I had prepared for Bryan and Jo. Peter had built a dining-hut for his little bride. When I was getting the rooms ready for them I remembered how I had planned for Bryan and Jo. I felt Bryan was with me, sharing my excitement.

The children stayed with us until they could go to their own farm. Instead of mud huts, they started with two pre-fabricated rondavels, while their house was being built.

Chunga went with them. He has never got over his military training, everything is done on the salute-right-turn basis, which is very wearying, but Elaine is patient. When we called the other day Chunga was cleaning a side window, and all I could see was an arm saluting.

Peter Muza was "saved life" and joined the police, but he

has never come to see us. Lupenga's son is Peter's right hand man, and Lupenga himself remains faithful. He works now in a beautiful new kitchen, and has an electric iron which he loves, and an electric washing machine which, in spite of gloomy foreboding, he has learnt to enjoy. As I have been writing this I have often called him in, asking him when certain things happened. He replied, "*Lo* time when *lo* dining-room was *lo* bathroom." He has seen many changes.

So history repeats itself, and Peter and Elaine have started from scratch as we did, but, thank God! with better chances.

And now ... it is you and I, Nkosi, who are walking into the sunset with a hard day's work behind us. Peter and Elaine are standing where we did twenty years ago. Peter so like his father, tall, strong, a hard worker. Elaine, so small and pretty, like Frances, yet infinitely superior to her in personality, brain, capability. She will work hard and take joy in the creating of her home. There will not be my mistakes and muddles, wild excitements and frantic fears. They will help carry Rhodesia on to a prosperous future, hard-working, happy in creating.

Dear Jo had said, "I wonder if people who marry in peacetime and are together always, know how lucky they are!"

Yes, I think some of us do.

I think the war has taught us to appreciate the present, although we naturally look to the future and plan, as all Rhodesians have planned, for NEXT YEAR.

ENVOY

"Where are you?"

The beautiful picture of Nkosi and me walking into the sunset is shattered. I blink away a tear and answer,

"Here! What do you want?"

"Come out for a bit, stuffing in there all day!"

"Half a moment."

We walk down the granite slope now bordered with bright flower-beds and turn among the tall trees planted over twenty years ago. Past the village of tobacco barns and buildings; past the tree still scarred with the nails that once held the washing fixture; past the one flat stone marks the site of the old sleeping-hut.

We climb the kopje, halt half-way for breath and look down. We see the neat rows of pigsties, the stable, the milling-shed, and to the left the borehole and the implements stacked in rows, and the shining wires of the Power which has brought such changes to our lives.

At the top we stand on the level granite and look at the farm stretching round us. The veld is now broken up with huge lands on every side, and we can see the wavey lines of the contour ridges. We hear the purr of the tractor and see it like a busy bee crossing the land. Far away to the left is the windmill of another borehole, which irrigates the tobacco beds and the vegetable garden which is no longer the sport of nature. On the fort kopje we can see the huts of an old native who tends the sheep, and these we can see like little black dots as they graze.

The spruit is still green-lined, and among the planted trees we see the glint of the weir we have built. Far away the Twin Kopjes stand as they did when we came. In the distance we can see new houses on land that has been lately taken up. Immediately before us is the precipice down which two small boys used to slide, and below is the paddock across which the oxen are plodding homewards. In the middle is the dam at which they will pause to drink.

Ahead through the trees, we see the huge earthworks of a new dam built by a powerful unit.

We sit on the warm granite as the sun sinks in the crimson sky, and the little evening wind blows softly as if it were bringing back words spoken long ago.

"I found these children . . . ."

"Daddy! do look at this caterpillar!"

Nkosi is speaking,

". . . . and when that dam fills up next year . . . ."

Salisbury,
Southern Rhodesia,
1946—1952